Stefan Hochrainer

Macroeconomic Risk Management Against Natural Disasters

WIRTSCHAFTSWISSENSCHAFT

Stefan Hochrainer

Macroeconomic Risk Management Against Natural Disasters

Analysis focussed on governments in developing countries

With a foreword by o. Prof. Dr. Georg Pflug

Deutscher Universitäts-Verlag

Bibliografische Information Der Deutschen Nationalbibliothek
Die Deutsche Nationalbibliothek verzeichnet diese Publikation in der
Deutschen Nationalbibliografie; detaillierte bibliografische Daten sind im Internet über
<http://dnb.d-nb.de> abrufbar.

Dissertation Universität Wien, 2006

1. Auflage Dezember 2006

Lektorat: Ute Wrasmann / Anita Wilke

Der Deutsche Universitäts-Verlag ist ein Unternehmen von Springer Science+Business Media.
www.duv.de

Umschlaggestaltung: Regine Zimmer, Dipl.-Designerin, Frankfurt/Main
Druck und Buchbinder: Rosch-Buch, Scheßlitz
Gedruckt auf säurefreiem und chlorfrei gebleichtem Papier
Printed in Germany

ISBN 978-3-8350-0594-5

Foreword

Looking back in history, we conceive the twentieth century as the century of wars. Most likely, we will conceive the twenty-first century as the century of (natural) catastrophes.

Wars can be avoided (unfortunately, it did not happen often in history), in contrast, most natural disasters are outside human influence. However, the consequences of disasters can be alleviated by means of risk management. For an effective risk management, information is needed about (i) the size of the risk (measured by the frequency and intensity of the hazard), and (ii) the degree of vulnerability of the economy and society. Stefan Hochrainer's thesis deals with measuring and modeling of both. While the physical risk modeling is a well developed area within statistical modeling (frequency analysis, point processes, extreme value theory, etc.), estimating the economic consequences is a more challenging task. The author studies economic effects of catastrophes by statistical analysis of macroeconomic data. One interesting finding is that disasters can decrease the absolute level of economic performance, such as the GDP, while keeping growth levels nearly the same (at least after some years) as in the pre-disaster years.

The boom of new products in the financial markets, especially of new derivative instruments, has led to new risk hedging instruments such as catastrophe bonds. CAT-bonds transfer the risk to the market of investors. In this volume, such instruments as well as insurance and credit arrangements are compared within the decision problem of optimally using limited funds. For this purpose, the software tool CATSIM was developed, which determines the effectiveness of proactive risk management instruments for the long-term economic development of a country by simulation.

It is hoped that this book will contribute to its goal: To create more stable and robust economic conditions and to avoid disruptions and stress on our planet, especially in view of the fact that this planet will be even more exposed to natural hazard events in the near future.

o. Prof. Dr. Georg Pflug

Preface

With pleasure I like to take this opportunity to thank all those who direct or indirectly helped me to write this book.

Special thanks go to my doctoral thesis supervisor Dr. Georg Pflug, Professor of the Department of Statistics and Decision Support Systems at the University of Vienna, for his encouragement and advice. Additionally, I want to thank him for the inspiring talks and fruitful discussions we had. I also want to thank Dr. Andreas Futschik for being my second supervisor. Furthermore, I want to thank my colleagues in the Risk and Vulnerability program at IIASA, where I have been continuing my scientific research since February 2005, especially Dr. Reinhard Mechler, for the many interesting discussions we had and constructive critics he gave and Dr. Joanne Linnerooth-Bayer, head of the program, for providing the environment for research and workshops. The work was funded by a doctoral stipendium of the University of Vienna and also was financially supported by IIASA.

I also want to thank all of the people who read and corrected the manuscripts in all stages: Michaela Krohn, Robert Birnecker, Stephanie Krohn, Elisabeth Sterrer and Sonat Hart. As always, the author retains sole responsibility for any remaining errors. I also want to express my gratitude to my parents Hubert and Dorothea Hochrainer for their constant support. Finally, I would like to thank Matthias and Michael Bodenstein for exciting discussions about professional as well as personal matters.

I dedicate this book to Katharina Stigler who has been at my side supporting me and this effort from the very beginning.

Stefan Hochrainer

Contents

List of Figures

List of Tables

Chapter 1

Introduction

1.1 Background

A natural disaster can be defined in its broadest sense as a serious disruption of the functioning of a community or a society due to the occurrence of an abnormal or infrequent hazard which causes losses that exceed the ability of those affected to cope with (UNISDR 2004: 17, UNDP 2004: 98). Usually, the disaster management literature distinguishes between sudden-onset and slow-onset events (Benson and Clay 2004: 6). Sudden-onset events, including extreme geotectonic events such as earthquakes, volcanic eruptions or slow mass movements and extreme weather events like cyclones, floods or winter storms, cause immediate losses and disruptions. Slow-onset events are either periodical or permanent in nature, like drought or desertification.

Losses due to natural disasters seem to exhibit an upward trend, both in human and economic terms. Over the last 50 years, the number of reported natural disasters and their impact on human and economic development has been increasing (Munich Re 2005b: 13). Between 1980 and 2000 some 75 percent of the world's population was living in areas that were affected at least once by natural catastrophes (UNDP 2004: 10). Furthermore, between 1980 and 2004 more than 15400 loss events caused by natural disasters occurred, 46 percent of these events happened in high-income countries, while 35 percent and 18 percent happened in middle- and low-income countries, respectively. The total death toll during this time period amounts to more than 1 million. Only 6 percent happened can be attributed to high-income countries whereas 35 percent and 59 percent occurred in middle- and low-income countries (Munich Re NatCatSERVICE 2005). Today, about 19 percent of the Earth's land area and more than half of the world's population are relatively highly exposed to at least one hazard (Dilley et al. 2005: 2).

As the above numbers indicate, there are major differences on the human loss statistics between industrialized and developing countries. This is also true for direct economic loss statistics: while direct losses in absolute terms are higher in industrialized countries, losses measured in percentage of GDP are more than three times higher in developing countries. In detail, between 1980 and 2004 natural disasters caused direct economic losses of about 1.412 billion US$, 65 percent of these losses occurred in high-income countries, 26 percent in middle- and 9 percent in low-income countries. However, the losses measured in percent of GDP indicate that economic losses are much more drastic for middle- and low-income countries. While losses in percentage of GDP are about 3.7 percent for the high-income country group, the losses are two and three times respectively higher in the middle- (7.4 percent) an low- (12.9 percent) income country groups (Munich Re NatCat-SERVICE 2005). On the country level, natural disasters can have serious impacts on the overall economic performance, e.g. gross domestic product, balance of payments, level of indebtedness, inflation rate (Otero and Marti 1995). While most of the time a disaster has to hit the country with a sufficient magnitude to have an impact on macroeconomic performance measures, sometimes, in the case that the main economic activity is hit, also a small loss in a larger country can affect the macroeconomic performance in a negative way. Such a rare situation occured in Ecuador in 1987, when a major oil pipeline was destroyed by an earthquake.

Summarizing, richer nations do not experience fewer natural disasters than poorer ones but they do suffer less due to higher economic development (which provides implicit insurance against the nature's shocks) and higher-quality institutions (Kahn 2005). The observed increasing number of human and economic losses can in general terms be attributed to the interaction of several variables including: (i) the location of geophysical phenomena, (ii) the increased exposure due to the increased population growth and human activity in disaster-prone areas, (iii) the low use of mitigation and preventive measures, (iv) regional underdevelopment (v) limitations of government available resources, (vi) environmental degradation and unsustainable land use policies (Miller and Keipi 2005). Furthermore, there seems to be an increase in the frequency and intensity of extreme natural hazards like hurricanes. This increase is generally thought to be associated with the rise of the global surface temperature (Munich Re 2005a).

Today, also due to the International Decade of Natural Disaster Reduction (IDNDR) initiative, efforts in this field aim at a proactive approach of disaster risk management against natural disasters (Mechler 2004a, Gurenko and Lester 2005) to achieve sustainable development, including poverty reduction and economic stability. Nowadays, there is a growing awareness in the disaster risk management literature that after-the-fact approaches may be unsustainable in the long run and proactive risk management strategies have to be considered. Especially, the need of countries for emergency relief and assistance from the outside after a disaster is considered to be a major problem. This was also stressed by Kofi Annan, secretary general of the United Nations, at the end of IDNDR by stating(Ingleton 1999: v):

> *Natural disasters profoundly affect our efforts to achieve sustainable development. By their powerful impact on the supply of primary commodities, they disrupt market stability, leading to steep declines in national revenue [...] We can no longer afford, financially or socially, to rely on the expectations of emergency relief when disaster strikes. Much greater attention must be paid to*

preventive strategies aimed at saving lives and protecting resources and assets before they lost.

As this quotation indicates, the reliance on ex-post payments after a disaster event is seen as unsustainable in the long run. Furthermore, natural disasters can cause serious disruptions in the case of insufficient funds for loss financing. As a consequence development can be seriously hampered. Since the early studies on the economic impacts of natural disasters in industrialized countries no macroeconomic long run effects were found (Burby 1991, Rossi et al. 1978). Therefore, empirical studies are focused on developing countries nowadays. However, since the rapid increase in losses caused by mega-disasters in developed countries (like Hurricane Katrina) it is also likely that this topic will be more prominent in the near future.

On the macroeconomic scale, especially in developing countries, the public sector is an important factor that influences the economic performance. This has been recognized in a number of studies (Briceño-Garmendia, Estache, Shafik 2004, Calderón and Servén 2004a,b). The need of the public sector for infrastructure development in developing countries is still high. For example, a recent World Bank report about infrastructure in Latin America and the Caribbean states that governments remain at the heart of infrastructure service delivery (Fay and Morrison 2005). Furthermore, for many people in developing countries, the lack of access to infrastructure services means living in isolation from markets and services. This often results in a significant curtailment of economic opportunities which increases poverty. The public sector is also important to improve market functioning and therefore private sector activity (Meier and Rauch 2005).

In theory public sector risk in developed countries can be ignored because the government has the ability to spread the risk over the whole population, so that the individual risk can be neglected, and therefore the government can behave risk neutral (Arrow and Lind 1970). As a simple example, the Elbe river floods in Germany in 2002 caused about 9.1 billion Euros of direct losses, with 9.6 billion Euro being available for loss financing. The *Sonderfonds Aufbauhilfe* founded by the federal and state governments of Germany amounted to 7.1 billion Euro and was created by means of tax raises (Mechler and Weichselgartner 2002). Therefore, loss financing with only ex-post financial instruments was no problem. However, the situation is quite different in developing and emerging-economy countries[1]. Based on empirical case studies, Mechler (2004a) investigated conditions where governments should behave risk averse and therefore should incorporate public sector risk. While he concluded that risk neutrality more or less holds true for developed countries, developing countries should act in a risk averse manner (Mechler 2004a: 59). Additionally to the public sector risk, due to the role as a de facto insurer of last resort for private sector risk and relief payments for the poor, developing countries have a large extra burden to bear in the case of a natural disaster event.

[1]They are used synonymously throughout the text.

It seems to be difficult to establish risk management measures in developing countries because budget expenditures are already reduced to bare necessities. Therefore, it is important to assess the costs and benefits of a proactive approach against natural disaster risk. Unfortunately, the assessment of the benefits is not so straightforward and therefore:

> *Building a culture of prevention is not easy. While the costs of prevention have to be paid in the present, its benefits lie in a distant future. Moreover, the benefits are not tangible; they are the disasters that did NOT happen.*[2]

Summarizing, there is urgent need for proactive disaster risk management strategies, especially for developing countries, which also incorporate and solve the serious problems which arises when the future costs and benefits of the approaches used have to be assessed. Furthermore, to build a culture of prevention, key policy makers in the real world have to be addressed and informed about the risks due to future natural disaster events.

1.2 Research objectives

This thesis deals with the consequences of sudden-onset natural disasters on the macroeconomic level, especially for the public sector of developing countries, and proactive risk management strategies to lessen the (long term) impacts of such events. While risk management can be undertaken by various actors on various levels, the decision maker in this thesis is most of the times the national government of a developing country. Because a proactive risk management approach always has some trade-offs in terms of forgone opportunities of other investments, the costs and benefits have to be assessed. Generally speaking, stability and growth are connected reciprocally.

Most of the current risk assessment and risk management models against catastrophe risk today are built to assess direct risks of the private sector. The actors in this field include insurers, reinsurers as well as brokers and analysts in the financial market (Grossi and Kunreuther 2005). In the context of natural disaster risk management reinsurer usually are those with the most widespread interest in catastrophe models (Grossi, Kunreuther and Windeler 2005: 27). Most of the current risk management models do not incorporate long term analysis of economic effects due to natural disasters on the country level. Exceptions are Mechler (2004a) and Freeman et al. (2002a,b). During the last few years more and more interest in public sector economic vulnerability emerged due to the high losses caused by natural disasters there (see for example Kunreuther and Linnerooth-Bayer 2003). While the government is responsible for loss financing in the public sector, where infrastructure reconstruction can be seen as the most important part (Freeman and Pflug 2003), it usually acts also as an "insurer of last resort" (Swiss Re 2002: 19) for the business sector. Furthermore, in the case of a disaster the government is

[2] UN Secretary-General: Introduction to Secretary-Generals Annual Report on the Work of the Organization of United Nations, 1999 (document A/54/1).

responsible for helping those who cannot survive without help, namely the poor. Hence, governments have to bear high additional costs in the case of a natural disaster.

As already said, governments of developed countries can ignore public sector risk because of their risk spreading and risk pooling ability. They can *spread* the risk over the whole population (e.g by raising taxes, borrowing), so that the individual risk can be neglected (Arrow and Lind 1970) and they can *pool* a large number of independent risks, so that its portfolio is diversified (Markowitz 1959). As a result the government can behave risk-neutral, e.g. they can neglect public sector risk. However, risk spreading and risk pooling is not always feasible for a government. Especially for some developing countries[3] such options would not be very effective, e.g. raising taxes in poor countries with shallow markets is a fruitless task. Based on empirical case studies, Mechler (2004a) investigated under which conditions governments should behave risk-averse and therefore use proactive risk management instruments. However, a methodological approach to assess the current financial vulnerability on this macroeconomic level is missing. Even more important, an approach to compare different countries and their financial vulnerability within a consistent modeling framework, is not at hand. Furthermore, a model to assess the costs and benefits of risk management strategies on macroeconomic variables in the long run is needed. Last but not least, the key policy makers in the real world have to be addressed and informed about the risk due to future natural disaster events to build up a culture of prevention (from a top down perspective).

In addition to the need for an integrated disaster risk management modeling approach on the macroeconomic level which can be used for cross-country economic vulnerability analysis, the question of empirically observed long term negative economic consequences due to natural disasters remains. Some country case study approaches (see for example Benson and Clay 1998, Clay et al. 1995, Thomson, Jenden and Clay 1998, Benson 1997a, Benson 1997b, Benson 1997c, Benson 1998 and Clay et al. 1999) and cross-country analysis (see for example Murlidharan and Shah 2003, Otero and Marti 1995, Crowards 1999, Charvériat 2000) present overall negative impacts in the short (event year and one year after the disaster) and medium (2 and 3 years after the disaster) run, whereas Albala-Bertrand's (1993a) empirical analysis found overall positive impacts on macroeconomic performance measures. An empirical reexamination of Albala-Bertrand's approach is still missing. Furthermore, empirical examinations of long run negative development due to natural disasters are still in its infancy. The empirical investigations in this thesis should shed light on this issue too.

Summarizing the discussion above, (i) an integrated risk management approach was needed for the development of, (ii) a catastrophe simulation model, where (iii) risk measures are used to assess the costs and benefits of proactive risk management instruments on macroeconomic variables in the short and in the long run, and (iv) to build user in-

[3]Developing countries comprise in this thesis emerging economy countries as well.

terfaces (software) around this model to bridge the gap between scientific analysis and implementation and policy issues. The model should incorporate the following features[4]:

- Assessment of stock effects: The financial vulnerability due to natural disasters, especially for governments in developing countries, can be evaluated. In this respect, financial vulnerability is seen as a function of the direct risk the government is exposed to and its financial resilience which in turn determines the flow effects.
- Assessment of flow effects: The macroeconomic risk due to natural disasters can be evaluated. The financial vulnerability determines the macroeconomic risk in the long run. If the government lacks the funds to meet their obligations, this can have serious effects on the economy and its population's livelihoods.
- The trade-off between stability and growth for proactive risk management strategies can be assessed: To increase the financial vulnerability and, therefore decrease the macroeconomic risk of negative long term economic development, the government can use ex-ante risk financing instruments. However, such instruments come with a price in terms of forgone opportunities to other investments. Therefore, the costs and benefits of the ex-ante instruments have to be assessed and evaluated in the risk management process.
- The financial vulnerability and macroeconomic risks of different countries can be compared within the modeling framework.
- Furthermore, a user interface for the model should fill the gap between scientific analysis and applied science. It aims at key policy makers in the real world and should help them to understand the complex interrelationships between long term economic development and natural disasters.

Because of the importance of this last point above, a scientific non-governmental independent institution is needed to carry out such analysis and possible workshops. IIASA, the International Institute for Applied System Analysis, situated in Laxenburg near Vienna, specifically the author in collaboration with Prof. Dr. Georg Pflug (Department of Statistics and Decision Support Systems, University of Vienna), Dr. Reinhard Mechler (IIASA) and Dr. Joanne Linnerooth-Bayer (IIASA)[5] carried out this work. The model itself and the usefulness of the user interfaces for training workshops was validated by a stakeholder workshop sponsored by the World Bank's Hazard Management (HMU) and the ProVention Consortium, and jointly organized by the HMU and IIASA on The Financial Management of Disaster Risks in April 21-23, 2004 (Laxenburg). Furthermore, a technical workshop named "Management of Disaster Risk Through Fiscal and Budget

[4] A detailed description of the objectives for the model structure is given in section 6.2.

[5] All of them are members of the Risk and Vulnerability (RaV) group, formally known as Risk, Modeling and Society (RMS).

Planning", sponsored by the Caribbean Development Bank and Inter American Development Bank as a joint initiative on mainstreaming disaster risk management which was held in June 26-27, 2006 (Barbados) proved the usefulness of the model for applied analysis and mainstreaming disaster risk into development planning.

The name of the model is called **CatSim** which stands for **Catastrophe Simulation model**. It is based on modeling work done by R. Mechler and G. Pflug (see Freeman et al. 2002a,b). Because of the special modular structure of CatSim now which is presented in section 6.3 various analysis in different directions can be performed, e.g. climate change. Therefore, CatSim will be used and further developed continuously in the future for specific analysis in this field by the author in cooperation with R. Mechler, G. Pflug and J. Linnerooth-Bayer.

1.3 Outline

The book is organized as follows:

Chapter 2 starts with an overall introduction to the concept of risk (section 2.1) and puts this notion into the context of natural disasters events (section 2.2). Section 2.3 provides basic definitions and describes overall humanitarian and ecological effects of natural disasters. Section 2.4 summarizes the discussion by presenting a new comprehensive integrated macroeconomic risk management approach against natural disasters for governments as the decision makers.

Chapter 3 looks at the macroeconomic effects of natural disasters. In section 3.1 some global statistics are discussed. Section 3.2 presents a literature review of empirical studies on indirect and secondary effects caused by natural disasters. Section 3.3 presents a sample of 85 disaster events in 45 countries between 1960 and 2000 which are analyzed in section 3.5 by using the methodology described in section 3.4.

Chapter 4 introduces risk financing instruments for the private and public sector. While section 4.1 presents an overview of possible risk management instruments, section 4.2 investigates the financial instruments in the private sector in more detail. Afterwards, risk management instruments for the public sector are presented in section 4.3. Some first qualitative statements when governments should behave risk averse and, therefore, act proactive are discussed. An overall introduction to risk management strategies for the public sector is given and the current support in disaster risk reduction within departments is investigated. Furthermore, current government catastrophe programs are presented.

In chapter 5 the ex-post (section 5.1) and ex-ante measures (section 5.2) which a government may use for loss financing or prevention are presented. Ex-post measures include diversion, taxation, domestic and foreign credits as well as assistance from the outside. Ex-ante measures, including structural mitigation, reserve funds, XL-insurance, contingent credit arrangements and catastrophe bonds, determine the financial resilience of the public sector against natural disaster losses. Section 5.2.6 summarizes the costs and benefits of these ex-ante measures.

Chapter 6 presents the modeling part. Section 6.1 starts with a presentation of the state-of-the-art approach for catastrophe models today. Section 6.2 gives a summary of the features and objectives for the own modeling part and section 6.3 outlines the modeling in CatSim based on the discussions before. In the appendix the user interfaces for the model are shown.

Chapter 7 presents three country case studies (Honduras, El Salvador and Colombia) where the model is used to determine the financial vulnerability and macroeconomic risk due to natural disasters. The trade-off between stability and growth is investigated and risk management strategies are assessed. Furthermore, some interesting results are discussed.

The last chapter 8 summarizes the main results presented in this thesis.

Chapter 2

Natural disaster risk

This chapter will discuss the notion of natural disaster risk and present an integrated risk management approach against long term macroeconomic risks on the country level which can also be used for cross-country economic vulnerability analysis. The chapter starts with an overall introduction to the notion of risk and specifies the concept in the context of natural disaster events in section 2.2. Because disasters stem from the realization of risk, definitions, conditions and consequences of natural disasters are presented in section 2.3. Section 2.4 summarizes the discussion by presenting a new approach for catastrophic risk management on the country level.

2.1 An introduction to the concept of risk

Risk seems to be an intuitive subject as all of us have a sense of what risk is. This is due to the fact that risk is an ineliminable part of human existence. Risk pervades all human activity. In every human decision or action the question is actually not one of taking or not taking a risk, but rather which risk to choose. Therefore it is not possible to avoid taking risks, e.g. the risk of loss of face, status, money, accidents, economic disasters and so on. On the other hand, neither man nor the organizations he founds can survive without taking risks, simply because every decision bears a risk and decision making is essential (Wharton 1992). This chapter gives an overview of some approaches to the concept of risk which can be found in the literature. No attempts have been made to present an all-inclusive review. Instead, the focus is on a suitable introduction to the concept of risk which highlights the main directions in the various current approaches in natural, applied and social sciences. Therefore, the questions *why* we have an understanding of the concept of risk, *when* it is constructed from the very infancy to maturity, and *how* risk is perceived by different individuals is looked at first. Afterwards, the history of the word 'risk' and its meaning today is investigated. Next, the earliest methods to measure and quantify risk are presented. Finally, a short look at the philosophical debate about the concept of risk is taken.

Before starting to explain the evolution of risk, a first condition when risk in its broadest terms will exist is given. At the most basic level, risk "exists whenever more than one outcome is possible" (Moss 2002: 22). This implies that the concept of risk is "inevitably future-oriented" (Rescher 1983: 41, see also Adams 1995: 30). From studies on newborn animals and humans we know that every individual is confronted with the necessity of satisfying two contradictory needs right from birth on: the search for and avoidance of risk (Assailly 1994: 3). Animals have some concept of risk, they know when and if a situation is dangerous for them, e.g. wildebeests drinking from a river in which crocodiles are in it. This concept of risk is driven mainly by their instincts and therefore their possibility to manage (e.g. reducing) this risk in a rational manner is very limited. Furthermore, most of the animals can only live in certain areas, within a specific environment, e.g. tropical zones, where they have developed special techniques to survive in their habitats. These techniques are very specialized and under most circumstances useless in other regions, e.g. deserts. They cannot change their environment and if the environment changes, it changes the animals (through natural selection) and not vice versa (in the most cases). On the other hand, man is born virtually without any instincts, he has to learn through his ability to communicate, he can preserve information through culture and he can change his environment because of his understanding of cause and effect. He can live in every region of the world he wants to, he can adapt etc., but most importantly, he can create abstract ideas of the world, like the idea of risk.

There are at least two important characteristics of man which made him the dominant species in this world. First, his highly developed intelligence and secondly his ability to communicate (Wharton 1992: 2). Both of these attributes are interconnected. The primitive man was mainly driven by instincts, he had no language to communicate and was unable to exploit and change his environment. Through his ability to communicate, the modern man has been enabled to act collectively. Through his ability to learn from observation and experience, to understand cause and effect, the modern man has been able to anticipate, control and exploit his environment. Through communication man is able to preserve knowledge over generations. He can make decisions for himself by evaluating the different outcomes he may get and choosing his favorite one. This evaluation implicitly uses the concept of risk. Therefore, we will next discuss the formation of the concept of risk for individuals from their childhood to maturity. Based on a psychogenetic viewpoint we will emphasize the complexity of the concept of risk during the course of development and highlight the interrelationship with two other concepts, probability and chance.

Why is risk one of the most difficult concepts a child has to understand and handle during his development? The main reason is the interrelation between the cognitive construction and two other concepts, probability and chance, because the intrinsic nature of the concept of risk is probabilistic (Assailly 1994). Probability being an intermediary phenomenon is not immediately understood but is the subject of a long construction. Initially, the notion of chance does not make any sense for a child. The psychological functioning of the child can be compared to that of 'primitive' mentalities, where the absence of the notion of chance is one of the most essential characteristics. 'Primitive' thinking always attributes causes, known or unknown, to every event. Chance is derived secondarily because the search for order and law is primary. Only when order and law are sufficiently constructed (first phase: period from birth to 7 years)[1], the child will be able to integrate chance (second phase: period from 7 to 11 years). From the moment that the foreseeable is constructed (law and order), the unforeseeable can acquire meaning (chance). However, the child cannot yet integrate the notion of probability, which requires an exhaustive analysis of the favorable cases in relation to all possible cases, because it can only oppose the operatory (determined) and the fortuitous (undetermined). In the third and last phase (between 11 to 15 years), which also corresponds to the general stage of formal operations, probabilistic reasoning becomes possible. This short overview emphasizes the fact that the concepts of risk, probability and chance are not fundamentals for the child (and thus for every human) but are the subject of a long and difficult learning process. The notion/concept of risk is a methodological approach for decision making in an uncertain world.

The next question which is natural to ask is: If everybody has an understanding of what risk is, does everybody perceive risk equally? The answer is no. The concept of risk means different things to different people. For example, experts judge risk with technical estimates such as annual fatalities whereas laypeople relate their judgment of risk more to other (qualitative) characteristics, such as catastrophic potential, threat to future generations, etc. As a result their assessment of risk tends to differ significantly from the expert ones (Slovic et al. 1979). Also because of cognitive limitations, biased media coverage or misleading experience, risk can be misjudged and believed with unwarranted confidence (Slovic et al. 1979). Furthermore, sociological and anthropological studies have shown that the perception of risk has its roots in social and cultural factors. For example, in sociocultural theory at least three major theoretical perspectives on risk have emerged since the early 1980s. The cultural anthropological approach of Mary Douglas (Douglas and Wildavsky 1982), the sociological examination of risk by Ulrich Beck (1992) and the sociologist approach, similar to that of Beck, by Giddens (1991). They stand in clear contrast to scientific approaches to risk by taking the broader social and cultural contexts in which risk as a concept derives its meaning and resonance into account (Lupton 1999: 1). However, as this chapter is an introduction to the concept of risk, a detailed presentation of the various approaches is omitted here[2] and the history of the word 'risk' and the meaning today in some western countries is examined next.

It is not clear if the origin of the word 'risk' comes from the Latin word *risicum* or the Arabic word *risq*, but both definitions implicitly assume fortuitous events. The Latin word *risicum* originally referred to the challenge presented to seafarers by a barrier reef, and so implied a possible negative outcome. The Arabic word *risq* signifies 'anything that has been given to you (by God) and from which you draw profit' and has therefore connotations of a favorable outcome. There is also a Greek derivative of the Arabic word

[1]See the model from Piaget and Inhelder 1969.
[2]See for example Adams 1995, Renn and Rohrmann 2000, Caplan 2000, Lupton 1999.

risq which is related to chance outcomes in a general manner and therefore has neither positive nor negative implications. Today, the word risk has solely negative connotations in most western countries. For example the modern French word *risque*, the common English and German word *risk* or *Risiko* have definitely negative associations. This emphasis on the negative aspects can also be found in dictionaries like the Oxford English Dictionary (1970) or Meyers Encyclopedically Lexicon (1971).

Over time the meaning of the word has changed from one simply describing any unintended or unexpected outcome, good or bad, of a decision, to one relating to an undesirable outcome and the probability of its occurrence[3]. Girolamo Cardano, an Italian physician and mathematician in the mid 1500s, was one of the first who studied risk in a serious manner by assigning probabilities to possible outcomes. His breakthrough was in discovering that the likelihood of rolling a particular sum with two dices is exactly equal to the number of possible ways that sum could be obtained, divided by the total number of possible rolls. Whereas a gambler at that time would have known from experience that throwing a seven was more likely than throwing a twelve, Cardano could say with precision that the probability of throwing a seven was 16.7 percent (6/36) as compared to 8.3 percent (1/36) for a twelve. He was therefore (probably) the first one who treated chance in an systematic way.

The broader notion of *expected value* emerged in the 17th century. In 1657 Christiaan Huygens proposed a method for determining the expected value of a game: It is the sum of the weighted average of all possible outcomes. He observed that in a lottery with two equally likely payoffs, a and b, the "fair" price of a ticket was $(\frac{1}{2}a + \frac{1}{2}b)$. In these early days of probability theory it was assumed that expected value was the same as 'fair price' in the marketplace. Thus, the fair price of a game with a fifty-fifty chance of \$ 0 or \$ 10 was believed to be exactly \$ 5. Stated differently, the owner of a \$ 100.000 house should pay no more than \$ 1000 for insurance when the probability of loss is 1 percent (100.000*0.01+100.000*0=1000). A very interesting and important discovery in the history of economics was that most people are willing to pay more than the expected value to get rid of the risk. Economists call this *risk aversion*, a human characteristic that could be captured and handled through the use of *utility functions*.

Daniel Bernoulli (1700-1782), a Swiss mathematician, was one of the first who recognized risk aversion. He stated that it is wrong to equate expected value with fair price in the marketplace and demonstrated this with the famous St. Petersburg Paradox, which was originally introduced by his cousin Nicolas Bernoulli 25 years ago :

> A fair coin is to be tossed until a head appears. If it does so on the nth toss, the gambler is then to be paid 2^{n-1} ducats.

The question was how much should the gambler be willing to pay for the opportunity to play the game? The expected value of the game is clearly infinite $((\frac{1}{2} * \$1) + (\frac{1}{4} * \$2) +$

[3]A excellent guide through the history of risk was written by Bernstein 1996.

$(\frac{1}{8} * \$4) + ... = \infty)$ but no reasonable person would pay more than (say) $20 to play the game. Bernoulli believed that people determine how much to pay for the game not on the basis of expected value but rather of *expected utility* - that is, the amount of pleasure they expected to derive from the game. A so called utility function determines how much pleasure one gains from a certain dollar amount. Bernoulli argued that the sum of this expected value never got anywhere near infinity because individuals derived a progressively smaller amount of utility from each additional dollar, meaning that they value every additional dollar a little less than the one before. In modern economic terms, Bernoulli was describing the diminishing marginal utility of wealth. One implication of this notion is that individuals will place a higher value on losses than on equal sized gains. Thus, in evaluating risk situations the decision-maker replaces the monetary values of final wealth by the utility (function) of final wealth. Utility can thus be interpreted as a method of passing from a more objective level to a more subjective or psychological level: that of the amount of satisfaction achieved.

As discussed above, in the beginning of the quantification of risk the probability, the expected value and the utility concept were the main instruments to characterize risk in a rational manner: Probability is essential to weight the different possible outcomes, the expected value shows what will happen in the average, and the utility concept gives the tool to distinguish different types of decision makers in the same situation. These terms are frequently used to define risk in broad terms, as shown by the following citations: Lowrance (1976: 94) defines risk as "a measure of the probability and severity of adverse effects". For Rescher (1983: 33) risk is the "chancing of a negative outcome. To measure risk we must accordingly measure both of its defining components, the chance and the negativity". Mileti (1999: 106) defines risk as "the probability of an event or condition occurring". UNDHA (1992: 64) risk is defined as "Expected losses (of lives, persons injured, property damaged, and economic activity disrupted) due to a particular hazard for a given area and reference period". Wharton (1992: 5) points out that "A risk is any unintended or unexpected outcome of a decision or course of action". Adams (1995: 30) defined risk as " the product of the probability and utility of some *future* events". Banks (2005: 3) defines risk "as the uncertainty surrounding the outcome of an event".

Taking the wide diversity of phenomena that could be considered into account, risk can mean too many things if one (or all) of the above definitions would be used. This problem disappears as soon as risk is put in the proper context. However, this approach makes it difficult to communicate across the various disciplines. Shrader-Frechette (1991) offered a systematic classification for competing conceptions of risk. She distinguishes two positions: Positivists and Relativists. Positivists think that risk is a purely scientific concept. They interpret risk as referring objectively to the circumstances of the physical world. The Relativists think that risk is a purely subjective reaction to phenomena encountered in personal or social experience. In their opinion risk is a mental construct expressing emotional, moral or political reactions. Hornig (1993) offered a very similar dichotomous schema like Shrader-Frechette. Hornig's scientific view of risk is largely consistent with the Positivist view of risk by Shrader-Frechette, but Hornig offers a contextualist view in place of relativism. In this view, the most important dimensions of risk are determined in the social context in which issues or decisions arise. Thompson and Wesley (1996) argued that the dichotomous schemes presented by Shrader-Frechette and Hornig for classifying opposing views overstate and misidentify the points of contention. Thompson and Wesley (1996) propose that risk probabilism and risk contextualism represent the opposite ends of a *continuum* for conceptualizing risk and is the key dimension of controversy in risk issues[4]. Be as it may, the different concepts of risk in the natural, applied and social sciences have their cons and pros because the handling (e.g. reducing) of risk, which is the ultimate goal in every risk research, needs specification of the risk. As long as no unified approach to the definition of risk exists for all fields[5] (and probably never will for good reasons), the concept of risk which is used in a specific context or scientific area should at least be defined explicitly, so that other researchers from different fields can understand the *idea* behind this approach. This will lead to a fruitful controversial discussion within the community. Such approaches are currently underway in the integrated disaster risk management community. The next section presents a more thorough discussion of the current conceptualizations of risk in the context of natural disasters.

2.2 Risk in the natural disaster context

To deal with natural disasters[6] one (e.g. individuals, firms, governments) has to know the risk that a natural hazard will overwhelm its capacity to cope with it. Therefore, a concept of risk is needed. In this section, we explore some of the current approaches in this field.

Fournier d'Albe (1979) was one of the first scientists who formulated a novel definition of risk within the context of natural disasters[7]. His emphasis was not only on the severity of the natural phenomenon, but also on the vulnerability of the exposed elements. UNDRO (1991) extended the concept to all natural disasters. Basically, the three components which determine risk and are used in the context of natural disasters as a standard are: Hazard, Exposure and Vulnerability (Alexander 2000, Burby 1991; UNDRO 1991, Mechler 2004a).

$$\textbf{Risk=f(probability(Hazard),losses(Vulnerability,Exposure))}$$

Risk is the combination of probability and loss, the probability is a function of the hazard and the potential loss is a function of vulnerability and the elements at risk. These

[4]However, Shrader-Frechette (1997) noted that these new labels are nothing new and articulated earlier by her.

[5]There are ongoing efforts, mainly in the economic literature, to find an unifying approach in expressing risk. See for example Aven et al. 2004.

[6]The word 'Catastrophe' and 'Disaster' is used synonymously throughout the text.

[7]Actually he was investigating volcano risk.

three components determine the risk. This definition does not represent a mathematical formula, instead it serves primarily to express the integration of these different dimensions in the evaluation of risk. For example, risk can be measured in different ways, e.g. through the expected value and the variance, by game-theoretic approaches (min-max criterium) or by more sophisticated stochastic dominance methods. Furthermore, hazard, vulnerability and exposed elements are not mutually exclusive and they are only separated for methodological reasons and to achieve a better comprehension of risk. Thus, when one of these three components of risk is altered, we alter risk itself. The following subsections discuss these three terms, address some terminology problems and try to evaluate this concept for natural disaster risk management.

2.2.1 Hazard

Hazard is completely physical defined and it is worth noting that a hazard and an event are distinct phenomenons. First, extreme events can be seen as events with relatively high variance from the mean (White 1974: 4)[8]. Second, a natural event is "nomen est omen" simply a natural occurrence, whereas a hazard is the potential danger to human life or property (Benson and Twigg 2004: 19)[9]. There is no potential threat to humans if the event happened in an uninhabited region, so the event cannot be a hazard. However, the concepts of event and hazard are not mutually exclusive. It is commonly accepted in the literature that the definition of a hazard has to include an interaction between humans and an event. This can be be seen by the following quotations: "A potential threat to humans and their welfare" (Smith 1996: 5). "A geologic hazard is a phenomenon associated with geologic processes that can produce a disaster when a critical threshold is exceeded and can result in significant loss in life or property" (Coates 1981: 257). "The hazard involves the human population placing itself at risk from geophysical events" (Alexander 1993: 4). "A natural hazard is a geophysical, atmospheric or hydrological event that has a potential to cause harm or loss" (Benson and Twigg 2004: 19).

The concept of "hazard" is used to refer to a latent danger to a system. This can be mathematically expressed as the probability of occurrence of an event of certain intensity in a specific region and during a determined period of time. To determine these probabilities a consistent inventory of historic events or pre-historic events is required. With these probability distributions further analysis can be done to assess the risk. Furthermore, this information can be used to create hazard maps. Computer science tools such as the geographic information system (GIS) have facilitated this method of identification and analysis. However, it is not possible to modify natural hazards in order to reduce risk.

There can be some ambiguity as to whether the probability of occurrence of a hazard, or the probability of a particular outcome is being referred to. This problem was addressed by Sarewitz et al. (2003). They define *event risk* as the "risk of occurrence

[8]For example, larger than the mean + 3 times the standard deviation.

[9]However, usually event and hazard are used synonymously in most of the literature today.

of any particular hazard or extreme event" and *outcome risk* as "the risk of a particular outcome". As the above formula implies, risk is defined in the terminology of Sarewitz et al. (2003) as outcome risk. The probability of occurrence of the specific hazard on the right hand side therefore could be called event risk. However, in this thesis, if not otherwise stated, 'risk' refers to outcome risk, the word 'event risk' is not used, instead the concept of probability for a natural hazard is preferred.

2.2.2 Elements at risk

The elements at risk, also called exposed elements, which are the second component in the definition of risk above, are not mutually exclusive from the concept of hazard. As already stated an extreme event can only be transformed into a hazard if there is an interaction with human life, values etc. Therefore, without any elements at risk there cannot be hazard and without a hazard there are no elements at risk. Furthermore, the exposed elements are not mutually exclusive with the vulnerability and hazard concept, because one cannot be threatened if the exposed elements are not vulnerable, implicating that no hazard exists as well.

Elements at risk can be include persons, building structures, objects of infrastructure (e.g. water and sewer facilities, roads and bridges), agricultural assets or economic activities, which can be impacted in the case of a disaster event. In theory, it would be desirable to create a map in which the spatial distribution of the exposed elements at risk are delineated. Such maps could be linked with a hazard map to determine in which extend these elements are exposed to the relevant hazard (Dilley et al. 2005). In practice, a thorough assessment is difficult and expensive due to the sheer number of the elements that should be considered. However, it is possible to look at the most important elements at risk and their spatial distribution (Frischknecht et al. 2003). Which elements should be seen as important is dependent on the view of the decision maker and is therefore also a subjective issue. There are also new methods like dasymmetric mapping where land use information is used to disaggregate census data for large-scale risk assessment (Thieken et al. 2006, Kleist et al. 2006)

To lessen the risk of a disaster, the equation above suggests that this could be achieved by reducing the elements at risk. To find out which elements are exposed to a natural hazard one has at least to know if and where the hazard could occur. As already stated, a hazard map would be the best instrument for determining which elements are exposed to a certain hazard.

There are at least three possibilities to lessen the risk by reducing the exposed elements. First, restricting building in hazard prone areas would lessen the future risk that an extreme event becomes a disaster, for example, this could be achieved through governmental incentives for people to build in less prone hazard areas (Hochrainer 2005). Second, there is the possibility to displace exposed elements (like local communities) in hazard prone areas to other, less prone, areas. The problem here is, that this is only feasible for small communities, because the displacement of the whole infrastructure and buildings from one place to another would be very expensive. On the other hand, if such a small community is heavily damaged through a natural catastrophe, the displacement could be feasible. Third, the degree of exposure within a system is also socially determined (Brooks 2003). Exposure depends on where populations choose (or are forced) to live, and therefore increase or decrease the elements at risk (infrastructure, business sector etc.). Thus, the change of the social perception on disasters could also change the willingness to live in disaster prone areas.

2.2.3 Vulnerability

The concept of vulnerability is a significant contribution to our understanding of natural disasters (Baird et al. 1975, Maskrey 1989, Turner et al. 2003). Vulnerability represents the susceptibility or predisposition of the exposed elements to incur damages.

> *"Vulnerability may be defined as an internal risk factor of the subject or system that is exposed to a hazard and corresponds to its intrinsic predisposition to be affected, or to be susceptible to damage."* (Cardona 2004: 37).

Generally speaking, vulnerability represents the physical, economic, political, institutional or social susceptibility or the predisposition of a community to damage in the case of a extreme natural event, although in one way or another all are actually related. Especially Whitman and Fournier d'Albe emphasized on the notion that damage was not only due to the impacts of the natural event, but also to the fragility or the vulnerability of the exposed elements.

The two main questions when talking about vulnerability should be: Who are vulnerable and to what are they vulnerable? As said before, if there is no hazard it is not possible to be vulnerable at all. There is no situation of a hazard threat to an element if it is not exposed or vulnerable to the potential phenomenon. It is important to make this distinction since at a certain moment in time the word 'vulnerability' might be employed in different ways in problem areas other than the field of disasters, e.g. psychology or public health (Cardona 2004).

Vulnerability can be analyzed from different perspectives and depending on the perspective different dimensions of vulnerability can be seen as important. This stems from the fact that different dimensions of vulnerability are linked together and the interaction between them is not yet (fully) understood. Some authors (e.g. Twigg 1998) argue that vulnerability is too complicated to be captured by models, frameworks and maps because there are so many dimensions included. However, this cannot be a reason to stop. In fact, one should develop models, frameworks and maps because vulnerability is not yet fully understood and scientists are searching for the driving forces of vulnerability to lessen the complexity of the subject and to find the main moments which constitute vulnerability.

This in turn allows us to handle vulnerability in a rational manner rather than guessing or giving up.

Different definitions of vulnerability exist, and it is not the purpose here to review them all[10], rather some different dimension of vulnerability are given here (Mechler 2004a: 19):

- Physical vulnerability: The susceptibility to damage of physical assets such as houses, dams, roads or bridges.
- Social vulnerability: The ability of a society to cope with the impacts of a natural disaster.
- Institutional vulnerability: It refers to the existence and robustness of institutions to deal with natural disasters.
- Economic vulnerability: The financial capacity to finance losses caused by a disaster and the ability to return to a previously planned activity path. This includes private individuals, companies as well as governments.

The approaches from the natural and applied sciences are concerned with physical and economic vulnerability most of the time. Physical vulnerability can be measured by the employment of damage matrixes, loss distribution functions, or fragility or vulnerability indices which relate the intensity of a phenomenon (the hazard) to the degree of harm or damage. For example vulnerability curves for different housing constructions for different impacts of an earthquake can be obtained by simulation or be based on empirical data (Altay et al. 2002, Erdik and Aydmoglu 2003). Economic vulnerability on the macro- and micro level can be measured by indices or a combination of indices (Murlidharan 2003: 23). One of the advantages of these approaches is that the results can be translated into potential losses and therefore used for further analysis, e.g. Cost-Benefit Analysis. Due to the fact that it is not possible to modify the hazard in order to reduce the risk, there are only the two possibilities to modify the conditions of vulnerability and the exposed elements. Emphasizes made in the technical literature on the study of vulnerability and vulnerability reduction as a measure of prevention mitigation can therefore be (indirectly) explained by efforts in risk reduction.

On the other hand, the social sciences are interested in social vulnerability and/or institutional vulnerability. In their view vulnerability has a social character and is not limited to the potential physical damage. From their point of view vulnerability cannot be defined or measured without reference to the capacity of a population to absorb, respond and recover from an impact of a natural event. Vulnerability is, therefore, socially constructed and is the result of economic, social and political processes. For example, Susman et al. (1984) define vulnerability as the degree to which the different social classes

[10]For a summary of definitions and approaches see for example Adger 1999, Brooks 2003, Siegel et al. 2003.

are differentially at risk. Thus, vulnerability is also established according to the political, social and economic conditions. In order to change vulnerability social, cultural and educational aspects should be considered (Anderson 1995).

There is an ongoing discussion about the concept of vulnerability in the literature (see for example Turner et al. 2003). At least one way to explain the difficulties behind the vulnerability concept should be pointed out here: The availability and quantification of information and subsequently the different methodologies used to define vulnerability. If information is available that is quantifiable and can be used to distinguish different vulnerabilities on the same scale, than vulnerability is most of the time defined by indices, (probability) curves or combinations of it. This approach is used to assess physical and economic vulnerability as the cause and effect relationship is quite clear. However, if the information is not quantifiable, as in the case of social and institutional vulnerability analysis, we are facing two problems: First, we cannot measure these vulnerabilities and therefore vulnerability is difficult to determine, which makes it difficult to argue with. Second, social and institutional vulnerability are much more complex than physical vulnerability for example, due to the dynamic interrelationship with other factors which determine these vulnerabilities, which again makes it difficult to understand what the driving forces and cause and effects of a given vulnerability are. Hence, the problem of quantification leads to different concepts of vulnerability because different authors and scientific fields have to use different methodologies (e.g. heuristic vs. mathematical methods).

This thesis is concerned with financial vulnerability and macroeconomic risk. State-of-the-art approaches in this field are probability based (Mechler 2004a, Freeman et al. 2004, Grossi and Kunreuther 2005). Hence, also in this thesis a probability based approach is used[11]. The link between the social sciences and implementation issues is established by user interfaces which are explained in the appendix. Next, the term *resilience* is introduced to distinguish in a clear way the concept and interrelationships between (direct and macroeconomic) risk and financial vulnerability. Because resilience is a rather new term in the disaster literature the origins are also presented.

2.2.4 Resilience

According to the Oxford English Dictionary (1970) resilience is "(i) the (or an) act of rebounding or springing back and (ii) elasticity; the power of resuming the original shape or position after compression, bending, etc". The origin of the word 'resilience' is Latin, where *resilio* means to jump back. The resilience of a material is the quality of being able to strain energy and deflect elastically under a load without breaking or being deformed. While resilience was first used in a pure mechanical sense, since the 1970s the concept has also been used in ecology and then gained ground in social science. A literature

[11]Probability based approaches are most of the time superior to limited information approaches due to various reasons, see for example Kramer 1995.

review about the conceptualization of resilience can be found in Klein et al. 2003. It is worth noting, that "resistance", and "resilience" do not have the same meaning. While resistance refers to the capacity to withstand external forces without change, resilience refers to the capacity to "bounce back" to a pre-disaster state (Etkin 1999: 74). A general definition of resilience is given by UNISDR (2006), for them **resilience** is:

> *The capacity of a system, community or society potentially exposed to hazards to adapt, by resisting or changing in order to reach and maintain an acceptable level of functioning and structure. This is determined by the degree to which the social system is capable of organizing itself to increase its capacity for learning from past disasters for better future protection and to improve risk reduction measures.*

Resilience has been discussed within ecological theory, adaptive systems analysis and natural disasters studies. It can be seen as a quality that enables an organization, ecological system, household or nation to recover quickly from disaster shocks. Its emphasis is on coping with disasters rather than promising to control or avoid their underlying physical energies (Pelling and Uitto 2001: 52). According to the above formulation of risk the new equation could look like (adapted from UNISDR 2004, see also figure 2.2):

risk=f(probability(Hazard), losses(Vulnerability,Exposure), Resilience)

While resilience is seen as a component aspect of the vulnerability concept, no general definition is yet accepted throughout literature. Therefore, resilience remains at the conceptual level and approaches to make the concept operational have not been provided yet (Alexander 1997, Klein et al. 2003). This thesis presents an approach how financial resilience and financial vulnerability can be connected and operationalized to determine macroeconomic risk. Section 2.4 can be seen as the summary of the discussion above and presents an approach to solve some of the mentioned problems. Before being able to do that it is necessary to discuss when it is legitimate to say that a disaster has occurred. Therefore, we have to study the various possible effects of natural disasters. Furthermore, it is important to find an acceptable definition when a natural hazard caused a disaster because this is also important to operationalize the terms presented above in an integrated manner.

2.3 Definitions and consequences of disasters

Disasters stem from the realization of risk. The section title should stress the fact that the definition when a natural disaster has occurred always has to rely on the consequences the disaster caused, as will be shown next. Basically, disasters are human-made and fundamentally are a social phenomenon. Natural hazards do not necessarily lead to disasters, they translate to disasters only to the extent that the population is unprepared to respond or unable to cope and is therefore severely affected. Social action is now a key component to understand natural disasters also due to the "International Decade for

Natural Disaster Reduction" (IDNDR). One of the important messages after the IDNDR was that "disasters were not acts of some divine force, but rather were the results of human intervention with the natural environment. [...] the critical factors explaining disasters were the ways that human-beings structured their societies and the ways that the allocated their resources. Human activities create the vulnerabilities that turn hazards into potential disasters." (Kent 1999: 293). This insight to understand disasters also in terms of social action, was also recognized nearly 75 years before:

> *Not even windstorm, earth-tremor, or rush of water is a catastrophe. A catastrophe is known by its works; that is, to say, by the occurrence of disaster. So long as the ship rides out the storm, so long as the city resists the earth-shocks, so long as the levees hold, there is no disaster. It is the collapse of the cultural protections that constitutes the disaster proper.* (Carr 1932: 211.)

Consequently, disasters can be seen as a result of human activities and not as an 'Act of God'. This in turn assumes that human societies have the capacity to recognize, control and manage the risks that could lead to disasters. Therefore, by regarding catastrophes as natural events that can be managed rather than acts of God that are responded to when necessary, it is made possible to allow for innovative development strategies to prevent or reduce the loss of life and the harm to the environment and the economy. Hence, concern with disasters (as with risk) is rather a sign of man's power than of his impotence.

There is a bulk of definitions of natural disasters from different organizations and institutions. As a rule, the impacts of a disaster are the guidelines for the various definitions. They can be split up into three categories: social, environmental, and economic effects (Mechler 2004a: 13) which can be further subdivided into direct and indirect effects (see figure 2.1). These effects implicitly constitute, in one way or the other, the various definitions of a natural disaster in the literature.

Social effects include the loss of life, people affected (people who need immediate assistance; displaced or evacuated people) and psychological post-disaster effects (e.g. traumatas). Secondary social effects include e.g. disruptions of the continuity of the structures and of the social processes as a whole. The ecological effects due to disasters include the loss of arable land, forests and damages to the ecosystem. The economic effects are normally grouped into three categories: direct, indirect, and macroeconomic (secondary) effects which also can be seen as stock and flow effects (Burby 1991: 64). In recent years flow losses become superior to stock losses in the damage estimation process due to the incorporation of the time dimension:

> *Attention to flow losses represents a major shift in the focus of hazard loss estimation - that losses are not a definite or set amount but are highly variable depending on the length of the "economic disruption" [...] This brings home the point that disaster losses are not simply determined by the strength of the stimulus [...] but also highly dependent on human ingenuity, will, and resources.* (Rose 2004: 19-20.)

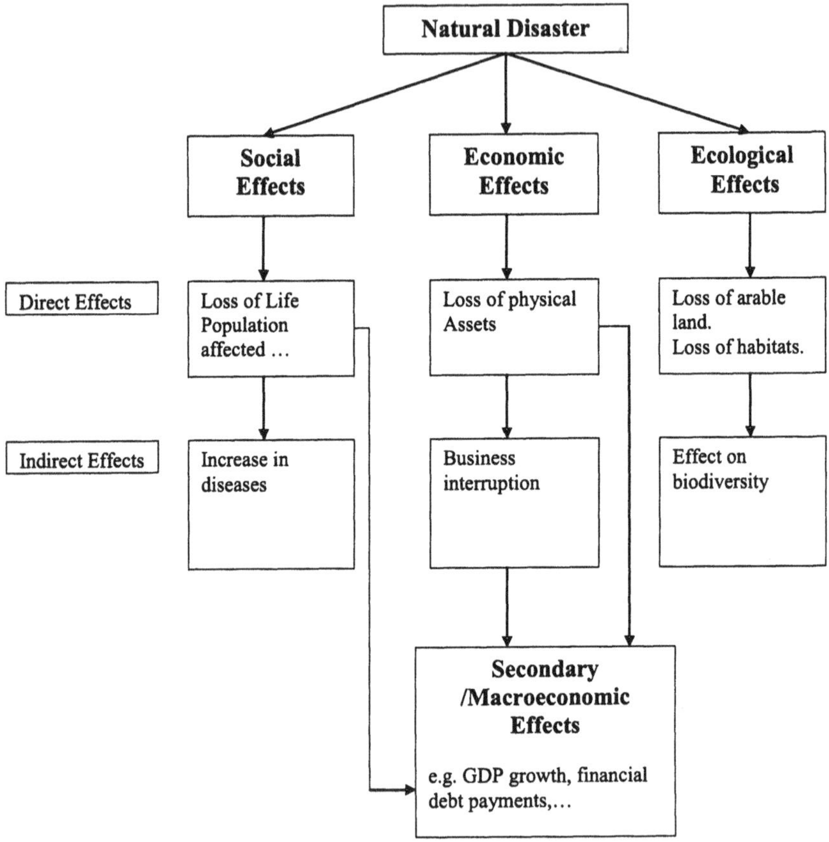

Figure 2.1: Possible effects of natural disasters. Source: Adapted from Mechler 2004a.

The direct losses, such as physical damage to infrastructure, buildings or agricultural assets due to the catastrophic event are roughly equal to stock impacts caused by the disaster itself or via consequential physical destruction. The direct stock losses have impacts on the flow of goods and services, e.g. business interruption. The macroeconomic impacts summarize the aggregate impacts on economic variables (GDP, consumption, inflation, trade, investment) due to the effects of disasters and reallocation of government resources to relief and reconstruction efforts. Table 2.1 shows some of the environmental and social effects of various sorts of natural disasters. The economic and macroeconomic effects are thoroughly investigated in chapter 3.

Type of Disaster	Physical environment effects	Social effects (immediate)
Volcanic eruptions	Air pollution from gas emissions; Changes to course of rivers, beach erosion and coastline alterations; Rubble and mud flows caused by snow and ice or by collapse of volcano walls; Contamination of water bodies; Fires; Earthquakes and tidal waves.	Loss of housing; Panic; Social disorder; Interruption of transport and communication systems.
Earthquakes	Land and mudslides on mountains, cliffs and coastal bluffs due to effects of vibration; Large land movements on hillsides with high water table saturation; these can lead to damming and alter the course of waterways developments that can produce further avalanches; Elevation or subsidence from earthquakes; Environmental damage from effects on basic service infrastructure, such as water, electricity, gas hydrocarbons.	Loss of housing; Interruption of transport and communications systems; Panic; Social disorder.
Floods	Erosion, soil destabilization and landslides; Sedimentation and washing of rubble and detritus into adjoining lands and bodies of water; Possible damming and subsequent avalanches; Contamination due to spills of water and sewage treatment tanks and the collapse of sewer and plumbing systems.	Temporary or permanent migration; Loss of housing, Interruption of transport and communication system.
Hurricanes and Cyclones	Coastal erosion, changes to the granulometry of beaches and bathymetric changes brought on by tides and oceanic turbulence; Changes to geographic characteristics; Erosion, landslides and avalanches caused by rains; Intrusion of salt water into surface and subsurface bodies of water.	Loss of housing; Interruption of communication systems; Panic; Social disorder.

Table 2.1: Environmental and social effects of natural disasters. Source: ECLAC 2003, Cuny 1983.

Given the three main categories, social, economic and environmental effects, as indicated above, there are several possibilities how a disaster can be defined. The World Bank defines an emergency as an "extraordinary event of limited duration or a natural disaster" that "seriously dislocates a country's economy" (World Bank 1995: 1). Hence, the focus lies on the economic impacts of a disaster. The definition promoted by the World Health Organization concentrates more on the human aspects of a catastrophe. For them a disaster is any occurrence that causes damage, ecological disruption, loss of human life, or deterioration of health and health services on a scale sufficient to warrant an extraordinary response from outside the affected community or area. The working definition at the beginning of the International Decade for Natural Disaster Reduction (IDNDR) by the United Nations was "A serious disruption of the functioning of society, causing widespread human, material or environmental losses which exceed the ability of the affected people to cope using only its own resources." (IDNDR 1992: 21). Another widely used formulation goes back to Fritz (1961: 655). According to him, a disaster is "an event, concentrated in time and space, in which a society, or a relatively self-sufficient subdivision of a society, undergoes severe danger and incurs such losses to its members and physical appurtenances that the social structure is disrupted and the fulfillment of all or some of the essential functions of the society is prevented". There are also more formal definitions in which cases a outcome is called a catastrophe, usually utility concepts are involved there. For example, Peterson (2002: 528) defines a catastrophe as an "outcome of an act for which the utility is very low". As these few quotations indicate, the exceedance of the impacts above a given level (in a given dimension) is used to determine if the hazard caused a disaster. If the impacts are below this level, the event is usually called an emergency or a crisis. The definitions above implicitly refer to vulnerability and resilience. However, there is no conceptual and operational framework how this exceedance level can be measured. Sometimes indicators are used to determine if a disaster has happened. Smith (1996: 29) for example used the following indicators:

- Number of deaths per event - 100 or more.
- Significant damage - economic damage in excess of 1 percent of total annual GNP.
- Affected people - more than 1 percent of an impacted country's population harmed.

However, these numbers can differ from athor to author and institution to institution. For example, for a disaster to be entered into the EM-DAT database at least one of the following criteria must be fulfilled:

- Ten or more people reported killed.
- 100 people affected.
- Declaration of a state of emergency.
- Call for international assistance.

Such indicators can sometimes be useful for categorization issues but they do not reflect the complex situations and consequences which arise due to disasters. Specifically, absolute numbers of the effects of natural hazards are always a little bit misleading. For example, it is well known that natural events are causing more damage in absolute terms in developed than in developing countries because more property of higher value can be damaged. However, it was recognized more than 20 years ago that losses in relative terms (GNP) were 20 times higher in developing than in developed countries (Funaro-Curtis 1983). Hence, relative rather than absolute indicators should be used (if possible) when different disaster situations, responses and consequences are analyzed and compared. Next, an integrated approach of disaster risk management on the country level against natural disaster is presented, where the definition of a disaster is given by quantifiable variables, e.g. the occurrence of a financing gap.

2.4 An integrated risk management approach

In the past, risk management was rarely undertaken in a systematic and integrated fashion due to the enormous amount of information and complexity of the system (e.g. firms) under consideration (Meulbroek 2002). Today, integrated risk management is rapidly becoming the technique of choice by virtue of its many tried and tested attributes for bringing science, technology, and policy into confluence (Gopalakrishnan and Okada 2003). By applying integrated risk management one can benefit from new insights into the interrelation of financial decisions which are missed without a comprehensive framework. However, because benefits and costs of risk management vary for different cases, e.g. firms, the framework must be flexible enough to incorporate such differences.

In this thesis an integrated risk management approach against natural disasters for governments as the decision maker is presented. Therefore, public sector risk is the main focus here. However, the model is capable of extending the focus in order to include the private sector. The approach is flexible enough so that the studying of risk management strategies for different countries is possible (see chapter 7 and the appendix). The public sector (infrastructure), especially in developing countries, can be seen as an important factor for economic development (World Bank 1994, Calderón and Servén 2004b), poverty reduction (Fay and Morrison 2005) and the improvement of market functioning and therefore private sector activity (Meier and Rauch 2005). In the case of a natural disaster the government is responsible for repairing damaged infrastructure and providing financial assistance to households and businesses (see section 4.3.1). However, this can cause a significant drain on the budget especially in developing and transition countries. Furthermore, there is the possibility of a financing gap, which can be defined as the amount of funds lacking to repair and finance all losses the government is responsible for.[12] This situation has happened repeatedly in the past, prompting financial development organizations, such as the World Bank, to call for greater attention in reducing the financial vulnerability of the public sector (Pollner 2001, Gurenko 2004). Because of the importance of the public sector in developing countries such a financing gap can have serious consequences on long term development goals, e.g. economic growth, poverty reduction,

[12]Shortly: The shortfall between financial sources and obligations.

sustainable development. During the last years various advanced model approaches were developed to study these effects (Mechler 2004a, Freeman et al. 2004). However, a unified risk management approach and model was still missing. The following approach should fill this gap. It is used for analyzing and managing the (financial) macroeconomic risk and the financial vulnerability due to natural disasters for the public sector on the country level. While here the overall concept is introduced, the modeling and detailed discussion is done in chapter 5 and chapter 6 respectively.

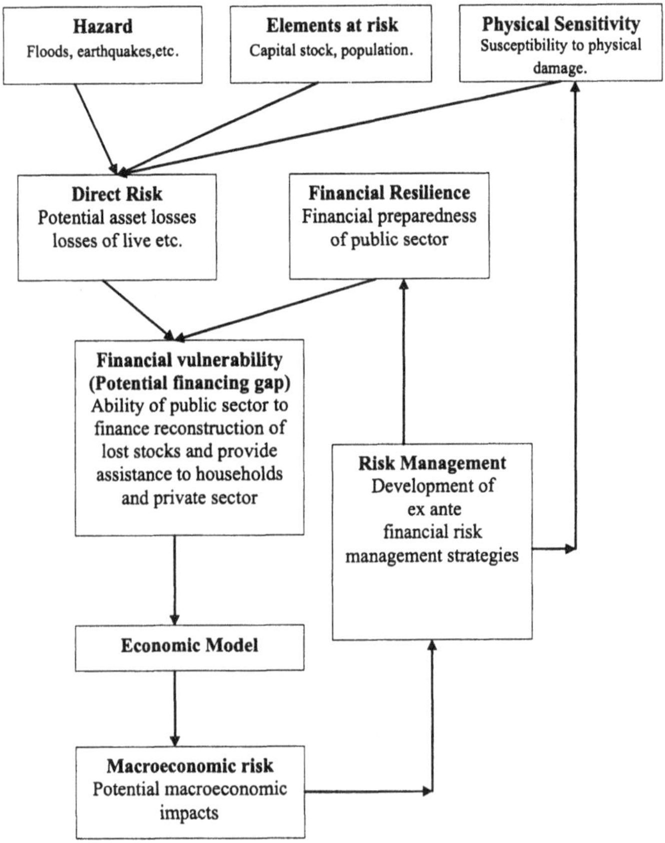

Figure 2.2: Macroeconomic risk management approach. Source: Adapted from Mechler, Hochrainer, Bayer and Pflug 2006.

As figure 2.2 shows[13] 'hazard', 'elements at risk' and 'physical susceptibility'[14] are determining the **Direct Risk**. The direct risks of potential asset losses are defined with

[13]The concept was built by four persons in the Risk and Vulnerability, formally known Risk, Modeling and Society, group in IIASA, see also Mechler, Hochrainer, Bayer and Pflug 2006.

[14]Which also could be called physical vulnerability but would intercept with the word financial vulnerability.

loss distribution functions (see section 6.3.1) describing the probability of specified losses occurring, e.g. a 50 year-event causes a loss of 70 million US$ of public assets, a 100-year event causes losses of 300 million US$ of public assets, and so on. The **financial vulnerability** is determined by the **financial resilience** of the public sector, e.g. the amount of ex-post measures and/or already committed ex-ante measures that can be used to finance the losses caused by the disaster (see chapter 5). Financial resilience depends in turn, on the economic conditions of the country. Therefore, direct risk and financial resilience combined gives the financial vulnerability of the public sector, e.g. the ability to compensate the losses the government is responsible for. The inability of the government to finance the losses results in a **financing gap** which can have serious impacts on the economy. Through an economic model the consequences on macroeconomic variables are calculated over a given period of time (e.g. 10 years). This indicators represent consequences to economic flows while the direct risk represents the consequences to stocks. Risk management strategies can then be developed and evaluated to strengthen the financial resilience and, therefore, to lessen the **macroeconomic risk** due to natural disasters on the public sector. The ex-ante measures were called financial, however, also structural mitigation measures were included for two reasons: first, mitigation is important by itself because it also saves lives and, therefore, has a new dimension decision makers want to incorporate. Second, mitigation can be coupled with insurance and the effects of mitigation on insurance premiums and the insurer can be complementary (e.g. see Kunreuther 1996, Kunreuther 1997, Kleindorfer and Kunreuther 1999). Therefore, mitigation which is actually a structural measure, is seen here also as an ex-ante option.

Figure 2.2 shows the overall concept of the risk management approach presented in this thesis. However, such an approach, while useful in its own terms for a better and more consistent understanding of the complex relationship between the various elements, is virtually useless for scientific and applied system analyses if those elements can not be operationalized. Hence, a modeling approach is needed. However, a detailed analysis of the various terms mentioned above has to be done first to incorporate all important issues for the modeling part. But before, because the main focus of this thesis is on the macroeconomic consequences due to a natural disaster, a literature review and additionally a statistical analysis to study some overall long term effects which clarify some important issues in this context is done.

Chapter 3

Economic impacts - Statistical analysis

Section 2.3 already presented an introduction to the overall social and environmental consequences of natural disasters. It was noted there, that the economic effects need a more thorough analysis due to the complexity of the topic and the importance for the risk management and modeling approach. Here, a number of issues and open questions about macroeconomic consequences due to natural disasters in the short and in the long term (until 4 years after the disaster) are statistically investigated using a sample of disaster events between 1960 and 2000. The chapter starts by grouping economic effects into three categories: Direct, indirect and macroeconomic effects[1](ECLAC 2003: (1)9ff, Charvériat 2000: 13ff, Rose 2004: 16f, Mechler 2004a: 31ff).

Direct damages comprise all damages to immovable assets and on stock (including final goods, goods in process, raw materials and spare parts). In the essence, direct damages occur right at the time of the actual disaster itself or by aftermath physical destruction. According to ECLAC (2003: (1)11) direct damages include the total or partial destruction of physical infrastructure, buildings, installations, machinery equipment, means of transportation and storage, furniture, damage to farmland, irrigation works and reservoirs. Direct losses are estimated post-event by institutions on the local, national or even multinational level and also by insurance companies like Munich Re and Swiss Re. There are four main sources for information on direct losses. The EM-DAT database from the Centre for the Epidemiology of Disasters (CRED) of the University Catholique de Louvain in Brussels, where also information about the type of event, event magnitude, fatalities, people affected etc. were collected on a worldwide basis dating back to 1900. The two biggest reinsurer Munich Re and Swiss Re (Swiss Re 2004a: 19) which are annually publishing data on the worldwide direct economic and insured losses and finally, ECLAC, the Economic Commission for Latin America, which has been estimating the impacts of natural disasters in Latin America and the Caribbean since 1972.

Indirect damages occur as a consequence of the direct stock losses. They refer to the loss of potential production and wage losses due to the disturbed flow of goods and

[1]Macroeconomic effects are also called secondary effects (Benson and Clay 2000: 12, Murlidharan and Shah 2003: 21f)

services, lost production capacities, increased costs of production as well as loss of future harvest and industrial output. Indirect damages can be difficult to estimate, due to the "knock-on" effects, e.g. the disruption of telecommunications or water supply can have far-reaching implications (Benson and Clay 2000:12). They continue to occur until reconstruction is completed and the entire capacity is restored, which can take several years. Some indirect damages maybe less tangible but can also have serious economic consequences, e.g. destruction of school infrastructure (Martelli et al. 2004). Indirect losses are harder to identify and measure and no standard assessment framework exists. Nevertheless, for developing countries, the main source is ECLAC.

The **macroeconomic impacts** comprise the aggregate impacts on economic variables, e.g. gross domestic product, consumption, inflation, indebtedness, reallocation of government resources for relief and reconstruction (Mechler 2004a: 36). The macroeconomic impacts concern both the short- and long-term impacts on overall economic performance. However, the net effect on macroeconomic variables of a disaster is the final outcome of direct and indirect effects and cannot be added up without causing duplication (Rose 2004: 15, ECLAC 2003: (4)71, Otero and Marti 1995: 16-18). Furthermore, the positive and negative effects on macroeconomic performance measures cannot be quantified directly (Albala-Bertrand 1993a: 57ff).

The next section investigates some global loss statistics in the context of natural disasters. In section 3.2 a literature review of empirical studies on macroeconomic effects are presented. Afterwards in section 3.3 a sample of 85 disaster events in 45 countries between 1960 and 2000 is presented. All of these disaster events have a loss to GDP ratio higher than 1 percent and no disaster event has happened four years before and after the event. The methodology used for the analysis is presented in section 3.4 while the results are presented in section 3.5.

3.1 Statistics of losses

Between 1980 and 2004 more than 15400 number of loss events caused by natural disasters occurred. 46 percent of these events happened in high income countries, while 35 percent and 18 percent happened in middle and low income countries, respectively. The total death toll in this time period amounts to more than 1 million, whereas only 6 percent happened in the high income countries and 35 percent and 59 percent occurred in the middle and low income countries (Munich Re NatCatSERVICE 2005). The worst catastrophe in terms of victims in this time period was the tsunami on 26 December 2004 which hit twelve coastal states on the Indian Ocean (Swiss Re 2005a: 35). The number of dead and missing persons are at least 280 000 (January 2005), however, the precise number will probably never be known (Swiss Re 2005a: 3). According to Munich Re (2005b: 9) 2004 was the costliest natural catastrophe year so far in insurance history, whereas the most expensive losses were those caused by hurricanes in the Caribbean and the United States and typhoons in Japan. Natural disasters in 2004 caused directly attributable financial losses totalling more than 145 billion USD (2003: 60 billion USD)(Munich Re 2005b: 2). Due to the high concentration of property assets in the industrialized nations, the major part of these losses occurred there. The estimate for the overall losses directly attributable to the December tsunami appears with a value of 14 billion USD rather moderate (Swiss Re 2005a: 5). This can be explained by the low level of property values in the economies affected. Insured losses rose to 44 billion USD (previous year: 15 billion USD) (Munich Re 2005b: 2) whereas annual average lies around 23 billion USD(Swiss Re 2005a: 6). A discrepancy can be found between the developed and developing countries by the numbers of fatalities and the insured losses in 2004: While 96 percent of the fatalities due to catastrophes happened in Asia (290.412 Victims, 24.9 percent of losses insured), 68 percent of the insured losses are in North America (with only 7342 Victims or 2.4 percent) (Swiss Re 2005a: 7). This is not an exceptional case. Using again a timeframe between 1980 and 2004 the average losses per GDP were quite different for high, middle and low income countries. According to figure 3.1, the losses in percent of GDP are more than 4 times higher in low income countries than in high income countries. As the above numbers suggest, the lack of capacity to limit the impact of hazards still remains a major burden for developing countries, where over 90 percent of natural disaster fatalities occur (UNISDR 2004: 45) and 2 percent (on average) of the population each year are affected due to natural disasters (Rasmussen 2004: 4).

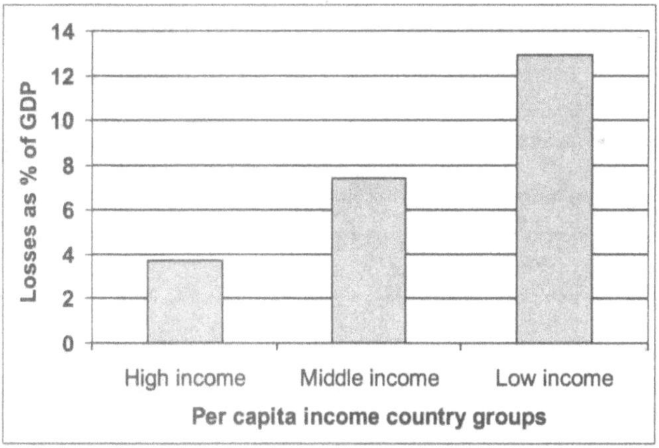

Figure 3.1: Average loss per GDP vs. income country groups (according to World Bank classification using GNI per Capita). Source: Munich Re NatCatSERVICE 2005.

One of the major questions today is, if there is a long-term trend of increasing natural disaster events. As figure 3.2 indicates there seems to be a clear upward trend. However, the question remains *why* there is a increase of natural disasters? No easy answer has been found, but there is evidence that the increase of vulnerable elements (human or property) in high risk areas is one of the major factors contributing to this increase.

Furthermore, there seems to be an increase in the frequency and intensity of extreme natural events. Such increase is generally thought to be associated with the rise of the global surface temperatures (Munich Re 2005a). Broadly speaking, the increased losses both in human and economic terms can be attributed to the interaction of several variables (Miller and Keipi 2005) including: (i) the location of geophysical phenomena; (ii) the increased population growth and human activity in disaster-prone areas; (iii) the low use of mitigation and preventive measures; (iv) regional underdevelopment (v) limited government available resources (vi) environmental degradation and unsustainable land use policies. Furthermore, there is the possibility that development paths are themselves exacerbating the problem by influencing in a negative way all points above (excluding (i)).

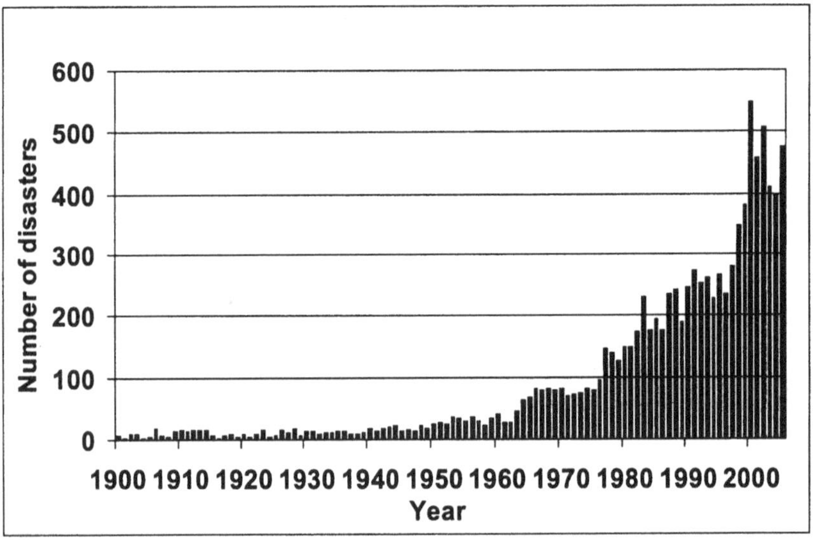

Figure 3.2: Total number of natural disasters reported: 1900-2005. Source: EM-DAT 2006.

As already said also large reinsurance companies have their own databases to assess long term loss trends. For example Munich Re, apart from time serious analysis, compared different decades and found evidences that losses are increasing (table 3.1). For example a comparison of the last ten years with the 1960s reveals a dramatic increase. While the numbers of events more than doubled, the economic losses are now 7 times higher and the insured losses 15 times higher than in the 1960s. A trend towards higher catastrophe losses has emerged since the late 1980s. Between 1987 and 2002 the average annual insured loss in property insurance caused by natural catastrophes was 14.1 billion USD (Swiss Re 2004b: 9). This increase can, for the most part, be explained by economic, demographic and geographical factors. Specifically in industrialized countries between 1970 and 2003

Decade	1950-59	1960-69	1970-79	1980-89	1990-99	Last 10 years
Number of events	20	27	47	63	91	63
Economic losses[2]	44.9	80.5	147.6	228.0	703.6	566.8
Insured losses	-	6.5	13.7	28.8	132.2	101.7

Table 3.1: Comparison of aggregate economic losses of decades. Source: Munich Re 2005b.

there was a rapid rise in insured values, such as residential, industrial and office buildings (Swiss Re 2004b: 13) and exposed elements at risk.

3.2 Macroeconomic effects: A literature review

Natural disasters can have serious impacts on the overall economic performance of a country (e.g. negative effects on growth levels, the balance of payments or the level of indebtedness). Most of the time the specific disaster has to hit the country with a sufficient magnitude (e.g. the loss ratio to GDP has to be at least over say, 1 percent for a small country) to have an impact on performance measures, but sometimes, if the main economic activity is hit, also a small loss in a larger country can affect the macroeconomic performance. For example, in 1987 an earthquake destroyed the most important oil pipe in Ecuador (loss ratio to GDP of 1.8 percent), cutting down the oil exports for several months (Albala-Bertrand 1993b: 1419). However, such situations are rather rare.

Since the early studies on economic impacts in developed countries no aggregate macroeconomic short or long run effects were found (see for example Burby 1991, Rossi et al. 1978) and the literature focuses generally on direct and indirect impacts and regional economies (Mechler 2004a: 36). The study of macroeconomic effects caused by natural disasters can therefore be restricted to developing countries. However, since the rapid increase in losses of mega-disasters in developed countries (like Hurricane Katrina in the U.S.) it is also likely that this topic will be more prominent in the near future there too. Therefore, the risk management and modeling approach presented here is capable of addressing such problems for both, the developed and developing countries.

A disaster will affect different sectors in varying degrees and thus will be reflected in the macroeconomic performance of the country's economy. Table 3.2 illustrates some potential impacts of a disaster event and its possible timeframe.

Empirical research on macroeconomic effects caused by natural disasters was done mainly for developing countries. The focus there was not only on significant short term and medium term effects but also on long term effects, e.g. economic growth, develop-

Macroeconomic Indicator	Expected change
GDP	Immediate drop in GDP growth in the year of the event. Rise in GDP growth in the year after the event. Slow down in second and/or third year.
Agricultural Sector	Significant fall in production (if hurricane, flood or drought).
Manufacture Sector	Decrease in activity due to disruption of transportation, reduced production capacities.
Service Sector	Decrease due to disruption of transportation and payment system.
Exports of goods	Reduction in the rate of growth in the year of the event. In the year after return to previous levels. In subsequent years continuation of the year after.
Imports of goods	Considerable increase in rate of growth in the event year. A return to pre disaster level a year after. In subsequent years a further drop, possibly caused by reduced incomes.
Gross Formation of Fixed Capital	Sharp increase in the year following the disaster.
Inflation rate	Short increase caused by the disruption of production and distribution and increasing transportation costs.
Public finances	Worsening of deficit due to a shortfall in tax revenues and increase in public expenditures.
Trade balance	Deficit due to decrease in exports and increase in imports, associated with the decline in production capacities and strong public and private investment for reconstruction.

Table 3.2: Effects of disasters on macroeconomic indicators. Adapted from Otero and Marti 1995, Charvériat 2000:16 and ECLAC 2003: (4)75.

ment and poverty (Benson and Clay 2004: 1). The findings of these empirical studies are presented below.

Benson and Clay published 2004 a synthesis report of a country case study approach for exploring economywide disaster impacts, including work on drought in Sub-Saharan Africa (Benson and Clay 1998, Clay et al. 1995, Thomson, Jenden, and Clay 1998), countries in the Asia and Pacific and Caribbean countries, including Fiji (Benson 1997a), the Philippines (Benson 1997b), Vietnam (Benson 1997c), Zimbabwe (Benson 1998) and Monserrat (Clay et al. 1999) as well as Bangladesh, Dominica and Malawi. They found that major natural disasters can, and do, have severe negative short run impacts (e.g. the fall of GDP and tax revenue, an increasing fiscal deficit due to the spending for relief and reconstruction, higher trade deficit, because of a reduction of exports and an increase of imports). They also found negative long term consequences for economic growth, development and poverty reduction if the disasters occur frequently, although these effects are difficult to isolate and quantify. They emphasize that the two broad categories of hazard - hydrometeorological and geological - are associated with distinct patterns and forms of economic vulnerability. Furthermore, they see the economic vulnerability of a country to natural hazards determined by various factors which interact dynamically, including the economic structure, the stage of development and prevailing economic and policy conditions. At last, in their opinion catastrophic events can induce conscious responses that may increase an economy's resilience.

Charvériat (2000) provided empirical evidence on the impact of disasters on GDP growth. She analyzed 35 disaster cases between 1980 and 1996 in 20 Latin American and Caribbean countries, whereas all disaster situations had a loss-to-output ratio superior to 1%. 28 cases out of 35 have shown a growth deceleration in the year of the disaster. Interestingly, in 5 of the 7 cases in which the GDP growth accelerated, the loss to GDP ratio was inferior to 5%. The growth rates accelerated during the two years following the disaster in 30 cases and 21 cases respectively(Charvériat 2000: 18).

Crowards (1999) found similar results. He studied 22 cases of hurricanes occurring between 1970 and 1997 in Caribbean Development Bank's borrowing member countries and found that GDP growth slowed down by 3% on average in the year of the disaster and rebounded by 3% in the subsequent years (however, looking at the median would yield probable different results because of they wide deviation of the average). He found also that exports are reduced by 9% in the year of the disaster while imports increased by 8.2% and therefore caused a substantial increase in the trade deficit. No patterns in the variation of government expenditures were found, but because of the increase in external debt during the disaster, it could be argued that this is caused due to emergency borrowing. He also did not find any response of consumer prices due to the disaster event.

Murlidharan and Shah (2003) concentrated on post-1970 catastrophic events and analyzed 169 events. They used extensively the annual loss as percent of GDP for their investigations. They found negative correlations of the loss with the post event economic growth, negative impacts on inflation, interest rates and savings. However, their empirical findings were based on regression analysis and the results had most of the time small R^2 values, but on the other hand the main directions of changes in economic performance measures were found to be as the literature before predicted, and therefore strengthened these hypothesis.

Otero and Marti (1995) analyzed macroeconomic effects of natural disasters in some Latin America and Caribbean regions. They found similar results on the macroeconomic effects as in the other case studies above, e.g. a decrease in GDP growth, an increase in the fiscal deficit, and increase in the balance of payments deficit.

Rasmussen (2004) provides some overall cross-country comparisons of natural disaster incidences between 1970-2002. He also investigates the short and medium term macroecomic impacts of 12 natural disasters in the ECCU (Eastern Caribeean Currency Union) since 1970. He founds a median reduction of the GDP growth in the event year of 2.2 percentage points, as well as with a large decline in agricultural production and an offsetting increase in investment. The exports declined and imports increased, which resulted in a staggering median increase in the current account deficit equal to 10.8 percent of GDP. The impacts on the government included a increase in expenditure and a small reduction in total revenue as well as and median public debt-to-GDP ratio increase by a cumulative 6.5 percentage points over three years. However, because of the small sample size no formal statistical analysis was done.

Auffret (2003) analyzed the impact of natural disasters on macroeconomic variables for a sample of 16 countries, where 6 came from the Caribbean region and 10 from Latin America. The impact of the disaster on macroeconomic variables was estimated using dynamic panel data models which were based on the generalized methods of moments. The author found a fall in output consumption and investment growth as well as a fall in private consumption growth and a more moderate decline in public consumption growth.

Albala-Betrand (1993a) analyzed 28 disaster situations in 26 different countries from the period 1960-1979. He comes to very different conclusions than the rest of the literature, and therefore he started fruitful discussions about some assumptions and some estimating issues in the literature. However, his findings were relativized theoreticaly by various other authors (e.g. Benson and Clay 2004: 21f, Mechler 2004a: 38f) and empirically by the results presented in section 3.5.

Taken into account that the empirical literature has found negative effects of disasters on the macroeconomic performance of a country, it is also necessary to look at the elements that determine the (economic) vulnerability. The current (different) views on this issue in the literature are therefore summarized below and some of the indicators presented here will be needed for the empirical investigation of the sample presented in the next section.

Unfortunately, there are no predetermined patterns as to the consequences of different disasters, rather the resulting pattern of effects is determined by the combination of many factors, including the economic situation prevailing in the country before the event, the productive structure of the country, the extent of damages sustained, the severity of the disaster's consequences, the time of the occurrence, the very nature of the phenomenon, the institutional reactions, the reconstruction phase, the indebtedness level before the disaster and so on. Hence, the vulnerability of an economy to natural hazards depends on a complex set of influences. However, some main factors which contribute to macroeconomic vulnerability can be determined (Benson and Clay 2004: 15ff, Pelling et al. 2002,

Benson and Clay 2000: 11ff, Charvériat 2000, Otero and Marti 1995): The type of natural hazard, the economic structure, the geographical area and scale of impact, the stage of development and the prevailing socioeconomic conditions.

1. **The type of natural hazard**

   The economic vulnerability differ for two broad types of hazard: 'Hydro- meteorological Hazards' (e.g. severe flooding, tropical cyclones and hurricanes) and 'Geophysical Hazards' (e.g. earthquakes, volcanic eruption). Severe flooding is likely to damage infrastructure and productivity capacity as well as directly reduce output due to the disruption of the economic and social activity and the destruction of standing crops. Tropical cyclones and hurricanes have devastating impacts on a productive economy. The impacts may be less widespread than those of drought or flooding, but can also destroy and disrupt whole regions. They likely have localized impacts in larger economies but can be overwhelmingly devastating in smaller economies. Earthquakes are more localized impacts and have the greatest risk of macroeconomic consequences if they occur in a major urban center or in the metropolis. Volcanic eruptions and tsunamis usually have localized direct impacts. Table 3.3 shows some immediate economic and social effects for different natural disaster types.

Type of Effect	Earthquake	Volcano	Flood	Tsunami
Loss of Industrial Production	x		x	x
Loss Business Production	x		x	x
Loss of Agricultural Production (plant crops and harvest)		x	x	x
Damage to Infrastructure	x		x	x
Disruption of Marketing Systems	x	x		
Disruption of Transport	x		x	

Table 3.3: Type of hazard vs. economic effects. Source: Adapted from Cuny 1983: 48.

   Major differences are between earthquake and flood impacts. As one can see earthquakes affect constructions (factories, public and social buildings), roads, bridges and underground structures, but causing only minimal damages to agriculture, while floods do minor damage to structures and lifelines, but heavily impact agriculture. However, these general statements must be viewed with caution and depend on various other factors, e.g. intensity, location.

2. **Overall structure of the economy**

   Stated in broad terms, the interaction between the type of natural hazard risk to which a country is exposed to and the basic structure of its economy at a particular moment in time plays a significant role in determining broader macroeconomic vulnerability. For example, the case studies from Benson and Clay (2004: 18f) for Dominica and Bangladesh showed how reductions in broad macroeconomic vulnerability are related to structural change, specifically, to a relative decline in agriculture which is commonly the most vulnerable sector. For example, Antigua, a small country which is dependent upon agriculture and tourism (two productive sectors with high vulnerability to disasters) had losses of about 66% of GDP due to Hurricane Luis in 1995 (Gibbs 1997). Countries with a large informal sector are likely to suffer more because they are poorly covered by insurance and reconstruction assistance and have limited access to private financing. In the case of countries with a large capital-intensive extractive sector which features significantly in the trade account, but which is only weakly linked with other sectors of the economy, the economic impact of a disaster will differ significantly depending on whether the extractive sector is affected or not. Also the composition of the manufacturing and service sectors are important in determining (economic) vulnerability.

3. **Geographical area and scale of impact**

   Natural disasters will have stronger impacts on a country's economic performance if the size of the damages *compared* with the size of the economy is high. Therefore, most of the time loss as a share of GDP is used to illustrate the scale of impact on a country's economy, because this makes it much easier to compare the impact of a disaster on an economy as absolute values of losses would do. Obviously, smaller countries are more likely to experience a sharp decrease in GDP in the short term, as there loss-to-output ratios are substantially higher on average. Therefore, a distinction between very small countries, where the hazard impact may be economywide, medium sized countries, where substantial areas can be directly affected and larger countries that only experience disasters in geographically limited areas should be drawn (Benson and Clay 2004: 22). Localized disasters tend to produce only limited aggregate impacts.

4. **Stage of development**

   The stage of development of an economy is also related to its economic vulnerability to natural disasters. Factors which can be seen as measures of economic development are the degree of sectoral, geographical and financial integration, levels of economic specialization and government revenue raising capabilities. Even though least developed economies are perceived as most vulnerable, economic development per se may not reduce vulnerability (Anderson 1995: 52, Benson and Clay 2004: 18). For example, the following factors can also be associated with an *increase* in vulnerability: The transformations of resources (e.g. nonrenewable), effluent production, production of dangerous substances and invention of dangerous techniques, population growth, the use of marginal land and urbanization (Anderson 1995). Interestingly, an economy at an intermediate stage of development is sometimes more vulnerable than in here less developed times, because in the former the economy is typically more integrated, sectorally and geographically, than the later one, which increases the multiplier effects of adverse performance in a particular sector or region. Also, due to the breakdown of traditional coping mechanisms (e.g. familial support, community, replacement of more hazard tolerant traditional crops with cultivation of cash crops) vulnerability increases, till other forms of coping mechanisms are available (e.g. insurance). However, in the later stages of development, due to the decline of the share in GDP of the particularly hazard vulnerable agricultural sector, and its decreasing importance as a source of employment, the relative scale of the economic impacts of disasters is likely to decline.

5. **Prevailing socioeconomic conditions**

   These summarizes other factors which can be both coincidental and deliberate, offset or amplify the economic impacts of a natural disaster, wether explicitly or implicitly. For example, countries which already experienced other adverse economic shocks are typically more vulnerable. The external policy environment, to the extent that it influences the pattern of productive activities, can also affect vulnerability. Other factors, like domestic macroeconomic and sectoral policies, as well as coincidental fluctuations in primary export and import prices may exacerbate or lessen the impacts of the natural hazard (Benson and Clay 2000: 15, Benson and Clay 2004: 19).

The next section presents a sample of natural disaster events which fulfill some specific requirements to ensure that the results of the statistical analysis done afterwards are reliable. It was created to (i) investigate empirically some overall (average) effects of natural disasters on macroeconomic variables, (ii) explain some of these results with indicators mentioned above, (iii) analyze if the observations made by Albala-Bertrand (1993a) also can be found in this sample (or not), and last (iv) show empirically that *long term economic development*, measured through the GDP level, can be hampered/affected negatively due to the occurrence of natural disaster events.

3.3 A sample of natural disaster events

The sample was constructed under the following considerations. Due to the fact that governments in lower income countries cannot spread their risk and/or losses from natural disasters sufficiently over the population (e.g. by taxation) and also because governments of indebted countries have limited capabilities to borrow from the outside (Mechler 2004b) which in turn means that in disaster situations, the government is less able to meet their obligations in loss financing, countries which are considered as severely/moderately/less indebted and also countries with low/lower middle/upper middle income where taken first as potential candidates (the candidates are taken from World Bank 2004). Afterwards, natural disasters in these countries between 1960 and 2000 were examined and those were taken which had economic significant damages according to Munich Re (2002) or the EM-DAT Database. The time span from 1960 until 2000 was chosen, because real world (macroeconomic) Data was needed after the disaster event occurred. The losses were calculated to 2000 USD and the loss per GDP ratios were calculated afterwards. Then, only those disaster events were taken, which had at least a 1 percent of loss per GDP ratio. With this procedure 217 disaster events were found. In the last step, only those events were taken, where no disaster events happened 4 years before and after the event, which means, only those disaster events were considered with a relative stable period (in terms of natural disaster occurrences) before and after the event was observed or in other words, no overlapping of the time horizon occurred for disaster events in the same country and no major disaster event happened four years before. Finally, all those disaster events were taken out which happened in a time period where other dramatic changes also took place, e.g. Brazil flooding in 1984 were, because of the adjustment program, exports were about double the imports; Chile earthquake in 1971 because of an almost 40 percent increase in imports of intermediate goods; the volcanic eruption in Colombia 1985 because of the structural adjustment program and the Nicaragua earthquake in 1972 because of the unusual high world prices for coffee and cotton. At the end the sample consisted of 85 disaster events in 45 countries (see table 3.4).

Table 3.4: Disaster Sample

COUNTRY	MONTH	YEAR	EVENT TYPE	LOSS as share of GDP %
Algeria	10	1980	Earthquake	28.02
Argentina	10	1985	Flood	1.48
Armenia	7	1997	Earthquake	1.83
Bahamas	8	1992	Hurricane	8.75
Bangladesh	9	1998	Flood	4.54
Bangladesh	4	1991	Cyclone	9.69
Bangladesh	8	1980	Flood	1.36
Barbados	9	1987	Hurricane	6.86
Bolivia	3	1982	Flood	19.80
Bolivia	1	1986	Flood	1.26
Bolivia	3	1992	Flood	1.63
Chile	3	1985	Earthquake	7.41
Chile	3	1965	Earthquake	1.32
China P Rep	7	1976	Earthquake	11.45
China P Rep	9	1991	Flood	3.98
China P Rep	9	1998	Flood	3.24
Colombia	11	1970	Flood	1.87
Colombia	1	1999	Earthquake	2.33
Costa Rica	12	1970	Flood	1.99
Costa Rica	2	1996	Flood	2.11
Costa Rica	4	1991	Earthquake	8.87
Dominica	8	1979	Hurricane	76.49
Dominica	10	1984	Hurricane	1.74
Dominica	9	1989	Hurricane	11.84
Dominica	9	1995	Hurricane	1.52

Dominican Rep	9	1998	Hurricane	12.08
Dominican Rep	9	1979	Hurricane	2.73
Ecuador	3	1987	Earthquake	17.28
Ecuador	11	1982	Flood	3.31
Ecuador	12	1997	Flood	1.15
Ecuador	4	1993	Flood	3.32
El Salvador	5	1965	Earthquake	2.80
Fiji	9	1972	Cyclone	7.10
Fiji	1	1985	Cyclone	4.47
Grenada	8	1980	Hurricane	5.90
Guatemala	9	1982	Flood	1.39
Guatemala	10	1998	Hurricane	4.32
Guatemala	2	1976	Earthquake	25.92
Haiti	9	1988	Hurricane	4.09
Honduras	9	1974	Hurricane	65.99
Honduras	10	1998	Hurricane	68.24
Honduras	5	1982	Tropical Storm	4.68
Honduras	9	1969	Hurricane	3.73
Honduras	11	1993	Flood	1.67
India	7	1975	Flood	1.44
India	8	1990	Storm	1.01
Indonesia	7	1976	Earthquake	1.25
Iran Islam Rep	7	1981	Earthquake	3.49
Iran Islam Rep	6	1990	Earthquake	5.90
Jamaica	8	1980	Hurricane	2.39
Jamaica	5	1991	Flood	6.62
Macedonia FRY	7	1995	Flood	12.26
Mauritius	2	1994	Cyclone	4.56
Mauritius	1	1989	Cyclone	3.03
Mexico	9	1985	Earthquake	1.55
Mozambique	1	1984	Cyclone	6.82
Nepal	8	1988	Earthquake	1.72
Nepal	8	1993	Flood	5.46
Nicaragua	5	1982	Tropical Storm	16.78
Nicaragua	10	1988	Hurricane	15.20
Nicaragua	9	1992	Earthquake	1.36
Pakistan	9	1992	Flood	2.05
Pakistan	8	1976	Flood	3.79
Panama	10	1988	Hurricane	1.23
Papua	9	1994	Vulcano	5.64

Paraguay	2	1983	Flood	2.57
Peru	1	1983	Flood	4.14
Peru	5	1970	Earthquake	7.05
Philippines	9	1995	Storm	1.23
Philippines	7	1990	Earthquake	1.51
Philippines	11	1964	Typhoon	10.93
Romania	7	1991	Flood	1.52
South Africa	9	1987	Flood	1.03
Sri Lanka	11	1978	Cyclone	3.78
Sri Lanka	6	1992	Flood	2.70
St Vincent and The Grenadines	9	1967	Tropical Storm	19.45
St.Kitts and Nevis	9	1995	Hurricane	85.42
Swaziland	1	1984	Cyclone	13.14
Thailand	8	1978	Flood	2.60
Thailand	11	1993	Flood	1.42
Thailand	1	1984	Flood	1.27
Tunisia	10	1982	Flood	1.58
Tunisia	1	1990	Flood	2.23
Tunisia	9	1969	Flood	9.41
Viet Nam	7	1996	Typhoon	1.58

3.4 Methodology

In this section the methodology and notation which is used to study the macroeconomic effects of the sample is explained. Generally speaking, time frames no longer than 5 years after the disaster are investigated in practice (ECLAC 2003: (4)72) but it should be mentioned that natural disasters can seriously hamper the economic development for longer time periods. In this analysis time frames up to 4 years after the disaster are looked at.

The impact year is denoted with t_0, the subsequent years with t_1,t_2,t_3 and t_4. The pre-disaster years are denoted with t_{-1}, t_{-2} and so on. The real growth rate in year t is denoted by $g_r(t)$. One possibility to answer the question in what way natural disaster events effect macroeconomic variables is to compare the growth rates in the pre-disaster years with that of the disaster year. Therefore the growth rates are analyzed according to the following three criteria[3]:

- **Counting criterion:** This criterion gives a first impression of the directional change of growth rates due to natural disasters. The sample is divided into two distinct

[3]The notation and methodology used for the growth rate analysis is similar to that of Albala-Bertrand (1993a). Also because the results should either support its findings or not.

groups: In the first group all cases of the sample with higher growth rates than in the year before are held, the second group contains all cases where the growth rate is lower than the year before. The number of cases in each group are compared so that some qualitative statements can be made. For comparison reasons this procedure is used for t_{-1}, t_0, t_1 and t_2. Stated differently, for each year the total number of cases in the sample with a higher growth rate than one year before, e.g. $(g_r(t-1)-g_r(t)) > 0.002$, is recorded and called 'Up'. Furthermore, the total number of cases in which a lower growth rate than one year before, e.g. $(g_r(t-1) - g_r(t)) < -0.002$, is also recorded and called 'Down'. The number of cases which cannot be attributed to one of these groups is called 'Neutral'. Also, for each group the sign of $g_r(t)$ for each case is recorded and the total number of cases with positive and negative sign is also shown for each group.

- **Average variation criterion:** While the counting criterion is used as a qualitative measure, the average variation criterion quantitatively compares the averages of the growth rates for different years. Not only the mean and standard deviation for each year is calculated, also the median is computed to account for outliers.

- **Medium and Long term criterion:** For each case in the sample, the geometric mean of the pre-disaster years and the post-disaster years are computed. Afterwards, like with the counting criterion, the cases with a higher growth rate and cases with a lower growth rate are counted and called again 'Up', 'Down' and 'Neutral' respectively. In detail, the medium term criterion compares the geometric mean of $g_r(t_{-1})$, $g_r(t_{-2})$ with the geometric mean of $g_r(t_1)$,$g_r(t_2)$, the long term criterion compares the pre disaster geometric mean of $g_r(t_{-1})$, $g_r(t_{-2})$ with the geometric mean of $g_r(t_3)$, $g_r(t_4)$.

While, the criteria explained above[4] give overall empirical results about the average effects of natural disasters to macroeconomic growth rates, the loss as a share of GDP, the type of hazard, the area of the country as well as the decade[5] when the disaster occured are used to explain some of the variation of the results (motivated by section 3.2).

Furthermore, the long term macroeconomic consequences of natural disasters are investigated by comparing the absolute values of GDP (in constant 2000 USD terms) of a country with projected values without the disaster event. Figure 3.3 shows the possible effects of a disaster on the GDP level in the future.

One can distinguish here conceptually between stock and flow effects. At the beginning the natural disaster destroyed stocks and caused indirect effects. As a consequence GDP drops in the disaster year which was already shown for the GDP growth rate and

[4]A detailed description how the tables for each criterion have to be read is given for the GDP analysis in subsection 3.5.1

[5]Because there is the possibility that the results of some decades are not indicative for another decade (see for example Charvériat 2000: 20) this variable is also introduced for separated analysis.

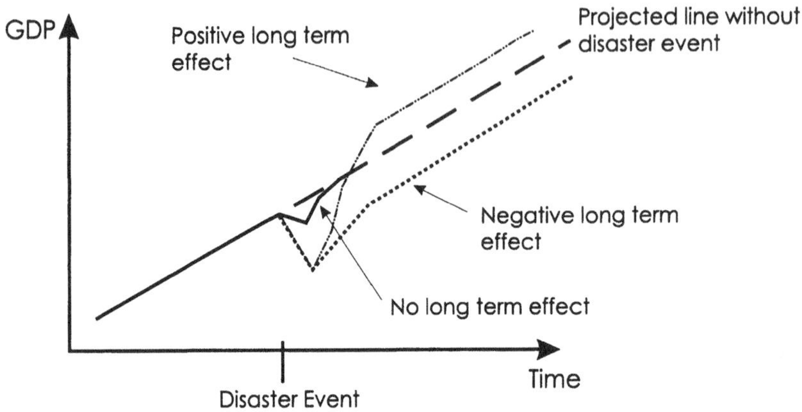

Figure 3.3: Possible trajectories of GDP after a disaster.

will be shown for the GDP level using the sample. The observation that GDP is negatively affected in the disaster year is generally accepted in the literature. Due to the lost stocks and also dependent on various factors of the countries pre-economic condition already presented in section 3.2, various flow effects can influence the pattern of the GDP performance, measured either by the growth rate or by the GDP level. In principle there are three possibilities for the GDP level. First, GDP can move back to the projected line which means the disaster had no effect on the macroeconomic variable. This can either happen shortly after the event or it could take some time. Second, GDP moves above the projected line, which means that the disaster had positive effects on the macroeconomic performance (the main protagonist of this view is Albala-Bertrand). Third, GDP moves up but stays below the projected line, which would indicate that the disaster had negative long term effects on the macroeconomic variable. Figure 3.3 is a stylized version, in reality the patterns are much more complex and more nonlinear as the figure suggests. Furthermore, positive effects on a country's economic performance due to a natural disaster are rather the exception than the rule according to the relevant literature. Be as it may, due to the construction of the sample, the following approach should give some robust average results about long term economic performance in the future in the case a disaster event has happened.

The biggest challenge is to estimate GDP in the future. The simplest approach to forecast GDP is to estimate its historical growth rate and assume that the same rate will hold in the future. A variant of this approach involves disaggregating the GDP into its major sectors whereas the projection is then a weighted sum of the sectoral forecasts derived from the historical growth rates for each of the sectors. There are also advanced techniques to project potential GDP in the future. However, such approaches are also controversial and are not feasible for large data sets. Therefore, a very simple approach is used. Because the events in the sample have a relative stable period of 4 years before the disaster, the geometric mean of these growth rates is taken for the projections four years after the event for each case. Hence, for each event in the sample the average growth rate is computed and used for the projection. The projections of absolute GDP are calculated through the formula:

$$GDP_t^i = GDP_0^i(1 + r_i)^t \qquad \begin{array}{l} i = 1, ..., 85; \\ t = 1, .., 4; \end{array}$$

where GDP_t^i is the GDP at constant 2000 USD prices at time t for case i of the sample; r_i is the growth rate of the sample event i and is kept constant for the projections; GDP_0^i is the GDP of disaster event i one year before the disaster event and t the time. The projection is done till year four. GDP is measured in constant USD for every country. For every country GDP before the year event is seen as the baseline, e.g. 100 percent. Then, increase or drop of GDP in subsequent years are measured as a percentage increase or drop to this baseline level. The difference of the percentage between the observed values and the projected values are then calculated and called $d_{po}(t)$[6]. For example, if in year four the projected percentage above the baseline would be 4 percent and the current percentage would be 3 percent, then there would be a difference of minus 1 percent between the observed and projected level. Various analysis with some indicators are performed with the data afterwards for each scenario, e.g. splitting the sample into subsamples according to indicators explained above (e.g. decade, loss per GDP, type of hazard). This method is used only for GDP because this is seen as the main indicator for economic development.

The proposed method is not used to analyze specific events in the sample, rather the average behavior is investigated. However, it is implicitly assumed that the average economic performance in the past of each case of the sample would be continued in the future if the disaster event did not occur. Because this assumption is certainly not true in general, the disaster sample was created in such a way that the above statement should hold true in the average.

3.5 Empirical analysis of macroeconomic effects

The following macroeconomic variables motivated by table 3.2 are investigated: (real) GDP growth and absolute GDP in constant 2000 USD , agriculture (real growth), production (real growth) and service (real growth), export (real growth), import (real growth), and government consumption (real growth). The macroeconomic data is taken from World Bank (2004, 2005b).

3.5.1 Gross domestic product

The GDP (real) growth rate can be seen as a main indicator of economic performance. Except of Albala Bertrand (1993a,b) the literature expects an immediate drop in the

[6]This stands for, difference of projected and observed in year t

disaster year, an acceleration one year afterwards and a slow down in the second and/or third year. As shown in table 3.5 growth decelerates in 53 cases out of 81 (65 percent) in the disaster year and accelerates in 56 cases out of 82 (68 percent) one year later. In the pre-disaster year and two years after the disaster the number of cases with increasing or decreasing growth rates is nearly equally distributed. Furthermore, from the 53 cases in the disaster year which have shown a deceleration, more than 43 percent showing a fall (e.g. a negative growth rate). This result supports the hypotheses that natural disaster events have a negative impact in the disaster year and a positive one afterwards on the growth rate.

Change[7]		t_{-1}	t_0	t_1	t_2
Up		41	28	56	40
	pos	39	23	52	38
	neg	2	5	4	2
Down		40	53	26	41
	pos	30	30	20	37
	neg	10	23	6	4
Neutral		3	4	3	4

Table 3.5: Counting criterion: GDP (real growth).

The hypotheses above is strengthened when the averages of the growth rates in the pre-disaster, disaster and post-disaster years are compared. In the disaster year a drop of the average growth rates of more than 51 percent compared with the pre-disaster year was found. As table 3.6 shows, the standard deviation is higher in the disaster year than in the other years which can explained partially by the different amount of total losses caused by the events. Therefore, also the median should be looked at. Also here, the growth rate drops down by more than 38 percent in the disaster year compared to the pre-disaster year. However, it can be noticed (see figure 3.4) that the average growth rate shows a dramatic acceleration one year afterwards back to the pre-disaster years level. In fact, the average growth rate is a little higher in the post-disaster year compared with the pre-disaster years, but this effect diminishes when the averages three year later are compared with the pre-disaster growth rates.

The findings of a positive effect on the growth rate in the medium term is supported by table 3.7. The median of the post average rates is more than 8 percent higher than in the pre-disaster year. Furthermore, 46 cases out of 78 (58 percent) are showing a higher

[7] Explanation of the table for the counting criterion: Each row of the table represents one year and is analyzed according to the specific criterion. For example, in the disaster year (t_0) 28 cases of the sample have had a higher growth rate in the disaster year compared to the growth rate one year before. 23 of this 28 cases showed a positive growth rate, while 5 cases showed a negative growth rate in the disaster year. 4 cases of the sample showed such a small difference of the growth rate between the disaster year and the year before, so that these cases were called neutral. The remaining 53 cases (which sum up to the total number of 85 cases) showed a smaller growth rate in the disaster year compared to the pre-disaster year. From this 53 cases, 30 cases showed a positive growth rate, while 23 cases showed a negative growth rate in the disaster year.

	t_{-2}	t_{-1}	t_0	t_1	t_2	t_3	$t_0/t_{-1}\%$
Mean	3.68	3.77	1.82	4.23	4.55	4.26	-51.65
Median	4.51	4.38	2.69	4.41	4.62	4.21	-38.50
Std. Dev.	4.38	4.73	5.44	4.10	3.42	3.97	

Table 3.6: Average criterion: GDP (real growth).

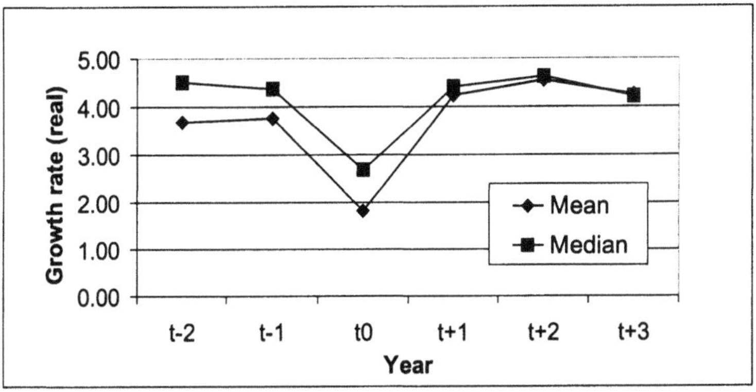

Figure 3.4: GDP (real growth), Average variation.

growth rate than in the pre-disaster year. However, for the long term, the findings are not supporting any hypothesis of a positive or negative trend. Equal number of cases show a higher or lower growth rate compared to the pre-disaster year. While the mean show a positive average trend, the median shows a negative one.

Medium Term Effects[8]			
	Pre	Post	Post/Pre
pos	70	76	
neg	14	8	
Up			46
Down			32
Neutral			6
Mean	3.70	4.37	17.95%
Median	4.27	4.65	8.71%
Std.Dev.	4.09	3.14	

Long Term Effects			
	Pre	Post	Post/Pre
pos	70	75	
neg	14	9	
Up			39
Down			39
Neutral			6
Mean	3.70	3.93	5.98%
Median	4.27	3.96	-7.30%
Std.Dev.	4.09	3.65	

Table 3.7: Medium and Long term criterion: GDP (real growth).

[8] Explanation of the table for the medium term criterion: 70 cases in the sample showed a positive geometric mean in the pre-disaster years while 14 cases showed a negative geometric mean. In the post-disaster years 76 cases in the sample showed a positive mean whereas 8 cases showed a negative one (1 case is missing due to missing values). If the geometric mean of the pre-disaster years is compared with the geometric mean in the post-disaster years (here year t_1 and t_2) for each case 46 cases of the

One interesting question is, if there can be found a trend of negative or positive long term economic development, when the method explained in section 3.4 is used, e.g. projecting the GDP (measured in constant 2000 USD) four years into the future, by using average GDP growth rates 4 years before the event and comparing this values with the real GDP levels. As mentioned above, while this method is very rough, the sample was chosen under restrictions which lessens the impacts of this estimation process and it should be feasible to find some general results.

Table 3.8 shows the overall results of the proposed method. The mean and median are showing for all years a negative value, indicating that the observed values are less than the projected ones (in the average). However, the standard deviation is high and gets even higher in the future which means that around the average behavior the cases vary widely. Also the skewness and the kurtosis, as well as histograms suggesting the view that the average results are showing a too mixed picture for a general statement yet. A usual procedure is to use the loss as a share of GDP as a impact indicator on a countries economy. Furthermore, the land area of a country should also be incorporated. Last but not least, also the type of hazard can have explanatory power.

Year	Median	Mean	Std. Dev.	Skewness	Kurtosis
Event	-1.42	-2.08	5.2	-0.392	0.833
+1	-1.07	-1.57	8.57	0.498	3.692
+2	-0.76	-0.8	12.54	0.838	5.383
+3	-0.33	-0.58	17.65	0.094	4.879
+4	-1.9	-1.19	23.13	-0.429	5.805

Table 3.8: GDP projection: Overall results.

Due to the high variation in the results above, classical Pearson correlation with the loss as a share of GDP (%) gives no significant results. Therefore, 6 different groups with different range of losses are created: 1-2%(18), 2-3%(10),3-5%(16), 5-10%(14), 10-20%(11) and greater than 20% (6) of loss as a share of GDP[9]. Table 3.9 shows the median of $d_{po}(t)$ for each year according to the categories explained above. Interestingly, it seems that especially losses above 10 percent have negative long term effects, while losses between 5 and 10 percent show no effects. The cases with losses between 1 and 5 percent gave no consistent view yet.

As already said, bigger countries should have less problems with disaster events. Therefore, the countries are grouped according to their land area. 5 groups were created: $<$

sample showed a higher mean in the post-disaster years compared to the pre-disaster years, 32 cases showed a lower mean in the post-disaster years compared to the pre-disaster years and 6 cases showed no significant differences. If the mean of all pre-disaster geometric means for each case in the sample is taken, then this will give a value of 3.70 and for the post-disaster a value of 4.37, which means a increase compared to the pre-disaster mean (of all cases) of 17.95 percent. Also the standard deviation and the median is shown for comparison reasons and to lessen the influence of outliers.

[9]The numbers in brackets are the number of cases in each group

Year/Loss	1-2	2-3	3-5	5-10	10-20	>20
Event	-0.95	-1.26	-1.26	-2.13	-5.64	-7.39
+1	-0.54	-1.6	-1.45	0.46	-4.52	-8.15
+2	-0.50	0.11	-2.1	0.46	-2.21	-5.57
+3	1.44	1.32	-0.72	0.03	-4.77	-6.75
+4	-0.2	0.39	-2.34	-0.12	-3.06	-6.62

Table 3.9: GDP projection results (Median): Year vs. Losses.

100000 sq km (28), 100001-200000 sq km (19), 200001-500000 sq km (11), 500001-1000000 sq km (8) and > 1000001 sq km (19). Also here, some interesting results were found. Table 3.10 shows again the median $d_{po}(t)$ for each year. While the patterns for countries with land area smaller than 500000 sq km seem to indicate that the disaster events higher than 1 percent of loss per GDP have negative impacts on long term economic development in the average, all subsample of those countries with land area higher than 500000 sq km showed no negative long term effects in the average.

Year/Area (10^3sq km)	<10	100-200	200-500	500-1000	>1000
Event	-2.24	-1.99	-3.44	1.05	-1.4
+1	-1.22	-5.52	-1.77	1.46	-0.52
+2	-0.44	-2.92	-3.5	0.14	1.00
+3	0.65	-1.54	-4.77	2.13	2.52
+4	-2.25	-1.9	-3.20	6.57	4.74

Table 3.10: GDP projection results (Median): Year vs. Land Area.

So, while no average negative long run effects where found for the subsample of countries with land area higher than 500000 sq km, e.g. the size of Thailand, smaller countries showed a trend of increasing negative impacts on the economic development with the loss per GDP ratio. Especially for countries with land area smaller than 100000 sq km, a overall relationship between economic development and losses can be found (see figure 3.5). Two different effects on the performance measure dependent on the loss to GDP ratio can be distinguished: While a disaster event seems to have a positive impact on the economic development if it causes direct losses below 3 percent as a share of GDP, it has *increasing negative impacts* for long term economic development if losses are higher than 3 and 4 percent respectively. However, as one can see there are exceptions.

Also for the other country groups with land area above 100000 sq km, patterns were found, but only general statements can be given because the relationship with the losses is not so straightforward (see for example figure 3.6). While on the right hand side of figure 3.6 a relationship with the losses could be imagined, the lower left hand side seems to have no distinct pattern. While the results are interesting by itself, they do not explain why these patterns occur. It seems that for smaller countries the loss per GDP ratio can be used as an indicator to determine if the direct damages caused by the natural disaster

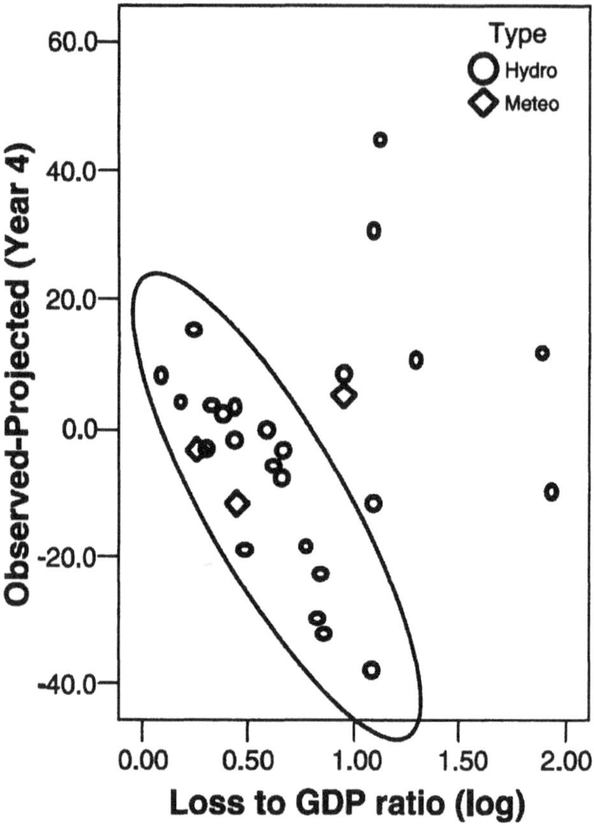

Figure 3.5: GDP projection (Year 4) vs. loss as a share of GDP (log) for countries with land area below 100000 sq km (28 cases).

will have negative long term economic consequences. However, this statement must be viewed with caution, because the losses are only one of the determinants which influence the economic performance after the natural disaster (see section 3.2) and it seems that they are more important for bigger countries. Especially, indirect effects play a vital role, when long term economic development is investigated. To address this topic, catastrophe models have to be created, which are using economic models and advanced sampling techniques to estimate the important flow effects.

In what follows, various other macroeconomic variables are investigated with the already introduced criterions. This should give some more empirical results about disaster effects. One important task is now, to check if the patterns of Albala-Bertrands' (1993a) studies can also be found in this sample. If not, these results can be seen as another argument against the view of positive effects of natural disaster events. However, as we have seen before and will see later on, the situation is not so straightforward.

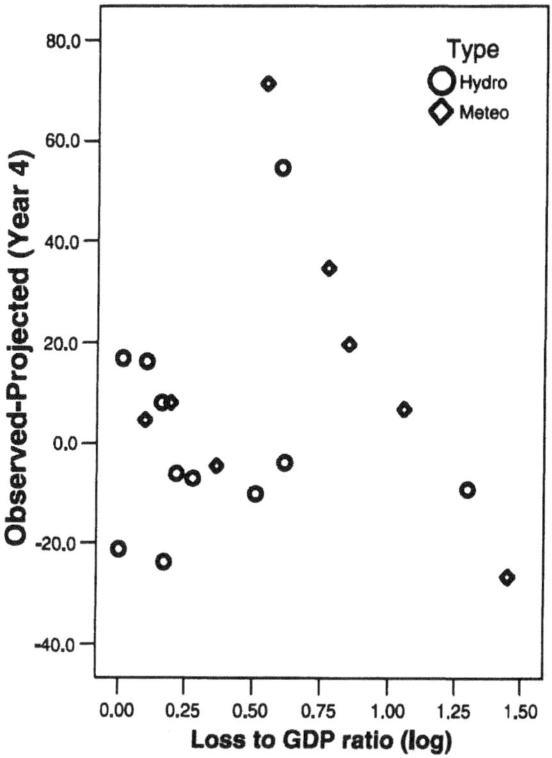

Figure 3.6: GDP projection (Year 4) vs. loss as a share of GDP (log) for countries with land area greater than 1000000 sq km (19 cases).

3.5.2 *Agriculture*

The agriculture (real) growth rate should be affected negatively especially by hydro-meteorological type of hazards. Table 3.11 is showing a deceleration of the growth rates in the disaster year in 49 cases out of 69 (62 percent) and a acceleration one year afterwards in 49 cases out of 80 (61 percent). More than 60 percent of the cases with a deceleration were of hydro-meteorological type. Furthermore, in the disaster year there are more cases with a fall (a negative growth) than in the other years. Therefore, it seems that the agriculture growth rate is negatively effected by the disaster event in the disaster year, but goes back to the pre-disaster year at least two years later.

Change		t_{-1}	t_0	t_1	t_2
Up		35	30	49	38
	pos	33	26	45	38
	neg	2	4	4	0
Down		44	49	31	41
	pos	27	20	15	26
	neg	17	29	16	15
Neutral		2	3	2	4

Table 3.11: Counting criterion: Agriculture (real growth).

These first findings are supported by table 3.12 and figure 3.7. Clearly the average growth rates in the disaster year are quite lower than in the pre-disaster years. Compared to the average growth rate one year before the event, in the disaster year the average is more than 62 percent lower. One and two years later, the average growth rates are higher than in the pre-disaster years.

	t_{-2}	t_{-1}	t_0	t_1	t_2	$t_0/t_{-1}\%$
Mean	2.52	3.10	0.72	3.66	4.19	-76.91
Median	3.37	3.01	1.12	3.83	3.67	-62.83
Std. Dev.	7.95	9.60	7.52	6.99	6.41	

Table 3.12: Average criterion: Agriculture (real growth).

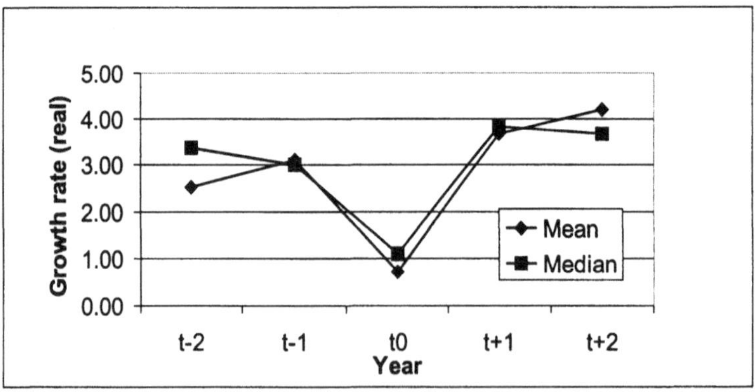

Figure 3.7: Agriculture (real growth), Average variation.

Looking at the geometric mean in the medium term, the majority of cases (41 out of 77) are showing a deceleration compared to the pre-disaster year (table 3.13). However, the mean and median are indicating a positive effect of the disaster event on the growth rates. No patterns were found if those results were analyzed by the type of hazard. For the long term effects the mean and median show a negative effect due to the disaster event. Also, more cases with a deceleration were found but the difference is not high.

Medium Term Effects			
	Pre	Post	Post/Pre
pos	68	69	
neg	13	12	
Up			36
Down			41
Neutral			4
Mean	2.55	3.79	48.70%
Median	2.99	3.56	18.93%
Std.Dev.	5.50	3.98	

Long Term Effects			
	Pre	Post	Post/Pre
pos	68	63	
neg	13	18	
Up			38
Down			43
Neutral			0
Mean	2.55	2.40	-5.72%
Median	2.99	2.73	-8.71%
Std.Dev.	5.50	4.02	

Table 3.13: Medium and Long term criterion: Agriculture (real growth).

Summarizing, it seems that the agriculture growth rate is affected negatively in the disaster event year, especially by hydro-meteorological type of hazards, but bounces back to the pre-disaster period growth rates after one and two years. While the growth rates are a little bit higher in the post-disaster period, no patterns that indicate a long term effect could be found.

3.5.3 Production

A decrease in activity due to the disruption of transportation and reduced production capacities are expected for the production sector. As table 3.14 indicates, the disaster event has negative effects on the growth rate in the disaster year for the majority of cases (53 out of 72). One year later the growth rates are accelerating in 48 cases out of 77 (62 percent). Looking two years after the disaster event, a majority of cases (47 out of 81) showed a deceleration. Furthermore, in those cases with a deceleration in the disaster year the growth rates were negative, indicating serious impacts of the disaster event on the production sector.

Change		t_{-1}	t_0	t_1	t_2
Up		37	29	48	34
	pos	33	26	43	31
	neg	4	3	5	3
Down		42	53	29	47
	pos	31	30	21	38
	neg	11	23	8	9
Neutral		2	0	5	2

Table 3.14: Counting criterion: Production (real growth).

Table 3.15 and figure 3.8 are showing a high decrease in the average growth rate in the disaster year compared with the pre-disaster years. In detail, according to the median, there is a decrease of more than 25 percent in the growth rate, compared to the pre-disaster year. Furthermore, two years after the event, the average is lower than in the pre-disaster year, while it is higher one year after the event.

	t_{-2}	t_{-1}	t_0	t_1	t_2	$t_0/t_{-1}\%$
Mean	4.47	4.89	2.02	5.41	4.85	-58.69
Median	4.83	4.52	3.38	5.07	4.01	-25.08
Std. Dev.	7.77	8.64	8.30	7.14	5.60	

Table 3.15: Average criterion: Production (real growth).

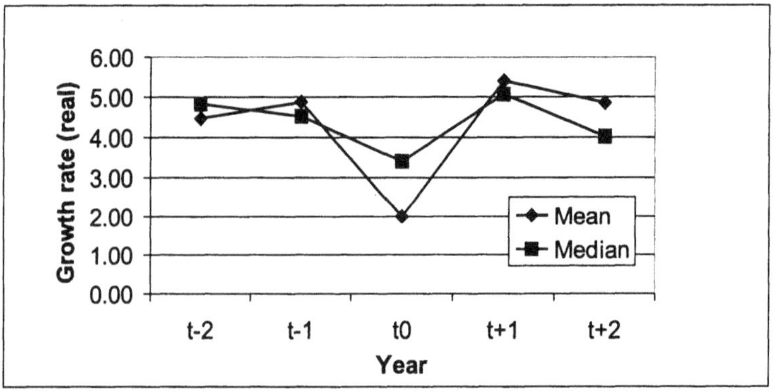

Figure 3.8: Production (real growth), Average variation.

Table 3.16 is showing no clear trends for the medium term effects. While there are equal number of cases of acceleration and deceleration of the growth rates compared to the pre-disaster period, the mean and median are showing an increase of more than 9 percent, probably due to reconstruction efforts. However, the table for the long term effects supports the hypotheses of a more negative effect to the growth rates due to the disaster event. A small majority of cases showed a deceleration (56 percent), and the median of the average growth rate is more than 2 percent lower compared to the pre-disaster period. However, these numbers are to small for any general statement of positive or negative effects on the production growth rate in the long run due to natural disaster events.

In summary, the production growth rate is clearly affected in a negative way by natural disasters in the disaster year but increases sharply one year after due to reconstruction efforts. However, it seems that in the following years the growth rates are still affected by the disaster event in a more negative way.

Medium Term Effects			
	Pre	Post	Post/Pre
pos	68	70	
neg	13	11	
Up			38
Down			37
Neutral			6
Mean	4.61	5.05	9.48%
Median	4.56	4.98	9.02%
Std.Dev.	7.35	4.86	

Long Term Effects			
	Pre	Post	Post/Pre
pos	68	65	
neg	13	16	
Up			35
Down			45
Neutral			1
Mean	4.61	4.22	-8.48%
Median	4.56	4.43	-2.87%
Std.Dev.	7.35	7.12	

Table 3.16: Medium and Long term criterion: Production (real growth).

3.5.4 Service

The disaster events seem to have only negative effects on the service growth rate in the disaster year (table 3.17). 53 out of 78 cases showed a deceleration in the event year (68 percent) whereas 68 percent of the cases with a deceleration also had a negative growth rate indicating a serious impact of the disaster onto the service growth rates.

Change		t_{-1}	t_0	t_1	t_2
Up		45	25	42	41
	pos	44	25	39	39
	neg	1	0	3	2
Down		29	53	29	38
	pos	22	36	25	34
	neg	7	17	4	4
Neutral		5	2	10	3

Table 3.17: Counting Criterion: Service (real growth).

Also table 3.18 and figure 3.9 are indicating only a sharp drop in the disaster year and a return to the pre-disaster level one year later, however, the averages are now a little bit lower. This indicates that the service sector growth rate is not very vulnerable to disasters. However, in countries were the service sector is important because of tourism, negative effects can be more dramatic. On the other hand it is known that disaster events are perceived from individuals after some time as very unlikely to happen to them (see the work of Slovic 2000) which could partially explain the observed results.

	t_{-2}	t_{-1}	t_0	t_1	t_2	$t_0/t_{-1}\%$
Mean	4.91	4.88	3.10	4.42	4.81	-36.49
Median	4.66	4.83	3.59	4.40	4.72	-25.72
Std. Dev.	4.36	4.02	4.68	3.99	3.38	

Table 3.18: Average criterion: Service (real growth).

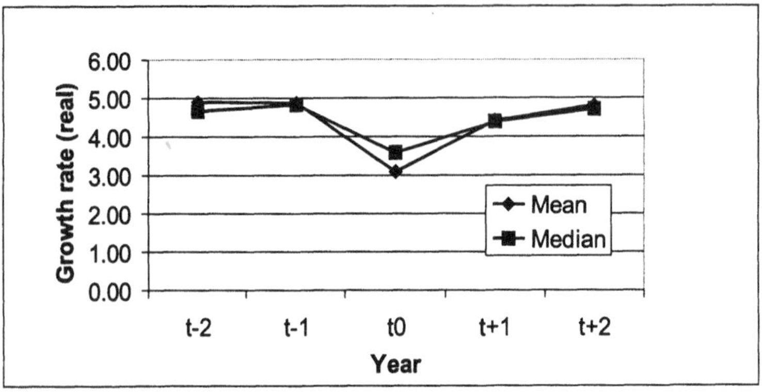

Figure 3.9: Service (real growth), Average variation.

The results for the medium and long term effects are not straightforward (table 3.19). In the medium term the majority of cases are showing a deceleration compared to the pre-disaster average growth rate. However, the median and mean of the pre-disaster and post-disaster growth rates are not very different in absolute values, indicating no medium term effects, but are showing different signs, indicating that some of the cases performed after the event extremely badly. For the long term effects the situation is quite similar. A majority of cases (55 percent) showed a deceleration compared to the pre-disaster period, but while the mean is showing a negative the median is showing a positive trend. Again, these results can be explained by outliers. Furthermore, the difference of the absolute values of the pre and post-disaster period are not high.

Medium Term Effects			
	Pre	Post	Post/Pre
pos	74	71	
neg	5	8	
Up			33
Down			42
Neutral			4
Mean	4.87	4.60	-5.53%
Median	4.41	4.64	5.21%
Std.Dev.	3.45	3.21	

Long Term Effects			
	Pre	Post	Post/Pre
pos	74	69	
neg	5	10	
Up			33
Down			41
Neutral			5
Mean	4.87	4.25	-12.66%
Median	4.41	4.77	8.29%
Std.Dev.	3.45	3.46	

Table 3.19: Medium and Long term criterion: Service (real growth).

In summary, the service sector growth rates are effected negatively by natural disasters in the disaster year, but those effects diminish at least after two years later.

3.5.5 *Exports*

According to the literature, there should be a reduction in the rate of growth in the year of the event and a return to the pre-disaster years afterwards. Table 3.20 shows a deceleration of the growth rates in the disaster year in the majority of cases (60 percent). Also, more cases than in the other years are showing a fall in the growth rate. One year after the event, the growth rates are accelerating in the majority of cases (62 percent) while two years after the disaster the numbers are similar to those of the pre-disaster period.

Change		t_{-1}	t_0	t_1	t_2
Up		39	30	46	39
	pos	37	23	43	36
	neg	2	7	3	3
Down		34	45	28	36
	pos	19	21	18	22
	neg	15	24	10	14
Neutral		2	1	2	1

Table 3.20: Counting Criterion: Exports (real growth).

As table 3.21 shows, the standard deviation for the mean is high, so that general statements are difficult to obtain. However, it seems from figure 3.10 quite clear that the average growth rate is in the disaster year lower than one year before (-52 percent if the median is used) and higher later on.

	t_{-2}	t_{-1}	t_0	t_1	t_2	$t_0/t_{-1}\%$
Mean	4.58	4.88	3.63	7.63	7.59	-25.77
Median	5.01	7.33	3.52	6.12	7.01	-52.00
Std. Dev.	13.98	13.62	11.98	14.65	11.65	

Table 3.21: Average criterion: Exports (real growth).

As with the average criterion, the medium and long term effects are difficult to interpret because of the high standard deviation. On the other hand, this is not surprising because the behavior of the growth rates is depending on various factors which are not controlled for here. What can be said about the medium term is that there seems a higher average growth rate than in the pre-disaster period. Also a majority of cases have higher growth rates than in the pre-disaster period (39 cases out of 72). This statement is not so evident for the long term. 39 cases out of 71 showed a decreased average compared to the pre-disaster period. While the mean shows an increase compared to the pre-disaster years of about 11 percent the median shows a decrease of 3 percent (table 3.22). Therefore, no general statement about the medium and long term effects can be made, however, it seems that natural disasters have at least two years after the disaster some negative effects on the production growth rate.

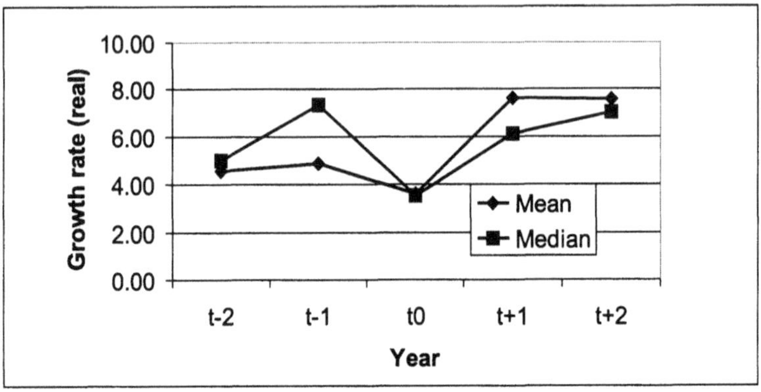

Figure 3.10: Exports (real growth), Average variation.

Medium Term Effects			
	Pre	Post	Post/Pre
pos	54	62	
neg	20	12	
Up			39
Down			33
Neutral			2
Mean	4.33	7.28	68.12%
Median	5.17	6.75	30.48%
Std.Dev.	11.59	9.05	

Long Term Effects			
	Pre	Post	Post/Pre
pos	54	55	
neg	19	18	
Up			32
Down			39
Neutral			2
Mean	4.42	4.93	11.34%
Median	5.24	5.06	-3.39%
Std.Dev.	11.64	9.53	

Table 3.22: Medium and Long term criterion: Exports (real growth).

Summarizing, there is empirical evidence that the export growth rates are negatively affected in the event year. However, while it seems that average growth rates are higher in the post-disaster period, which is difficult to explain, in the long run no clear trends could be found, however, a more negative than positive direction was found.

3.5.6 Imports

According to the literature, there should be an increase in imports in the disaster year and a decrease in subsequent years due to lower income. Interestingly, the majority of cases showed a deceleration of the growth rate in the disaster year, while the other years are showing no clear trend (table 3.23).

Looking at table 3.24 the interpretation of the results is not straightforward, also due to the high standard deviation of the mean. From figure 3.11 one can see that the average growth rate goes down in the disaster year, which is not expected from the literature. If the median is used, the post-disaster period growth rates are lower than in the pre-disaster

Change		t_{-1}	t_0	t_1	t_2
Up		38	32	39	39
	pos	32	30	34	36
	neg	6	2	5	3
Down		36	43	37	36
	pos	16	25	19	17
	neg	20	18	18	19
Neutral		1	1	0	1

Table 3.23: Counting Criterion: Imports (real growth).

period. While in the medium term there is a majority of cases with a higher growth rate than in the pre-disaster period and in average the growth rates are 17 percent higher, there seems to be a decrease in the growth rate in the long term. Here the average growth rates are more than 23 percent lower compared to the pre-disaster years. However, the number of cases with an acceleration are nearly equal with those with a deceleration. Furthermore, looking at table 3.25 one can see that the pre-disaster averages are quite different, which is not very good for robust interpretations of the results.

	t_{-2}	t_{-1}	t_0	t_1	t_2	$t_0/t_{-1}\%$
Mean	4.75	6.96	4.63	6.19	7.86	-33.54
Median	5.55	7.49	6.98	5.70	5.94	-6.75
Std. Dev.	18.50	13.20	15.48	14.08	12.63	

Table 3.24: Average criterion: Imports (real growth).

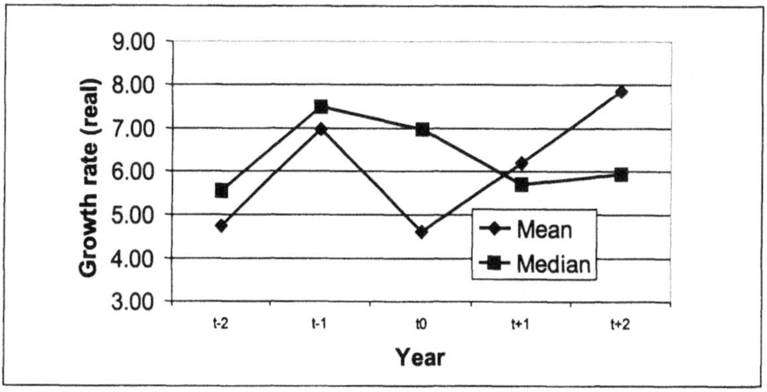

Figure 3.11: Imports (real growth), Average variation.

Summarizing, different to the literature survey, in this sample the import growth rate is affected negatively in the disaster year. For the medium term (e.g. two years after the event), the growth rate seems to be below the pre-disaster period. No general statements

Medium Term Effects			
	Pre	Post	Post/Pre
pos	47	61	
neg	27	13	
Up			41
Down			31
Neutral			2
Mean	5.34	6.52	22.10%
Median	5.55	6.51	17.24%
Std.Dev.	11.93	8.30	

Long Term Effects			
	Pre	Post	Post/Pre
pos	46	51	
neg	27	22	
Up			35
Down			38
Neutral			0
Mean	5.23	4.53	-13.24%
Median	5.50	4.21	-23.43%
Std.Dev.	11.97	11.85	

Table 3.25: Medium and Long term criterion: Imports (real growth).

can be concluded for the long term period. However, one interpretation of the results is, that, while the imports are higher one and two years after the event because of assistance from the outside, later on this assistance diminishes which lead to smaller growth rates.

3.5.7 Government consumption

Another interesting question is, if governments consumption growth rates are affected by natural disaster events. As shown in Table 3.26 growth accelerates in 39 cases out of 74 (52 percent) in the year of the disaster while 40 cases out of 75 (53 percent) showed a deceleration. However, most important, two years after the event, growth accelerates in 47 cases out of 75 (62 percent). Furthermore, in this year the least amount of cases with a negative growth rate can be found. This could be explained by the outside help usually governments get after a disaster but takes some time to transfer it.

Change		t_{-1}	t_0	t_1	t_2
Up		34	39	35	47
	pos	30	35	25	42
	neg	4	4	10	5
Down		36	35	40	28
	pos	22	13	27	19
	neg	14	22	13	9
Neutral		4	2	1	1

Table 3.26: Counting criterion: Government Consumption (real growth).

Looking at table 3.27 and figure 3.12 one can see that the mean and median are showing a deceleration of the growth rates in the disaster year and one year afterwards and an acceleration two years after the event. In detail, compared to the pre-disaster year there is an average drop of the growth rate of more than 12 percent (median used) in the disaster year. However, it is not quite clear if the average growth rates are higher in the pre-disaster period.

	t_{-2}	t_{-1}	t_0	t_1	t_2	$t_0/t_{-1}\%$
Mean	5.67	3.71	2.89	2.67	5.76	-22.25
Median	3.81	4.40	3.84	2.99	3.81	-12.67
Std. Dev.	12.93	9.92	11.42	10.92	9.24	

Table 3.27: Average criterion: Government Consumption (real growth).

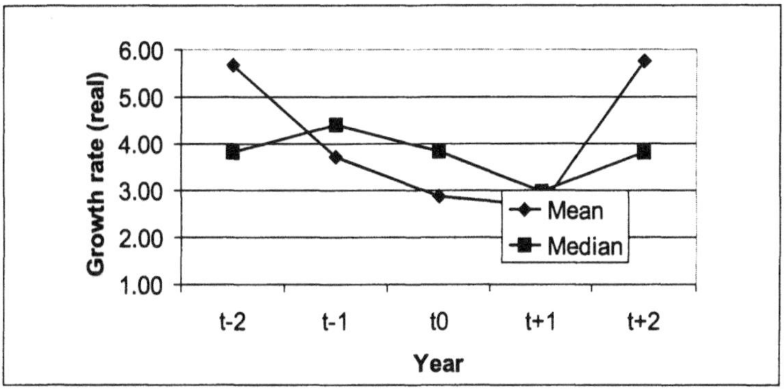

Figure 3.12: Government Consumption (real growth), Average variation.

In the medium term, the growth rates seem to be under the pre-disaster level. If the median is used an average decrease of more than 33 percent compared to the pre-disaster period was found. However, only a small majority of cases (53 percent) showed a deceleration (3.28). For the long term a small majority of cases (55 percent) showed an acceleration compared to the pre-disaster period. However, if the averages between the post and pre-disaster period are compared, the average growth rate lies under the pre-disaster level.

Medium Term Effects			
	Pre	Post	Post/Pre
pos	57	55	
neg	16	18	
Up			32
Down			36
Neutral			5
Mean	4.33	3.93	-9.21%
Median	4.50	3.00	-33.22%
Std.Dev.	6.83	6.94	

Long Term Effects			
	Pre	Post	Post/Pre
pos	56	61	
neg	15	10	
Up			39
Down			31
Neutral			1
Mean	4.55	4.04	-11.21%
Median	4.64	4.41	-4.88%
Std.Dev.	6.75	5.52	

Table 3.28: Medium and Long term criterion: Government Consumption(real growth).

Summarizing, there seems to be a drop of government consumption in the disaster year compared to the pre-disaster years. However, one and two years after the event, the average growth rates indicating higher government consumption, probably do to reconstruction and financing efforts in the public and private sector. In the long run two years after the disaster event the government consumption stagnates below the pre-disaster year levels, which could be explained by fiscal problems of the government due to loss financing.

3.5.8 Summary

One of the main findings of the empirical analysis is the observed relationship between losses due to natural disasters and negative short and long term economic development measured by the GDP level. Especially countries with land area smaller than 100.000 sq km and loss per GDP ratios higher than 3 percent showed negative long term effects. In more detail, two different impacts of natural disasters on the economic development measured by the GDP level for countries with land area smaller than 100.000 sq km in the sample were found: While a disaster event seems to have also some positive impact on the economic development if it causes direct losses below 3 percent (as a share of GDP), it has *increasing negative impacts* for long term economic development if losses are higher than 3 and 4 percent respectively. Similar results are obtained also for bigger countries, however, it seems that in these cases other variables become increasingly important for the overall economic performance over the post-disaster years. Especially, indirect effects play a vital role, when long term economic development is investigated there. Furthermore, the question remains *why* some countries behave better than others after a disaster event. As seen above, losses and land area have some explanatory power, but they did not reflect the complex relationships mentioned in section 3.2 which constitute the economic vulnerability of ab country due to a natural disaster. Also, the reason why no negative effects for smaller events were found is still missing and the results above could be misunderstood by saying that natural disasters can also be seen as 'good' events which can also increase the economic development: It should be stressed the fact that natural disasters per se have to be seen as 'bad' events. They destroy stocks which must be rebuild and even if the stock is replaced with better equipment, it is not rational to rely on a natural disaster to get rid of them or to rely on believes of positive effects because of luck. For example, also small events can seriously hamper the economy if they occur frequently. The analysis also showed the limits of an empirical study if large cross-country data sets are used. In a macroeconomic context, pre-conditions of the country, the impact of the disaster, indirect effects and the financial vulnerability are the overall parameters which influence the economic development in the long run (see figure 2.2). Therefore, to address this topic a modeling approach is needed.

The various other macroeconomic variables analyzed in this chapter showed trends which were expected in the literature (see table 3.29). Therefore this results can be used as an empirical example against the hypotheses of Albala-Bertrand (1993a). First, there is a fall in the *Gross Domestic Product* growth rate due to natural disasters; secondly, there is a decrease in the GDP growth rate; thirdly, nothing can be said about these

Variable	**Change**
GDP	Growth rate drops in disaster year, increases in year afterwards back to pre-disaster level. Long term negative effects were found.
Agriculture sector	Growth rate is affected negatively in disaster year. Bounces back to pre-disaster levels one and two years later. Hydro-meteorological hazards had worst impacts.
Production sector	Growth rate falls in disaster year. No clear trends in post-disaster year found (more negative trends).
Service sector	Growth rate falls in the disaster year. Fast recovery to pre-disaster levels at least two years later.
Export	Decrease of the growth rate in the disaster year. Increase one and two years later. No clear trends later found
Import	Growth rate negatively effected in disaster year. Below pre-disaster years one and two years afterwards.
Government consum.	Drop in the disaster year. Increase one and two years later. Stagnates afterwards.

Table 3.29: Summary of empirical analysis.

rates in the long run if no other information is available. The *agriculture* growth rate was affected negatively in the disaster event year, especially by hydro-meteorological type of hazards, but bounced back to the pre-disaster period growth rates after one and two years. While the growth rates are a little bit higher in the post-disaster period, no patterns that indicate a long term effect could be found. Also the *production* growth rates are negatively effected by natural disasters in the event year. While the average growth rates are higher than in the pre-disaster period one year after the event no clear trends for the medium and long term were found. However, it seems that in the following years the growth rates are still affected by the disaster event in a more negative way. The *service* growth rates were effected negatively by natural disasters in the disaster year, but those effects diminish at least two years later. The *export* growth rates are negatively affected in the event year. However, while it seems that average growth rates are higher in the post-disaster period, which is difficult to explain, in the long run no clear trends could be found, however, a more negative than positive trend can be shown. Different to the literature, the *import* growth rate is affected negatively in the disaster year. For the medium term (e.g. two years after the event), the growth rate seems to be below the pre-disaster period. No general statements can be concluded for the long term period. However, one interpretation of the results could be, that, while the imports are higher one and two years after the event because of assistance from the outside, later on this assistance diminished which lead to smaller growth rates. *Government consumption* growth rates experience a drop in the disaster year compared to the pre-disaster years. However, one and two years after the event, the average growth rates indicating higher government consumption, probably due to reconstruction and financing efforts in the public and private sector. In the long run government consumption stagnates below the pre-disaster year levels, which could be explained by fiscal problems of the government due to loss financing.

As already mentioned this empirical analysis gave evidences of serious negative effects of natural disasters to the macroeconomic performance of a country, however, it also showed the limits of the empirical study for a more detailed analysis due to the complexity of the issue. As a consequence to analyze and manage catastrophic risk, modeling approaches must be used. However, the risk bearers in the event of a natural disaster on the country level and the risk financing options in the private and public sector have to be investigated first.

Chapter 4

Natural disaster risk management measures

In this chapter an overview of risk management measures against natural disaster impacts is given. While section 4.1 gives an outline of risk financing instruments, section 4.2 introduces classical and new innovative financing instruments available today for the private sector on the household and business level. Afterwards, section 4.3 gives a more detailed introduction into public sector risk and risk management practices on the governmental level.

On the country level, the risk bearers in the event of a natural disaster can be the government, the domestic private sector, or international institutions such as the World Bank (Miller and Keipi 2005: 7). The private sector stakeholders include the property owners (households and businesses) as well as insurers, reinsurers and the capital market. On the household and business level the entities can choose between a range of risk management strategies, including risk reduction, risk transfer and/or keeping and financing the risk by themselves. However, the way in which particular entities decide their risk management strategies is often a function of their perception of risk they are exposed to (Loefstedt and Frewer 1998, Slovic 2000). Especially for low probability events, people are often not worried about the consequences. Kunreuther (1996) called the effect of limited interest in protection (e.g. insurance or structural mitigation measures) prior to a disaster and the resulting high costs to insurers and federal governments following an catastrophic event as the *Natural Disaster Syndrome.* Section 4.2 takes a closer look at this and related topics. While insurers provide protection to property owners for losses due to natural disasters, reinsurers provide protection to insurers (see section 5.2.3). The capital markets can be seen as a complement to reinsurance for covering large losses from disasters through new financial instruments, e.g. catastrophe bonds (see also figure 5.6).

Repairing damaged infrastructure and providing financial assistance to the business sector and households can be seen as the major (financial) issues the government is responsible for after a disaster. Section 4.3 identifies in detail the responsibilities of the government after a natural disaster, gives some qualitative statements when governments should behave risk averse and therefore adopt proactive risk management approaches, explains the general possibilities of the government to ease their financial burden in the context of natural disaster losses and examines the level of support in disaster risk reduction within relief and development departments. Last but not least, strategies that public agencies can adopt to effectively protect households and their members from the adverse impact of aggregate shocks are presented.

The private sector entities as well as the government can use a variety of financial instruments to manage catastrophe risk. Generally speaking, risk financing instruments can be categorized into risk transfer (e.g. insurance) and (intertemporal) risk spreading instruments (e.g. credits). Furthermore, those instruments can be separated into market and non-market instruments (Mechler 2005a: 109). There is also the possibility to separate market-based instruments into catastrophe hedges and non-insurance catastrophe hedges. For example, Freeman (2000: 51) distinguish six broad categories of non-insurance catastrophe hedges according to two dimensions: Whether they are issued as equity or debt or whether they are indemnity instruments or event hedges. In the following section those instruments as well as other non-market instruments are introduced.

4.1 Risk financing instruments: An overview

Risk financing instruments against disaster risks can be categorized into risk transfer and risk spreading instruments. While the dominant risk financing instrument is risk transfer by insurance and reinsurance, other non-market risk transfer instruments, e.g. collective loss sharing, are also available[1] (Mechler 2005a). Non-Insurance market based catastrophe risk financing instruments include catastrophe bonds, contingent surplus notes, exchange traded catastrophe options, catastrophe equity puts, catastrophe swaps and weather derivatives (Pollner 2001: 73). These instruments can be categorized whether they are issued as equity or debt or whether they indemnify against losses or trigger according to a specified physical event. (Freeman 2000: 51, Keipi and Tyson 2002: 11, Banks 2005). Contingent credit, catastrophe bonds and weather derivatives can be seen as important non-insurance market based financial instruments, while contingent surplus notes, catastrophe equity puts and catastrophe swaps are becoming less important. Therefore, these instruments are not considered here. Table 4.1 summarizes the instruments for financing disaster risks. While non-market risk transfer approaches usually have an ex-post character[2], market risk transfer and spreading instruments are ex-ante risk financing instruments.

Non-market risk transfer: Post disaster government assistance can be seen as one of the most important arrangements for transferring risk. The government plays a key role in loss financing after a disaster in developing and emerging-economy countries, and even in high-income countries. As the government acting as a "insurer of last resort", governments pool their risk across a wide geographical area. If a hazard realizes, the losses

[1] Especially for the government.

[2] But can be considered as ex-ante risk financing instruments if implemented before the disaster

Approaches	Examples of Instruments
Non-market risk transfer	Government assistance (taxes) for private and public sector relief and reconstruction funding Kinship arrangements, Some mutual insurance arrangements, Donor Assistance
Market risk transfer	Insurance and reinsurance, Microinsurance, Financial market instruments: Catastrophe bonds, Weather derivatives
Inter-temporal risk spreading	Contingent credit (financial market instrument), Reserve fund, Microcredit and -savings.

Table 4.1: Risk management approaches and instruments. Source: Mechler 2005a: 109.

are often financed with taxpayer funds, therefore, this collective loss sharing practice is based on solidarity from persons not at risk. However, a major concern with risk financing systems which depends on solidarity is "moral hazard". A more detailed analysis is done in section 4.3. There is also the possibility that households and businesses which have similar risk profiles create a pool by themselves. Such non-profit mutual insurance arrangements have a long tradition, however, they as well have limitations, e.g. the lack of technical and organizational know-how in running the schemes. Informal kinship arrangements are another traditional (based on social networks) coping mechanism which is characterized by financial or in-kind support of relatives (or neighbors) after a disaster. However, because natural disasters affect whole regions, a family has to diversify its livelihood to insure that some of their relatives are not affected by the disaster and can support them.

Market risk transfer: Households, businesses and governments can transfer their catastrophic risk by insurance and/or reinsurance. The principles and rationales for insurance and reinsurance are discussed in detail in section 5.2.3. Especially in developing countries where insurance is not available or unaffordable, microinsurance schemes are an alternative. Microinsurance schemes are organized by trade unions, municipalities, private insurance companies, micro-finance institutions, health service providers, NGOs and CBOs. Microinsurance can be defined as the pooling of a group or community's resources to share risks. The principles underlying microinsurance is the pooling of defined resources and risks, non refundable payment made in advance and a guarantee that the risks defined will be covered in case of bad fortune (International Labour Organization 2005: 2). However, one of the major problems of microinsurance, of which microcredit and microsavings are not exempted, is the smallness of the transaction, which results in high unit transaction costs for the institution (Pantoja 2002: 52). In addition to traditional insurance and reinsurance there is emerging interest in other alternative risk transfer instruments, e.g. catastrophe bonds and weather derivatives. Weather derivatives are index based, e.g. physical indicators such as rainfall measured at a specific location are used to define trigger events. Weather derivatives and index based insurance are seen now as promising risk transfer instruments for the developing and emerging economy countries, especially in the agriculture sector (World Bank 2005a). Catastrophe bonds emerged as instruments primarily for reinsurers, however, there are also governmental efforts in some countries (e.g. Mexico) to transfer their risk with this instrument. For a detailed discussion see section 5.2.5.

Inter-temporal risk spreading: On the household level risk spreading over time can be achieved in the form of savings. On the country level governments (e.g. Mexico: FONDEN) can establish catastrophe reserve funds, usually financed by taxes, which are depleted only in the case of an disaster event (see also section 5.2.2). Contingent credit arrangements allow to borrow money after an event whereas the post-event annuity payments are smaller in comparison to a regular credit. However, for contingent credit arrangements an annual pre-event fee has to be paid (see section 5.2.4). Borrowing is also a kind of inter-temporal risk spreading of losses, because payments will be made in the future. As one can see, a contingent credit is a mixture of saving and borrowing.

4.2 Financial risk management in the private sector

In this section we restrict our attention to the household and business level. The traditional method to manage catastrophe risk here is through **insurance**. However, there are problems on the demand as well as the supply side for this type of catastrophe coverage. As an overall consequence, insurance density for disaster risk is correlated with the economic development measured in terms of per capita GDP. Furthermore, even in the high income countries insurance density is far from its potential (figure 4.1).

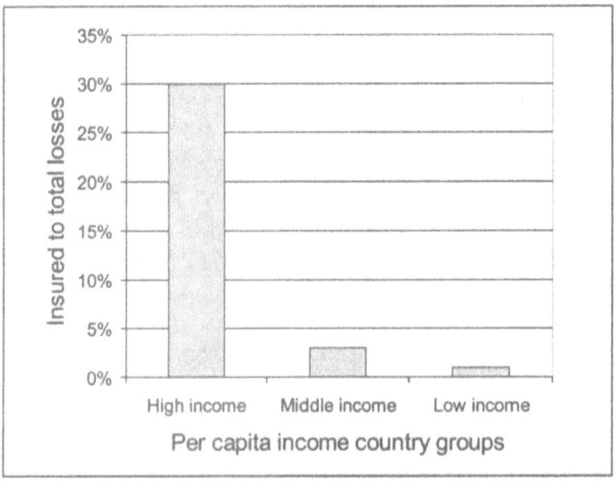

Figure 4.1: Catastrophe insurance density for losses 1980-2004. Source: Munich Re NatCatService 2005.

The low insurance density in high income countries cannot be attributed to insufficient supply, but rather must be found on the demand side. Two explanations arise: First, people have limited interest to voluntary purchase insurance because they perceive the risk of a disaster causing damage to their property as being sufficiently low but in fact underestimate their risk exposure. As a result they do not consider the consequences and therefore do not take preventive actions (Kunreuther 1996).[3] The second explanation seems more important. Victims to a great extent receive assistance from the government. For example, the Hungarian government fully financed the rebuilding of over 1000 homes that had been washed away after the 2001 flood on the Upper Tisza river. Only 12 percent of the losses from the Midwest floods in 1993 in the US where absorbed by the insurance sector, while 30 percent of the losses were covered by the US federal government (Linnerooth-Bayer et al. 1999). Other examples could be made. The main point is, since the emergency aid is usually based upon the actual loss of a victim, insurance and other sources of compensation are direct substitutes. Therefore, "the low demand for fundamental risk coverage and insufficient loss prevention can therefore be explained by the potential victims anticipation of (costless) non-insurance assistance" (Nell and Richter 2005: 336)

The low insurance density in the developing world is not surprising. On the demand side, for low income households, commercial insurance is unaffordable and has high opportunity costs. Many low income countries are highly exposed to natural disaster risk and therefore even fair premiums would be quite high. As a consequence, residents of such countries cannot pay the price for such risk transfers and therefore require support from the non-risk communities or internationally (Mechler 2005a, Linnerooth-Bayer, Mechler and Pflug 2005). On the supply side, insurers are reluctant to promote coverage because of the intrinsic problems of insurability of catastrophe risk (see section 5.2.3), the lack of formal titles to property of firms and individuals in developing countries, without which no formal proof of holdings can be established and therefore no premium calculations can be done, high transaction costs, unstable business environments and insufficient risk assessment and mitigation amongst others (Andersen 2001: 28). Hence, in developing countries, instead of insurance, households usually rely on family and public support. Furthermore, they use traditional coping mechanisms to protect themselves from the economic impacts of natural disasters: Diversification of crops and livelihoods, different sources of income, remittances from family members who are living abroad or spatial diversification of family members.

Recently, there is growing interest in **microinsurance** and **microfinance** arrangements to provide financing to poor individuals and households (Armendáriz de Aghion and Morduch 2005: 166). The basic idea is that the transaction costs, overhead and profits are kept as small as possible to provide low cost financing. The principle behind microin-

[3]The perceived risk is higher if a disaster occurred before, but diminishes after some years without a disaster event (Hochrainer 2005).

surance is the same as for insurance (e.g. law of large numbers), however, the distribution of such contracts and the providers are different. Microinsurance was started to cover funeral expenses, health and more recently death. Microinsurance schemes are also used for social protection of the poor, e.g. in the Philippines (International Labour Organization 2005). The providers of microfinance services are usually Microfinance Institutions (MFIs) which can be NGOs, commercial companies, and more important Alternative Financial Institutions (AFIs), which include state-owned banks and postal services, member-owned savings and loan institutions and low-capital local or rural banks. In some countries, e.g. India or Bangladesh, there are additional affords to couple microfinance and insurance schemes, however, some problems emerged, e.g. policyholders were instead from poor households from the middle class (Mechler 2005a: 120).

A promising alternative to traditional insurance are **weather derivatives**, especially index based weather derivatives (World Bank 2005a). These are weather contingent contracts whose payoff will be determined by future weather events. These contracts link payments to a weather index that is the collection of values of a weather variable measured at a stated location during a explicit period (Dischel and Barrieu 2002: 26). The two main advantages of such contracts are that, because the trigger event is defined physically, there is no moral hazard; on the contrary, policyholders have an incentive to reduce potential losses, e.g. farmer diversifying their crops (Linnerooth-Bayer, Mechler and Pflug 2005). However, one disadvantage is that there is a "basis risk", which means, that claims do not need to fully correlate with losses. Another disadvantage is, as with insurance, that the insured risk is dependent within a single region. Schemes based on weather derivatives have been proposed or are currently examined in Morocco and Ethiopia (Stoppa and Hess 2003) and pilot studies are done in India.

4.3 Financial risk management in the public sector

Throughout this thesis we refer to "the government". Therefore, the question what or who the government is should be treated first. We start with some differences between the public and private sector. Basically, there are two important differences between the 'government' and 'private institutions' (see for example Stiglitz 1999: 13). First, in a democracy the individuals who are responsible for the operation of public institutions are elected. In contrast, those who are responsible for administering a private institution are chosen by shareholders. Secondly, the government is endowed with certain rights of compulsion that private institutions do not have (e.g. taxes). Furthermore, in contrast to private institutions, the government restricts the rights of individuals to give to others similar powers of compulsion (e.g. the government does not allow someone to sell some of his organs). Table 4.2 shows the rationale for and examples of public intervention.

Unregulated monopolies tend to charge too much and produce too little. Thus, government intervention can lead to more production at a lower price. Traditionally, the solution has been to have a public enterprise which provide the good or service. However,

Rationale	Examples of Intervention
Natural monopolies	Franchise bidding, regulation, provision
Externalities	Taxes and subsidies, regulation, provision
Public goods	Provision if exclusion difficult; Subsidies or provision if exclusion is undesirable
Information failures	Regulation, taxes and subsidies, provision
Incomplete markets	Provision, taxes and subsidies, regulation
Equity objective	Subsidies, provision
Redistribution	Provision, subsidies
Merit goods	Regulation, provision

Table 4.2: Rationale for public interventions. Source: Belli 1997: 13.

there is also the solution to auction off the franchise to private firms or to regulate the private monopolies. In the case of externalities, e.g. private projects which use or destroy resources for which it does not pay, the government can intervene to produce the socially optimal quantity of goods through taxes or subsidies. There is also the possibility to set quality standards irrespective of cost considerations which must be fulfilled by the private sector entity. The private sector usually shies away from producing public goods , e.g. clean air in the city, or it produce too little or charge too much for them, which calls for public intervention, e.g. provision of public goods (Belli 1997). The remaining rationales in table 4.2 are discussed in more detail in the next section.

Most of the economies today are mixed economies in which there is both a private and a public sector. The core of the economy are profit-maximizing firms interacting with households in a competitive market. However, only under certain idealized conditions (e.g. perfect information) a competitive economy is efficient. If these conditions are satisfied, there would be no (or very limited) role for the government. Welfare economics is a branch of economics which focuses on normative issues (what should be?). The two most important results of welfare economics describe the relationship between competitive markets and Pareto efficiency. To answer the question how and why governments are exposed to natural disaster risk one has to take a closer look at these fundamentals.

4.3.1 Governments risk exposure

From an economic perspective the two main functions of governments are first, the *allocation* of goods and services and second, the *distribution* of income. The question how much the government should intervene in the countries economy is heavily debated in the literature. The rationale behind government intervention comes from the violation of the assumptions of the two fundamental theorems of welfare economics[4]: The first theorem states that any Walrasian (competitive equilibrium) is Pareto efficient. No distributional

[4]The two Fundamental Theorems of Welfare Economics, stretch back to Pareto (1906) and Barone (1908) and were proved graphically by Abba Lerner (1934) and mathematically by Harold Hotelling (1938), Oskar Lange (1942) and Maurice Allais (1943: p.617-35)(see also Abba Lerner (1944) and Paul Samuelson (1947)

concerns are included in this model. Its implication is that competitive markets will always be efficient, e.g. a Pareto-efficient outcome in a competitive market economy under certain conditions is possible *without* government intervention in this model. Violations are the cases of complete market failure with public goods and partial market failure, e.g. noncompetitive markets, imperfect information and the existence of externalities. The government therefore has to allocate or regulate the allocation of those goods. The second theorem states that an equitable Pareto-efficient market outcome can be reached by a redistribution of initial endowments. The inability to redistribute initial endowments calls for redistribution by governments e.g. through taxation or transfer payments.

In the context of natural disasters three sources of government risk can be distinguished (Mechler 2004a: 50):

- Because governments are responsible for allocating funds to the provision of public goods and services (e.g. public infrastructure), governments are exposed to the risk of losing it.
- In the case of partial market failure, governments also provide those goods and services (e.g. natural disaster insurance) because they are often the final entity that private households and firms can turn to in case of need. Therefore, due to the role as a de facto insurer of last resort for private sector risk, there is a large extra burden to absorb for government in times of a disaster.
- Because governments redistribute income to those members of society that are in need of help[5] after a disaster, the government is also responsible for relief payments to sustain a basic standard of living. Certainly, this is even more the case for developing countries which have a large proportion of the population living in poverty.

Repairing damaged infrastructure and providing financial assistance to the business sector and households can be seen as the major (financial) issues the government is responsible for after a disaster. However, it is also interesting how much of the total losses the government is responsible for. Dacy and Kunreuther (1969: 50-51) surveyed eight disasters occurring in the 1950s and 1960s. They found that damage to public facilities accounted for from 7 percent to 75 percent with a median of 25 percent of total damages experienced. Sheaffer et al. (1976: 24) calculated average annual flood damages to infrastructure (without public buildings) at about 25 percent of total damages from flooding in urban areas. Sheaffer and Roland (1981: 113) investigated 23 communities and estimated that flood losses to public facilities (without public buildings) would average 16 percent of total losses. Petak and Atkisson (1982) reports that public sector losses accounted for about one quarter of all losses. The types of losses to which state and local governments are exposed vary by the type of hazard (Burby 1991: 33). The most severe losses incurred by state and local governments can be associated with damages to highways, roads and streets. For example, half of all losses incurred by the government in US between 1980 and

[5] The poor as well as those that are in danger in slipping into poverty

1987 whereas clearance of debris and emergency protective measures ranked second and third (Burby 1991: 32). Talks with World Bank economic experts say that as a general rule 50 percent of the total losses in developing and emerging countries the government has to finance, whereas 30 percent of the losses come from the public sector, and 20 percent of the losses come from the private sector. This values are rough but they seem to be a good rule of thumb.

4.3.2 Governments risk preferences

Knowing the elements at risk on the governmental level due to natural disaster the next question is how the government should treat and deal with this risk. The ability to deal with risk is generally described as risk-preference. This term and the Arrow-Lind theorem is discussed next. The conclusion is that under some specific conditions, governments should behave risk averse. These conditions are most often satisfied for developing countries.

Arrow and Lind (1970) argued in their famous paper "Uncertainty and the Evaluation of Public Investment Decisions" that national governments are the entity best suited to deal with risk, mainly because they can spread the risk over the whole population, so that risk can be neglected in government decision making. Generally speaking, the Arrow-Lind theorem holds for developed countries. For example, in the USA although average annual losses caused by natural disasters are enormous, they fall far below the level of normal repair and replacement costs associated with the ongoing depreciation of public infrastructure. Furthermore, the disasters are manageable financially and only a few local governments (one in ten with losses) experience truly catastrophic damages to public property an those losses account for the lions's share of federal disaster relief costs (Burby 1991: 4). Also, earlier studies on long term consequences of natural disasters in America in 1960 to 1970 did not found any empirical evidence (Rossi et al. 1978). However, the situation is quite different in developing and emerging-economy countries. Mechler (2004a,b) investigated the assumptions underlying the Arrow-Lind result and compared it with empirical (macroeconomic) data[6]. He concluded that assumptions of the Arrow-Lind theorem of risk neutrality holds true for developed countries, but some developing countries should behave risk averse and therefore should incorporate public sector risk. He, concluded that under the following characteristics of a country, a government should behave risk averse (Mechler 2004a: 59):

- Countries subject to high natural hazard exposure.
- Countries subject to high economic vulnerability, - low tax revenue, small tax base, limited ability to borrow at favorable conditions, high indebtedness with little access to external finance.

[6]For some qualitative discussions see Freeman 2003.

- Small countries with few large infrastructural assets and high spatial correlation between those assets.
- Countries with concentrated economic activity centers exposed to natural hazard.

However, this characteristics should be seen as rather qualitative statements. To assess if a government should behave risk averse, a detailed analysis has to be done by assessing their financial vulnerability.

After this qualitative answers when a government should behave risk averse, the next question is, how the government should manage the risk. *Risk management* itself is an important element of the financial planning process of governments. Its objective is to conserve governmental resources from accidental loss. A successful risk management program therefore protects government assets, assures a safe environment for government employees and the general public, minimizes the interruption of essential public services, and reduces the financial impact of losses.

It should be noted that risk management strategies on the local level can have negative impacts on risk management strategies on the governmental level. For example, if local governments are able to transfer loss burdens to higher government levels, they may not be paying adequate attention to financial and physical planning measures. Case studies about earthquake events in the USA between 1980 and 1987 suggests that federal and state disaster relief provide a significant disincentive for localities to purchase insurance or to earmark contingency and other reserve funds specifically for disaster recovery. However, considering the time lag between when losses are incurred and relief payments arrive, local governments at risk from natural hazards need to have adequate contingency funds in reserve to act prompt (Burby 1991: 58). Also, there is an important distinction between individuals and a governmental entity. Unlike individuals, where experience with a disaster rather than perception of risk leads people to insure their property (Kunreuther 1996, 1997) for local governments perceptions rather than experience seems to be the key. That difference is probably due to the fact of turnover among local government personnel. The person making insurance purchase decisions today may not even be aware of the losses his or her government experienced in a natural disaster some years earlier (Burby 1991: 99).

4.3.3 Risk management strategies

Governments have principally four possibilities to ease their financial burden in the context of natural disaster losses: First, they can continue as before and recover from the effects of a disaster event as best they can using available resources. Second, they can eliminate the risk, e.g. by locating infrastructure out of hazard prone areas. Third, they can reduce the risk (mitigation), e.g. by retrofitting existing facilities and the last and fourth option is to transfer risk to other levels (Burby 1991: 1). However, the different measures should be chosen in relation to the frequency and the severity of the natural hazard, where losses would be least for low frequency/low severity events and greatest for high frequency/high severity events (see figure 4.2). While for the high frequency events it is easy to assess the risk by historical data, natural disasters are low frequency/high severity events so that estimates are much more difficult to obtain. Especially the identification of the exposure to risk is generally more difficult when assessing losses resulting from natural disasters than for other types of risks that governmental entities face because of the poor data on or lack an inventory of facilities and therefore the estimation is difficult and barely accurate. The problem arises also because governments usually do not keep detailed records of the value of its entire inventory of public facilities.

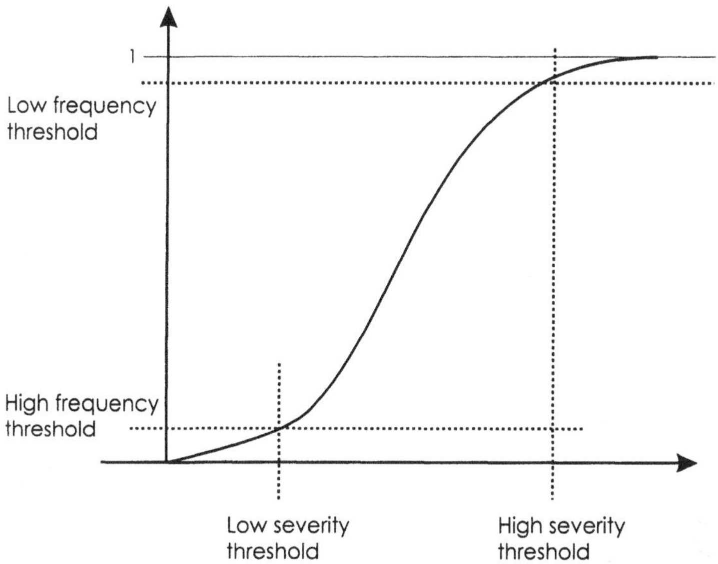

Figure 4.2: Loss distribution: severity and frequency thresholds.

The losses of greatest concern are those of the highest severity. Governments may eliminate those losses by various techniques, e.g. by discontinuing the service that is at risk or by moving facilities to an area that is less risk prone. However, the elimination of risks to public facilities from natural hazards is a limited risk management tool for governmental entities. A much more feasible strategy to reduce losses from natural hazards is to limit the susceptibility of facilities to damage through various hazard mitigation measures, such as retrofitting facilities and adopting appropriate land use regulations. Furthermore, land use changes can have impacts on the severity of natural hazards and therefore can increase or decrease damages. For example, modeling results of the Yasu basin in Japan indicated that the scattered land use transformation have resulted in increased flood peaks in the order of 7-18 percent. The increase in flood peaks were attributed mainly to changes in flow resistance due to different land use (Kimaro et al. 2003). On the other hand, appropriate land use changes can also decrease the impact of natural hazards, e.g. restoration of rivers and forests. For low severity/low frequency events the government can finance the losses through reserve funds or to the imposition of emergency taxes or surcharges on a one-time basis, or it might turn to the capital markets and issue debt to finance the losses. For the Low or low to medium severity/ high frequency events governments might be best advised to assume those losses through the use of contingency or reserve funds, provided that the funds have adequate levels of resources. For high severity events, borrowing may present an alternative source of funding those catastrophic losses, although a catastrophic loss may have eliminated resources to such an extent that the borrowing capacity of the governmental entity is severely constrained (Burby 1991: 74). Chapter 5 looks in more detail on the ex-post and ex-ante measures a government may use to increase its financial resilience and therefore decrease the risk of negative long-term macroeconomic effects due to natural disasters.

While there is a growing awareness of the negative impacts on the public sector due to natural catastrophes table 4.3 indicates a low level of support in disaster risk reduction within relief and development departments. Also the funding for risk reduction seems quite low: Only 7-8 percent (C$3.5 million) of CIDA's annual humanitarian assistance budget of C$40-50 million accounts for disaster prevention. The Inter American Development Bank's annual lending for risk reduction is between 5 and 10 percent (4 billion USD and 9.5 billion USD). SIDA spends only 1 percent of their total budget on risk reduction. The SDC spend 10 -20 percent of its overall humanitarian aid budget on disaster prevention and preparedness (around 20 million Swiss Francs). OFDA aims to allocate 10 percent of its emergency budget (10-20 million USD) to risk reduction, however, it can get pinched when a big emergency occurs. The World Banks total annual lending is 16-19 billion USD, of which $3-5 billion a year is spent on operations linked to emergencies (which also includes social crisis etc.) (Trobe and Venton 2003: 46f).

While government catastrophe (insurance) programs are very limited in developing and emerging economy countries, such programs are established more often in developed countries, especially after a major natural disaster has occurred. The various programs differ widely amongst each other and implicitly reflect the underlying exposures and the social milieu of each country. Some of this programs are presented next.

The **National Flood Insurance Program (NFIP)** in the USA was created in 1968 and covers damages caused by water. In order to benefit from the NFIP, communities must fulfill some requirements: risk has to be assessed, the area has to be mapped and most important risk control measures have to be designed and adopted. The maximum cover for residential buildings and contents is 250000 and 100000 USD respectively. The deductible is around 500 USD. The NFIP is funded by the government. The **California Earthquake Authority (CEA)** was created 1996 as a consequence of the Northridge earthquake and covers the houses but not other structures such as swimming pools or garages. If the capacity of the fund is exhausted settlements with policyholders are pro-

Organisation	Total No. of Staff	No.of Risk Reduction Staff in Headquarters	Location of Risk Reduction Staff
Canadian Government (CIDA)	1600	1 day a month, 1 full time	International Humanitarian Assistance, Policy
European Union (ECHO/ DIPECHO)	225 (relief sector)	5	DIPECHO/ECHO
Inter-American Development Bank (IDB)	1600	16	Environment, Finance and Infrastructure divisions
Swedish Government (SIDA)	650	18 (also on conflict)	Humanitarian Affairs and Conflict Department
Swiss Government (SDC)	619	No information available	-
UK Government (DFID)	2695	1 full time, 4 part time (with the ability to call upon a group of approx. 20 advisors with risk reduction knowledge)	Conflict and Humanitarian Affairs Department
United Nations (UNDP)	4000 (development sector)	5	Disaster Reduction Unit
US Government (USAID)	7912	No information available	-
World Bank	10000	5	Disaster Management Facility

Table 4.3: Risk reduction units within development departments. Source: Adapted from Trobe and Venton 2003.

rated. The contents coverage is limited to 5000 USD. A deductible of 15 percent on home and contents applied to the total loss is set. CEA is not funded by the government. The **Florida Hurricane Catastrophe Fund (FHCF)** was established in 1993 as a consequence of Hurricane Andrew. The fund reimburses a portion of insurers' losses after a hurricane is declared by the National Hurricane Center and therefore the fund is used for reinsurance. For insurers it is mandatory to purchase reinsure from the fund. The deductible is adjustable and was 4.9 billion USD in 2004 for the entire industry. The FHCF is not funded by the government. The **Catastrophes Naturelles** in France was created in 1982 as a consequence of floods in the southwest of France. It is used for reinsurance. The purchase of reinsurance from the fund by primary carriers is voluntary. It is funded by the government. The **Icelandic Catastrophe Fund** in Iceland was created 1975 according to the Iceland Catastrophe Insurance Act and act as a primary insurer. All property and contents insured against fire are automatically insured against direct losses resulting from earthquakes, volcanic eruptions, snow avalanches, landslides and floods. The fund is not funded by the government. The **Japanese Earthquake**

Reinsurance Company (JER) was started in 1966 and covers the following perils: Earthquake, tsunami and volcanic damage to residential properties. It is used for reinsurance. The purchase of reinsurance from the fund by primary carriers is mandatory. The JER is funded partially by the government because it is protected by an excess of loss retro program on which the major underwriter is the Japanese government. The **Earthquake Commission (EQC)** in New Zealand was established in 1994 to replace the Earthquake and War Damage Commission of 1944. It acts as a primary insurer and covers the following perils: Earthquake, tsunami, volcanic eruption and geothermal activity for personal property. The deductible is 1 percent of the loss. The EQC is not funded by the government. The **Norsk Naturskadepool** in Norway was created in 1980 and covers damages caused by floods, storms, earthquakes, avalanches, volcanic eruptions , and tidal waves to personal and commercial property. Purchase of reinsurance from the fund by primary carriers is compulsory in property policies which cover natural perils. The fund is not funded by the government. The **Consorcio de Compensacion de Seguros** in Spain was created in 1954 as an extension to the "Cosorcio de Compensacion de Motin" which covered war damages. It acts as a primary insurer and covers business interruption, direct damage to personal and commercial property as a result of earthquakes, tidal waves, floods, volcanic eruptions, and cyclonic storms, acts of terrorism, rebellion, insurrection, riots and civil commotion, and acts or actions of the armed forces in times of peace. The state guarantees unlimited coverage. The deductible is usually fixed at 10 percent of the claim with a maximum of 1 percent of the sum insured and a minimum of 150 Euro. In Switzerland the **Elementarschadenpool** which was created in 1939 covers damages from flooding, storm, hail, avalanche, snow pressure, landslide, rockfall and earthslip It acts as a primary insurer. The deductible is 15 percent of the claim per building. The Elementarschadenpool is not funded by the government. The **Taiwan Residential Earthquake Insurance Pool (TRIP)** created in 2002 acts as a primary insurer with no deductibles and is funded by the government. The cover responds only to a constructive total loss. Payment is provided when the damage ratio exceeds 50 percent. The **Turkey Catastrophe Insurance Pool (TCIP)** was created in the year 2000 and covers primary basic structures. The rates are calculated according to the location of risk. TCIP is not funded by the government. (Guy Carpenter 2003).

While this thesis is mainly concerned with the financial aspects of natural disasters in the public sector, there are however various other public sector interventions in response to natural disasters. An excellent review of some of the ex-ante and ex-post strategies that public agencies can adopt to effectively protect households and their members from the adverse impact of aggregate shocks is given by Skoufias (2003). Table 4.4 gives a summary of some of the instruments available to governments in the event of a natural disaster. The advantages and disadvantages of some of these instruments are discussed below.

Intervention type	Beneficiaries
Cash transfers	Poor families, women and children; Working poor including informal sector; Disabled; Poor elderly; other vulnerable groups
Public works	Poor unemployed and underemployed including informal sector; Poor agricultural workers during off seasons
Unemployment assistance	Formal sector unemployed
Wage subsidies	Formal sector unemployed, working age youth, usually poor
Commodity price subsidies	Poor and extreme poor families, especially the urban working poor
Targeted human development	Poor students; poor families with access to health services
Service fee waivers	Poor students; poor families with access to health services
Food and nutrition	Small children, pregnant and lactating mothers; children attending schools in poor communities
Microfinance	Poor microentrepreneurs, Poor women
Social funds	Poor families, women and children; poor unemployed and under-employed

Table 4.4: Government intervention types. Source: Adapted from Blomquist et al. 2002.

Cash transfers usually do not distort prices and can directly meet critical household needs. However they can distort incentives to labour market participation and the implementation of such cash transfers are usually very information intensive (e.g. "newly" poor). Public works (usually infrastructure development projects) can be implemented or adapted very quickly after crisis and the programme size can be easily reduced once the crisis is over. Also, needed infrastructure is created and maintained. However, such programs can distort incentives to labour market participation and they are difficult to administer. Unemployment assistance provides immediate assistance to eligible beneficiaries in the event of a crises and has automatic countercyclical financing characteristics. But, as with cash transfers and public work, they can distort incentives to labour market participation and the assistance is biased to urban formal sectors. Wage subsidies can be implemented quickly after crises onset and can reach individuals with a variety of skills and experience. However, it has substantial negative incentive effects for employers and it is also biased to urban formal sectors. Commodity price subsidies have potentially (depending on the delivery mechanism) low administrative costs and can be implemented or expanded quickly after the crises. But one of the problems with such programs is, that they are difficult to remove once established due to interest group pressures. Also, they are often biased to urban populations and distorts commodity prices and use. Microfinance promotes physical capital accumulation in poor communities and may increase household income and benefits of public resources may be enhanced by multiplier investment effects. But such intervention types are administratively costly and biased to rural populations (limited beneficiary group). Also there is only limited application to economy wide crises because of procyclical demand for microcredit. Social Funds may promote human and physical capital accumulations in poor communities and there is a high degree of community involvement in project selection and implementation. However, they are difficult to implement or adapt quickly after crisis onset and are again often biased to rural populations (Blomquist et al. 2002: 319-320).

As this chapter has shown the risk management measures and the principles behind it to lessen the impacts of a natural disaster can vary widely. For the risk management and modeling approach a detailed analysis is needed and the main focus is now on the government and its financial resilience.

Chapter 5

Financial resilience of the public sector

In the last chapter an overall introduction to risk management measures against natural disasters from the individual to the country level for the private and public sector was given. However, for a further development of the financial vulnerability concept (e.g. financing gap) as well as for modeling purposes presented in the next chapter a more in-depth discussion about the financial resilience of the public sector is needed.

A government has two options for loss financing after a disaster. It can rely on *ex-post* financing sources which is the most common praxis today or it arranges *ex-ante* risk financing strategies before the event occurs. Table 5.1 shows the ex-post and ex-ante financing sources for assistance and reconstruction the government may use. The need for a proactive approach in loss financing is now recognized in the literature (Mechler 2005a: 130). However, it is also recognized that a proactive approach has trade-offs in terms of forgone opportunities to other investments. Therefore the cost and benefits of such approaches have to be considered. The framework presented in this thesis (figure 2.2) is the starting point to analyze the benefits and costs on a macroeconomic scale. Generally speaking, the trade-off between **stability** and **growth** has to be analyzed.

Ex-ante financing instruments	Ex-post financing instruments
Reserve fund	Diversion from budget
Insurance	Taxation
Catastrophe bonds	Foreign reserves
Contingent Credit	Domestic bonds and (central bank) credit
	Multilateral borrowing
	International borrowing
	Aid

Table 5.1: Ex-ante and ex-post financing sources. Source: Adapted from Mechler 2005a: 130.

The next section introduces ex-post financing options available for the public sector. Section 5.2 presents new ex-ante financial instruments as well as mitigation measures which can be part of a proactive macroeconomic risk management strategy for governments in developing and emerging countries. The concrete modeling approach of each of the instruments is presented in chapter 6.

5.1 Ex-post financing options for governments

This section describes the options governments may have for financing relief and reconstruction through ex-post measures following a major disaster. It is kept rather short because these options have already been discussed heavily in the literature (Freeman 2000, Charvériat 2000, Freeman et al. 2003, Mechler 2004a). Generally speaking, there are four ex-post sources of financing disaster relief and recovery (Benson 1997a, Fischer and Easterly 1990) (table 5.2). All of these options have their own costs and constraints (e.g. availability) which are important to analyze before planning to use them.

Type	Source
Decreasing government expenditure	Diversion from budget
Raising government revenues	Taxation
Domestic Deficit financing	Central Bank credit Reserves Domestic bonds and credit
External Deficit financing	MFI borrowing International bonds Assistance

Table 5.2: Ex-post financing sources.

Diverting funds from other budget items may appear first to have little direct costs to the government. However, there *are* some costs: First, there are costs in terms of the foregone returns or benefits of the budgeted projects and services. Second, there may be high political costs since ministries are often reluctant to reduce their expenditures even in times of crises. Third, there are also costs in terms of the disruption of government planning. However, in times of catastrophes, money is needed and it is common in developing countries to divert resources from the budget to finance the losses following a disaster. For example, the Philippines diverted 3.5% of spending after the 1991 Mt. Pinatubo outbreak. Also, the Fiji government diverted 5.3% of its budgeted expenditures following the 1993 cyclone Kina (Benson 1997a, 1999). However, the option of diversion is mainly constrained by the fact that budgetary expenditures are most of the time already reduced to bar necessities and furthermore are often under pressure to reduce budget deficits. For example, Bolivia, Colombia and El Salvador have all experienced difficulties in reallocating current budgets to finance reconstruction projects due to these problems (Freeman et al. 2002b: 43). But still, the benefits of using budgetary resources to finance lost assets and undertake relief can outweigh the costs.

Establishing **additional taxes** is always problematic, especially after a major disaster when the economy is typically in a low-growth situation (see section 3.5). A catastrophe tax can have high administrative costs and/or will further compress consumption thus adding to recessionary tendencies. In recent years, many developing countries have initiated tax reforms that have lowered many types of tax rates, while increasing efficiency of the tax collection methods. For example, through the increasing efficiency in tax collection and reducing tax exemptions El Salvador had additional tax revenue even after the earthquakes in 2001. The reconstruction after the 1999 earthquake in Colombia was primarily financed by the creation of a new tax a few months earlier. This tax was not originally intended for disaster relief (Freeman et al. 2003: 55).

If sufficient funds cannot be raised through diversion or taxation, the government must turn to other options. Typically deficit financing comes into play. The instruments include credit from the central bank or the private sector (commercial banks and private households), tapping into the foreign reserves of the central bank, taking out loans from MFIs or selling bonds abroad. In comparison to private corporations, governments have an additional alternative which increases their financial resiliency which is not available to private corporations: The access to external financing (Freeman 2000: 55). However, from the standpoint of macroeconomic policy, one key question is how much and how rapidly the government can afford to borrow the finances of the reconstruction costs, while keeping fiscal policy on a sustainable path (IMF and WB 2001).

A **central bank credit** is usually obtained by the government selling bonds to the central bank. This results in money creation, which can lead to inflation if the money growth is not in proportion to real GDP growth (Fischer and Easterly 1990). The use of foreign exchange reserves of the central bank is problematic. There is the risk of provoking a balance-of-payment crises due to the lack of needed reserves for imports. Hence, the World Bank and International Monetary Fund have strongly recommended against their use (IMF and WB 2001). These instruments are particularly problematic in developing countries where inflation and external debt issues are important policy issues (Ferranti et al. 2000). Therefore, in most Latin American and Caribbean countries, central bank borrowing is constitutionally permitted only in the case of natural disaster (Linnerooth-Bayer, Mace and Verheyen 2003: 16ff).

Also **borrowing** domestically or abroad is problematic. Domestic borrowing, if at all possible, may also compress consumption domestically, particularly in shallow credit markets. This could result in a rise of the interest rate and a crowding-out of domestic investment. Borrowing abroad increases future debt service obligations and thus the potential for a fiscal and debt crisis if large portions of the revenue have to be used or insufficient foreign exchange is available to service the external debt (Fischer and Easterly 1990).

The costs of either issuing **bonds** or taken a **credit** differ. The capital market conditions for issuing bonds are contingent on sovereign ratings from rating agencies such as Moody's or Standard & Poors . The lower the rating, the higher the risk premium and total interest on bonds will be. The constraints for external credit come from the demand side as well as the supply side whereas demand is restricted by external debt sustainability. The Highly Indebted Poor Countries Initiative (HIPC) assesses on a regular basis the debt sustainability for developing countries. The main indicator used in the initiative is the ratio of the net present value of debt to exports. A ratio of less than 150% is generally regarded as a sustainable value for this indicator. Another important indicator is the debt service/exports ratio for which a value above 20% signals a problematic debt situation. On the supply side, MFIs offer loans at more generous terms than borrowing at market conditions. Whereas the supply of international loans is potentially unconstrained for the purposes of reconstruction financing, the availability of MFI loans is limited by the willingness of the donor community to grant subsidized credit. MFI loans come at high and low concession conditions. Eligibility for high concession loans is determined by per capita income. The World Bank through the International Development Association (IDA) offers high concession loans to the poorest low-income countries with a per-capita income of less than 885 USD. Countries with higher incomes have to borrow on significantly higher terms.

Assistance from abroad after a catastrophe includes private and public donations from private institutions, government agencies and inter-governmental agencies. Aid inflows come in the form of relief, technical assistance, grants, commodities and money. The amount of assistance is dependent on the event and on the will of the donors to grant assistance which is furthermore dependent on the media attention of the event. International aid to countries after major catastrophes appears to be dependent on both the will of the donor communities and the size/publicity of the disaster. Thus, there is a considerable uncertainty as regards to the amount of aid obtained.

Table 5.3 gives a summary of the risks and costs of ex-post financial instruments available for the government.

5.2 Ex-ante instruments for governments

In this section ex-ante (financial) instruments for governments which can be used to increase their financial resilience or decrease their financial vulnerability and therefore also decrease its macroeconomic risk due to natural disasters are presented. The following instruments were chosen: Mitigation, Reinsurance, Reserve fund, Contingent Credit and Catastrophe bonds.

Ex-post measure	Costs and Risks
Diversion	Costs of foregone returns Political costs Disruption of planning and development processes
Taxation	High administrative costs Compress consumption Political costs
Central Bank Credit	Inflation Balance-of-payments crises
Borrowing	Fiscal and debt crisis
Assistance	High uncertainty Probably decreasing in the future

Table 5.3: Disadvantages of ex-post instruments.

5.2.1 Mitigation

The concept of Mitigation can be seen as a bulk of various methods to lessen the direct impacts of a disaster.

> *Mitigation* is any action taken to minimize the extent of a disaster or potential disaster. Mitigation can take place before, during or after a disaster. Mitigation measures are both physical or structural ... and non-structural. (Benson and Twigg 2004: 21).

This thesis is concerned with mitigation actions taken before a disaster. Successful mitigation measures will lower the direct risk that an extreme future hazard event becomes a disaster. Two separate measures can be distinguished: Structural and non-structural mitigation. *Structural mitigation* measures are reducing the physical susceptibility of the exposed elements at risk or reducing the impact of an extreme event. Therefore, for different hazards, different structural mitigation measures have to be used, e.g. building earthquake resistant houses, building dykes against flooding. Furthermore, the consequences of such mitigation measures can be different for each hazard.

Structural mitigation measures can also increase the direct risk: First, because of the possibility that in the case of failure the impact is even more devastating (e.g. a dam breaks), and second because structural mitigation measures have the potential to provide people with a false sense of security, e.g. development in high-risk areas. Therefore structural mitigation measures should be accompanied by appropriate land-use planning and public awareness programs (Freeman et al. 2003: 4). *Non-structural mitigation* measures include the training of people who are living in hazard prone areas in disaster management and response, public education programs and/or the regulation of land use.

Especially, in development countries with only scarce resources the question if disaster mitigation or disaster recovery is more cost-effective, and how much of it to buy, is a very serious question. In an economic context, the amount of disaster mitigation that is warranted is the amount that can be bought for less than the cost of losses that are averted through mitigation efforts. However, some of the benefits and costs associated with a disaster are not quantifiable, e.g. loss of life, social or political costs. The focus is here to economic losses but the additional non quantifiable advantages of mitigation should be kept in mind. From a purely economic point of view the costs for investments in mitigation measures are sometimes quite lower than the benefits. For example, a cost-benefit analysis for eight cities in the Argentina Flood Rehabilitation Project found an internal rate of return of 35 percent. The Rio Flood Reconstruction and Prevention Project reduced total floodable areas by 40 percent through flood control dams and improved drainage. They achieved an estimated 6.5 benefit-cost ratio for seven subbasins of the Iguau and Sarapui Rivers (World Bank 2001: 172). Improvement projects and restoration works after the flooding in 1998 of the Abukuma river basin in Japan cost 80 billion yen and took one and a half years between 1998 and 2000 but reduced the inundation area by 70 percent and the number of inundated houses by 80 percent (Hiroki 2003). In the case of large scale infrastructure projects, FEMA estimated that the costs of including hurricane and earthquake resistant techniques increase the initial costs only by 0.5 to 2 percent (PAHO/WHO 1994: 82).

Figure 5.1 shows the relationship between the cost of mitigation and damage reduction whereas the three different lines conceptually representing different sizes of events because the efficiency of a mitigation measure is dependent on the impact (e.g. peak per ground acceleration) of the event. For events with lower impacts (upper curve) one can secure substantial reductions in damage at relatively little expenditure. However, at a certain point it generally becomes increasingly difficult and costly to achieve further reductions. Therefore, most of the time a ineliminable risk of damage will exists, e.g. it is not possible to build earthquake resistant houses for all possible earthquake impacts.

Structural mitigation measures did not have to be very expensive, even on the household level. For example in the USA after Hurricane Andrew, studies of the added costs of materials and labor for hurricane-resistant designs indicated that it will add no more than 4-5% to the cost of a new home. Furthermore, this additional expenses were not substantial relative to the added benefits of safety and security (Unnewehr 1994). The benefits are associated with a decrease of direct risk of damage, but it is crucial to understand that physical vulnerability reduction through structural mitigation measures is not a smooth function as will be explained in the following.

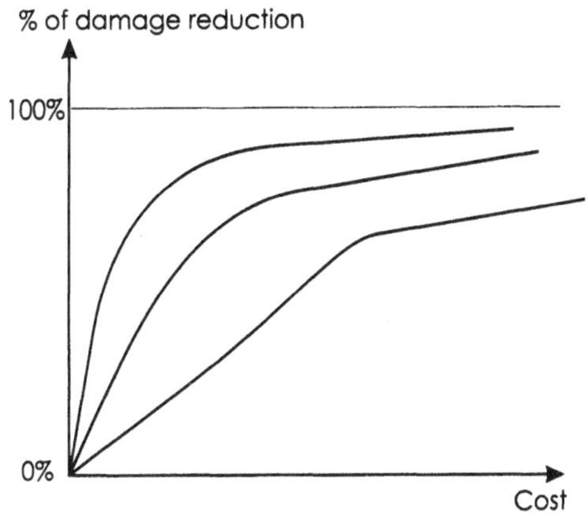

Figure 5.1: Decreasing marginal damage reduction. Source: Adapted from Rescher 1983: 137.

It is generally believed (Quarantelli 1991) that mitigation should be agent-specific, however, there are some similarities of the effects of mitigation measures that should be noticed. As stated before, constructing earthquake resistant houses makes them only resistant to some upper level of impact. It is impossible to build houses that are resistant to all possible impacts mainly because the financial expenses for the construction of such a house gets (exponentially) higher and higher. Assume now that an earthquake hits a strengthened house. If the magnitude exceeds the capacity of the house to withstand it the house gets destroyed. Therefore the expenses for mitigation are lost and the full damage, like in the case with no mitigation measures occur. This effect can be seen best through the use of fragility curves. For example, Altay et al. (2002) compared the effects of earthquake mitigation measures for apartment houses in Turkey. Figure 5.2 shows on the x-axis the peak ground acceleration (PGA) which can be seen as the severity of the earthquake and the y-axis shows the damage probability for four different types of damages (slight, moderate, major and collapse) for given PGA levels, e.g P(slight damage | PGA).

As one can see the fragility curves, corresponding to a given damage level, shift to the right as the structure is strengthened. Furthermore, after some impact level is reached the probability of damage can be seen as one and depending on the structural mitigation measures the full loss occurs, which usually indicates that the house has to be rebuild. The same logic can be used for structural mitigation measures against floods, like dams. For example, the flooding in Germany and Austria in August 2002 caused severe losses due to the fact that the embankments were not high enough. Hence, they were not useful anymore and were destroyed very fast. These examples can be applied on also for hurricanes or tsunamis (e.g. hurricane Katrina in the USA). For further discussions see

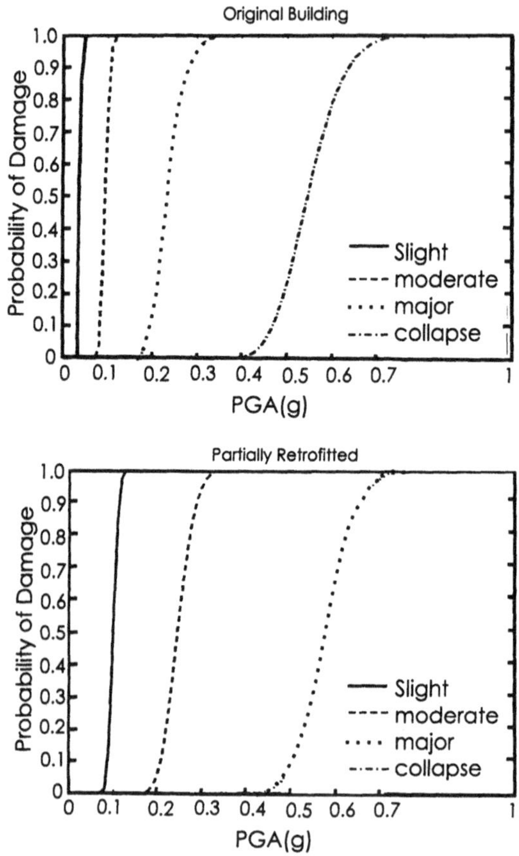

Figure 5.2: Fragility curves of partially retrofitted and original building. Source: Altay et al. 2002.

Quarantelli (1991). The point is, that mitigation effects ideally can be represented as a step function.

In figure 5.3 the y-axes represents the losses on assets for a given impact of a disaster (x-axis), e.g. strength of an earthquake vs. damage of a house, or flood level vs. damage of an entire area. If no mitigation measures were set, the full loss occurs, which is indicated through the hypothetical loss (pointed line). The bold printed line shows the loss as a function of the hypothetical loss. Up to a limit given by the invested mitigation no loss occurs. If the hypothetical loss is larger than this limit, the full loss occurs. As one can see such disasters have **two** negative effects at once. First, the expenses for mitigation are lost and second no reduction of losses could be achieved through the mitigation efforts.

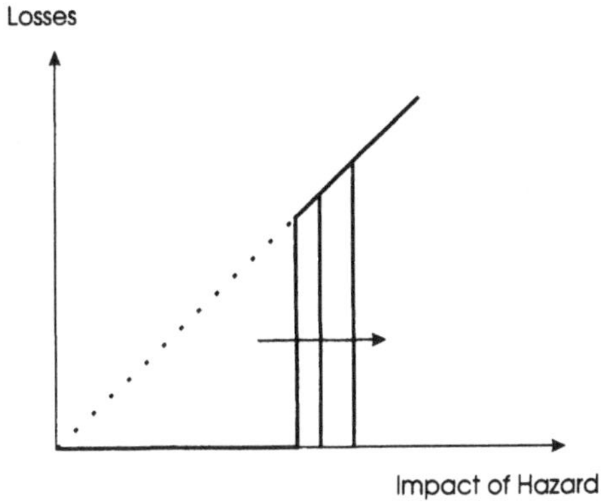

Figure 5.3: Mitigation efficiency seen as a step function.

5.2.2 Catastrophe reserve fund

The purpose of a catastrophe reserve (or calamity) fund is to establish a reserve to cover the potential costs of a disaster. The main principle here is risk capital accumulation. The fund accumulates in those years without catastrophes and is used only in the case of a catastrophe to finance the losses. The accumulation should be done on an annual basis. If the amount of funds are equal through the years they accumulate linearly (see figure 5.4).

Many countries have put into place reserve funds to decrease their dependency on debt financing. For example, state and local governments in the USA have historically relied upon reserve and contingency funds as a financial risk management tool for dealing with unexpected events (Burby 1991: 66). In 2001 the "Natural Disasters Fund" (FONDEN), was created by the Mexican government to prevent imbalances in the federal government finances derived from outlays caused by natural catastrophes. In Colombia, the federal government is obligated by law to dedicate a part of their budget to the constitution on a natural disaster reserve fund. Costa Rica, Nicaragua and Honduras are also interested in similar funds (Charvériat 2000).

There are two main problems which can be addressed to catastrophe reserve funds. *First*, when starting a reserve fund it takes some time to build up substantial capital reserves. If a disaster happens before the reserve fund has reached a substantial level, it is likely that the fund is insufficient for loss financing (figure 5.4: Scenario 1). Analysis in El Salvador showed, that reserve funds cost only the expected losses each year but provide less protection if compared with insurance or contingent credit arrangements. Only after an accumulation time of at least 22 years the reserve fund provide an equal level of protection (Mechler 2004a: 71). Furthermore, after a disaster the reserve fund will be depleted and it would again take some time for accumulation. Therefore, there is the risk

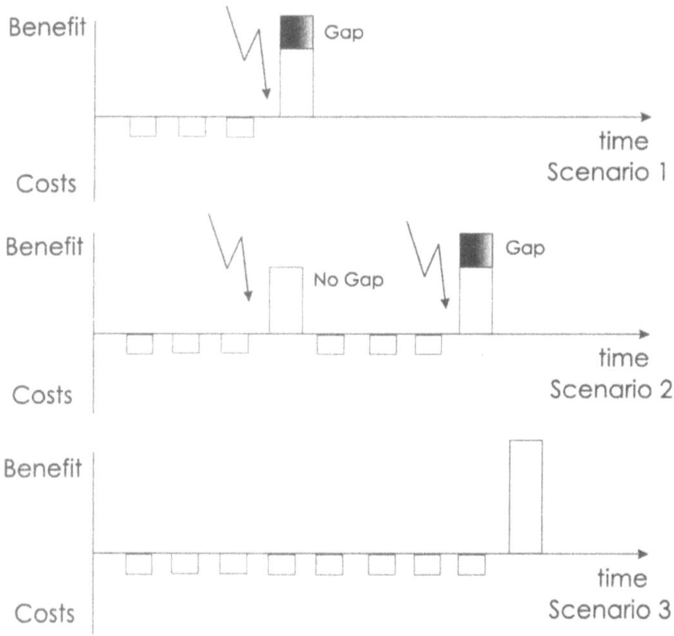

Figure 5.4: Catastrophe reserve fund: financial streams.

that the reserve fund is insufficient for loss financing if a second disaster happens in the near future after the first disaster (figure 5.4: Scenario 2). *Second*, the risk of depletion is relatively high, especially in capital-scarce economies. The trend is if disasters have not occurred for a longer while, the fund will be used for financing other important issues. Sometimes even the budgetary process does not allow to accumulate funds over budget years (Freeman et al. 2002b: 54). Additional problems with catastrophe reserve funds include changing government administrations and political priorities which can decrease or even stop the accumulation process. Also, because the value of resources increase with inflations, the size of the reserve fund may also need an increase over time (Burby 1991: 67).

However, there are also advantages of catastrophe reserve funds. First, the opportunity cost of a reserve fund is the interest foregone on the resources invested in the fund, but the accumulation capital is not lost in the case of no event (figure 5.4: Scenario 3). Secondly, in time of need the reserve fund could be used without any time delay.

5.2.3 Insurance and reinsurance

Losses caused by occurrences of unexpected events are serious problems for individuals, firms and the society as a whole. Insurance is a mechanism for spreading these losses. The insured party, usually called the policyholder, receives coverage indemnification against the loss from an uncertain event from the insurer. The insurer in exchange gets a certain payment from the policyholder, called the premium. The loss to be reimbursed based on an insurance contract is called a claim.

An insurance contract without some limitation as to maximum amount or maximum duration of benefits is virtually unknown. Therefore, by agreement between the insurer and the insured, contracts of insurance carry some form of limitation coverage. The basic limitations on coverage for a single loss are deductible or retention, maximum or limit and pro rata share. Combinations of these basic limitations are common (Hogg and Klugman 1984: 8). The most common form of loss exclusion on smaller losses is the **deductible**. This election reduces the cost of the coverage purchased and eliminates the need for the insurer to become involved in the processing of small claims, which is usually a relatively expensive and time consuming process. In the deductible, the policyholder agrees to absorb the full cost of losses which fall below an amount specified in the contract, furthermore, he has to absorb this agreed upon amount on all losses which exceed this deductible limit (figure 5.5: point A). In the **disappearing deductible**, the insured absorbs the full cost of losses that fall below the amount of the deductible. If the loss amount exceeds the deductible, the policyholder pays only a percentage of the deductible. The percentage decreases the higher the losses exceed the deductible until at some amount of loss the amount of the deductible is waived entirely (figure 5.5: point B).

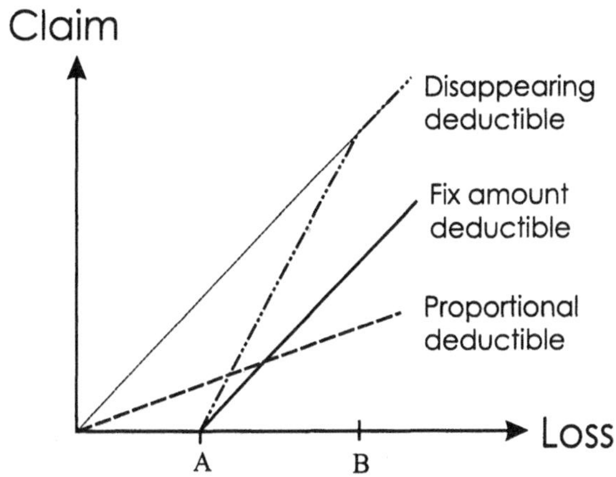

Figure 5.5: Payment function under disappearing, fix amount and proportional deductible.

As the size of the deductible increases, the terminology changes and the deductible becomes known as the **retention** (Hogg and Klugman 1984: 7). Hence, the retention is nothing more than the insurer's deductible in the event of a loss. The insured absorbs the amount of the retention and, furthermore, pays the amount of the retention on all losses that exceed the amount of the retention. The larger the value of the insured item, the larger the retention the insured is willing to assume. Retentions are common in contracts between an insurer and its reinsurer. Another method of coverage limitation is for the insured to assume some percentage of all losses. This participation by the insured is generally referred to as **pro rata** or **quota share** insurance or reinsurance. In this arrangement the insured has to pay a percentage of the losses himself (see figure 5.5). This type is used to reduce moral hazard.

The insurance market uses the pooling of risk in order to spread the losses. It is well know that the "Law of Large Numbers"[1] underlies the principle of risk pooling: For a series of independent and identically distributed variables the sample mean over the variables converges to the theoretical population mean. For insurance, this means that the variance of average claim payments decreases as the number of policyholders increases. This in turn increases the degree of confidence in the calculation of the premium. However, there are some important assumptions which must be fulfilled so that a risk is insurable (Berliner 1982, Freeman 2000, Moss 2002, Mechler 2004a, Swiss Re 2005b).

- **Uncertainty:** Insurance policies are designed for events that are unintended and uncertain. A risk is therefore uninsurable if the event can accurately be predicted in time, space and magnitude.
- **Low correlation:** The risks covered by the insurer must be independent of one another (like automobile accidents). This assumption is critical for using the law of large numbers which assumes independent and identical distributed random variables. However, this assumption is not always considered to be necessary, e.g. it is possible to diversify correlated risk into larger uncorrelated portfolios to reduce the insurers risk to an acceptable level (Dong and Grossi 2005).
- **Identification of losses:** The losses must be well defined in time and space. This assumption is critical to evaluate the expected losses over a given time period.
- **The probability of loss:** The probability distribution of the future losses should be accurately as possible estimable to calculate the expected losses and for setting the insurance premiums. The probability of losses can be estimated more accurately for high frequency events than for low frequency events which in turn influences the premium settings.

While the above points are more technical assumptions which must be fulfilled so that a risk is insurable, the following two points represent problems due to behavioral issues of people at risk:

- **Moral hazard:** Moral hazard relates to the fact that as the risk is insured, the insured party has less incentive to prevent the occurrence of the risk and therefore

[1] Also called "insurance principle"

the probability of loss may increase so that the premium will be too low. To avoid such behavior the insurance companies most of the time use deductibles and coinsurance so that the insured party is less reluctant to behave carelessly because they will have to pay some of the resulting losses by themselves.

- **Adverse selection:** Adverse selection occurs when the insured party knows more than the insurer about its own level of risk. For example, if the premium is based on the experience of a large population but only those in the highest risk category purchase coverage this risk is uninsurable. This can be seen in the following way: The insurer calculates his premium based on the average probability of the loss. Those at the highest risk will be most likely to buy insurance for that risk. But the premium is set on the average of risk, so the insurer will lose money because for a subpopulation with higher risk, the expected probability loss would be also higher, and therefore also higher premiums would be calculated. Therefore, the implicit assumption of adverse selection is that the purchaser of insurance knows more about the risk than the insurance company, e.g. he has more information on the probability of the loss. To avoid adverse selection it is necessary to estimate individual risks more carefully and charge premiums that reflect their risk position. This may be a costly process if the insurer has to bear the costs, but it may be feasible if each owner incurs this expense as a condition for obtaining the policy.

In the context of natural disaster risk, not all conditions above can be fulfilled. While the conditions on uncertainty, identification and estimation of the probability of losses and moral hazard are fulfilled the main problems are the low correlation assumption and adverse selection.

There is a general agreement in the literature that natural disasters are unintended and uncertain. In this context uncertainty means that a specific event cannot be predicted with absolute accuracy for a given area, only a probability for such an event can be calculated. Till now, no model exists which can accurately predict the timing, the location and the magnitude of natural hazards in the future. It seems that most of the natural hazards have such complex structures that an exact prediction is virtually impossible. Therefore the assumption of uncertainty is fulfilled in the context of natural disaster risk. However, the uncertainty must be measurable. The identification of losses and the estimation of loss distribution functions are difficult tasks due to the limited availability of past and present data. Therefore, estimating the probability and consequences of a natural disaster in a specific area are most of the time highly uncertain and ambiguous. Studies showed that insurers are quite averse to this uncertainty. This can be supported by comparing the variance of premiums from well-defined risks to ambiguous risks with the same expected loss (Kunreuther, Hogarth and Meszaros 1993). However, there is a growing awareness for the need of detailed spatial asset information both in the public and private sector. Furthermore, due to the rapid increase in highly qualitative computer based simulation models, more accurate predictions can be made. Overall, the identification and probability estimation of losses are problematic but can be solved. Moral hazard is not very problematic because nearly all policies against natural disaster losses include a deductible (Swiss Re 2005b: 19). Furthermore, especially in risk-prone areas, it is mandatory that mitigation measures have to be set before a contract can be underwritten (e.g. the National Flood Insurance Program (NFIP) in the USA).

Adverse selection is especially a problem in the context of natural disasters. Typically, in a country some people are at higher risk than others with respect to a natural hazard. As a result, those people at risk buy insurance while the others do not. This will result in higher premiums and therefore to thinner markets. Whenever the premiums are set so high as to compensate for adverse selection large numbers of people are not willing to pay for this actuarially fair rate. One possibility to prevent adverse selection is public intervention. For example, stakeholder approaches to establish such insurance schemes can be used (Linnerooth-Bayer and Kunreuther 2003). However, they are very time consuming but sometimes adequate on the long run perspective. A more serious problem for insurers is the low correlation assumption. The condition of independent events is not met. Therefore, the insurance principle cannot be used. The problem is, that natural disasters often impact entire regions and thus will affect all policyholders in that area. For the insurance company this means that their risk portfolio of losses is close to the variance of the individual losses if all policies are affected by the same event (Kunreuther 1998). This also may question the economic feasibility of national or regional insurance arrangements, because there is again no diversification of the risk portfolio (Swiss Re 2000). This issue apply as well to informal insurance arrangements that play a major role in developing countries. They also tend to collapse in the presence of dependent risk (Hoogeveen 2000).

While there are several problematic conditions for insuring catastrophe risk, there are also several means by which insurers can manage and diversify their catastrophe risk (Grace et al. 2003: 13):

- Reducing the geographic concentration of exposures in high risk areas.
- Modifying the terms of their insurance contracts.
- Encouraging risk mitigation.
- Purchasing reinsurance.
- Utilizing catastrophe-hedging financial instruments.
- Holding more capital, e.g. establishing catastrophe reserves.

Each of these measures have their own costs and constraints. Diversification of the risk exposure is sometimes not feasible. Modifications of insurance contracts to lower an insurer's risk may be undesirable to consumers. Risk mitigation needs ex-ante financial investments and is most of the times undervalued by homeowners (Kunreuther 1996).

In the private sector, reserves for future catastrophes are subjected to taxation. For example, Harrington and Niehaus (2001) showed that there are very high tax costs in the USA for setting aside capital for future catastrophe losses. Also, additional capital to fund catastrophe losses is subjected to expropriation through corporate takeovers or regulation. There are also some constraints on the reinsurers ability to assume a significant amount of risk, particularly at higher layers, however, most of the time insurer companies redistribute their risk to global reinsurer, and reinsurer redistribute their risk through capital market instruments like catastrophe bonds (see figure 5.6).

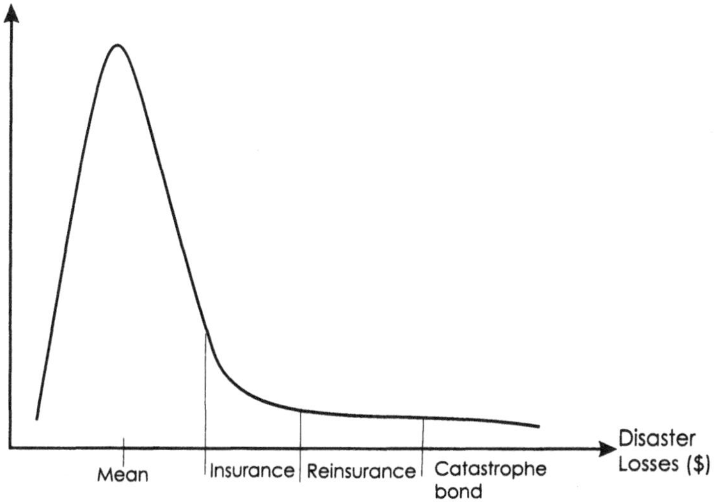

Figure 5.6: Probability distribution and financing instruments. Source: Adapted from Goes and Skees 2003.

As mentioned above, there are a number of ways how insurers can adjust their exposure of capital at risk: they may reduce their risk exposure, increase the amount of capital or use risk transfer themselves. The latter is usually done by means of reinsurance (Mechler 2004a: 75) and is presented next.

Through reinsurance, the industry's losses are absorbed and distributed among a group of companies. Therefore no single company is overburdened with the financial responsibility of offering coverage to its policyholder and a series of large losses that might be too great for an individual insurer to absorb can be handled through it (McIsaac and Babbel 1995: 1). Most of the reinsurance clients are primary insurers from all classes of insurance. The question how much business an insurer will reinsure depends on several variables, like insurer's business model, its capital strength and risk aversion, and prevailing market conditions. For example, insurers whose portfolios are exposed to natural catastrophic events have a strong need for reinsurance cover. Also small local players need more reinsurance coverage than larger insurers because they cannot diversify their insurance risk over a big client base. Furthermore, specialized insurers have a less balanced portfolio than insurers with many different lines of business. The main benefits of reinsurance are stabilization of underwriting results, financial flexibility and expertise (Swiss Re 2004a: 4-6).

The insurer is usually called the primary carrier, the ceding company, or the direct underwriter. The quantity of insurance which is ceded to a reinsurer is called the cession. If more of the risk is shifted to the reinsurer than it wants, the reinsurer may in turn reinsure a portion of risk, which is called retrocession.

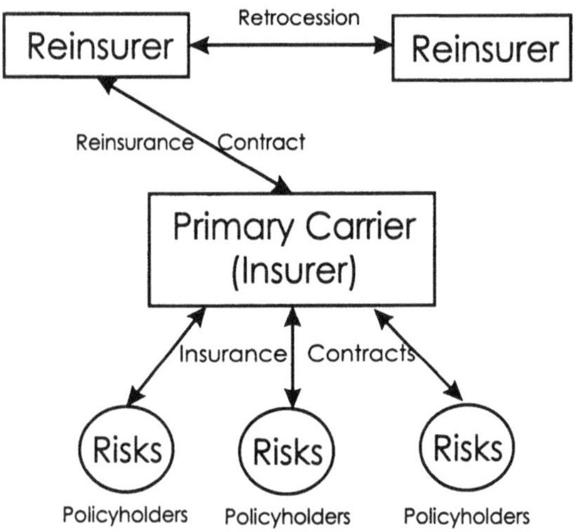

Figure 5.7: Policyholder, insurance, reinsurance, and retrocessions. Source: Adapted from McIsaac and Babbel 1995: 1.

The underlying principle for reinsurance is the same as for insurance. Therefore reinsurance is "insurance for insurers " (Swiss Re 2004a: 3). Reinsurance is essentially an international risk-sharing agreement that makes it possible to transfer catastrophic risk from the national insurance system to worldwide risk-sharing pools operated by multinational reinsurance companies. Table 5.4 shows the five biggest reinsurance groups in 2003. As one can see all companies have a financial strength rating of at least 'AA-', as measured by Standard & Poor's indicating that the credit risks are very small [2].

Similar as with insurance contracts, there are also different forms of reinsurance contracts (see McIsaac and Babbel 1995: 5) but for large unbalanced risks like catastrophe risks usually non-proportional reinsurance is used. One type of this non-proportional reinsurance is Excess-of-Loss (XL) reinsurance. It is the dominant reinsurance cover for natural disasters (Froot 1999: 2). In XL-reinsurance contracts, the ceding insurer bears

[2]The ranking has changed a little bit since 2005

	Rating (S&P 01/11/04)
Munich Re	A+
Swiss Re	AA
GE Insurance Solutions	A+
Hannover Re	AA-
Gen Re	AAA

Table 5.4: The five biggest reinsurance groups in 2003. Source: Swiss Re 2004a: 19.

the losses up to a certain point usually called the attachment point and the reinsurer pays the losses from the attachment point till to a maximum amount of loss, usually called the exit point. There are two basic types of XL-insurance: Per Risk XL where protection for only one risk is purchased and Per Risk Aggregate XL with protection for losses for a defined accumulation of individual risks.

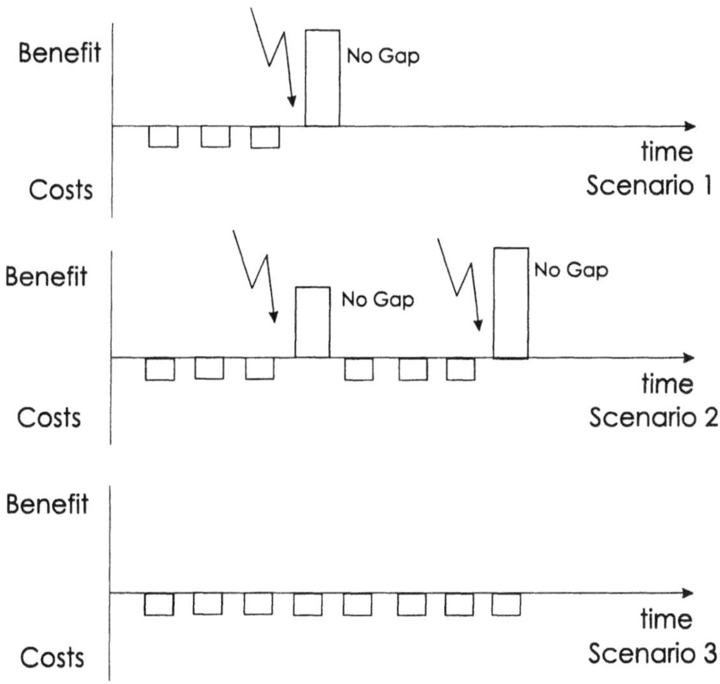

Figure 5.8: Financial streams of (re-)insurance.

The advantages and disadvantages of (re-)insurance can be seen in figure 5.8. While there are annual costs (premium payments) for holding the insurance policy which are foregone if no disaster occur (figure 5.8: Scenario 3), in the case of a disaster event the money needed for loss financing (claims) is provided by the (re-)insurance company in a short time period (figure 5.8: Scenario 1). Furthermore, no accumulation process is needed and the assets are insured right after the contract is signed (figure 5.8: Scenario 2).

5.2.4 Contingent credit

Contingent credit arrangements spread the risk inter-temporally instead of transferring the risk. The contingent credit options are most of the time grouped under alternative risk transfer instruments. The basic principle is that in exchange for an annual fee, the right is obtained to take out a specific loan amount after the event that has to be repaid at contractually fix conditions. Hence, a contingent credit has small annual administrative costs before the event but when an event occurs, large debt service payments after the event are necessary (figure 5.9: Scenario 1). This can increase the debt burden of a country significantly. On the other hand the funds are available in a matter of days, while diverting funds and acquire new loans would take several months (Freeman et al. 2003: 67). As with insurance, in the case of no disaster event the costs are foregone (figure 5.9: Scenario 2). However, the costs for a contingent credit are much lower than those for insurance.

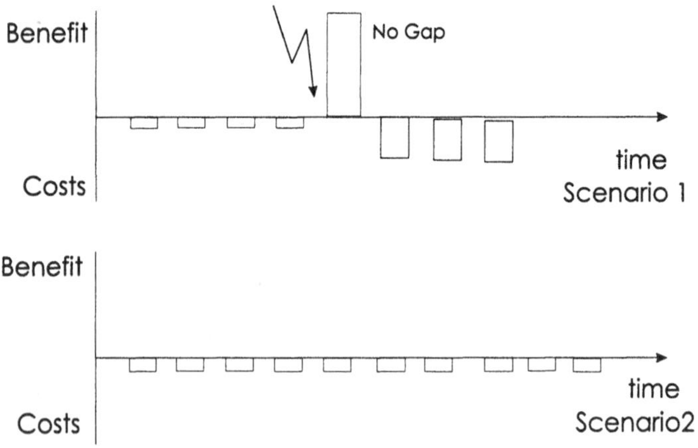

Figure 5.9: Contingent credit scheme.

Because of the annual payments for contingent credit arrangements ex-post borrowing is more attractive if interest rates are low. However, the negotiation process can take some time, whereas a contingent credit is there after the trigger event has happened.

5.2.5 Catastrophe bonds

Catastrophe bonds (cat-bonds) allow an issuing institution (e.g. insurer, reinsurer, companies) to transfer catastrophic exposures to investors. The bonds provide multi-year protection against catastrophic risks with no counterparty credit risk. Additionally, cat-bonds provide an alternative to traditional reinsurance when capacity is tight, especially for peak perils. To investors, cat-bonds offer high yield with low probability of default.

Cat-bonds have become an increasingly important part of the loss financing market. Catastrophe bonds are now a major segment of the insurance-linked securities (ILS) market. Since its inception, ILS has witnessed worldwide issuance in excess of 9.5 billion USD, were approximately 80 percent (7.5 billion USD) of these securities were cat-bonds. In 2003 over 2 billion USD worth of cat-bonds were issued. The market ended the year with over 4.3 billion USD, which is an increase of more than 50 percent from year end 2002 (Swiss Re 2004b). The primary drivers of the sector growth includes (i) the hardening of reinsurance pricing in recent years due to the high losses in the past and the lack of insurance capital, (ii) the increase of demand for fully collateralized protection in response to increased counterparty credit risk, (iii) the growth in hedge funds dedicated to the sector and furthermore (iv) the need for fixed income portfolio managers to diversify their credit exposure (Swiss Re 2004b).

A cat-bond is typically structured around a special purpose vehicle (SPV). This is an independent legal entity which is typically established in a tax favorable jurisdiction and acts as an issuance vehicle, e.g. selling notes to investors and providing an indemnity contract to the issuing company. The funds raised from the sale of the bonds are held in a collateral account. When the bond is to be redeemed either because of maturation or loss, the account is liquidated and payments are made to the issuer for loss payments and the remainder to the investor.

The basic cat-bond structure can be summarized as follows (Lane 2004) (see figure 5.10).:

- The sponsor (the insured) establishes a special purpose vehicle (SPV) as an issuer of bonds and as a source of reinsurance protection.

- The SPV sells bonds to investors. The proceeds from the sale are invested in a collateral account. The resources in the collateralized account are invested in risk free securities (e.g. British or American government backed securities).

- The sponsor pays a premium to the SPV; this and the investment of bond proceeds are a source of interest paid to investors.

- If the specified catastrophic risk is triggered, the funds are withdrawn from the collateral account and paid to the sponsor; at maturity, the remaining principal - or if there is no event, 100% of principal - is paid to investors.

A cat-bond can be viewed as a standard bond with and embedded contingent option giving the issuer the right to delay, or permanently withhold, principal and/or inter-

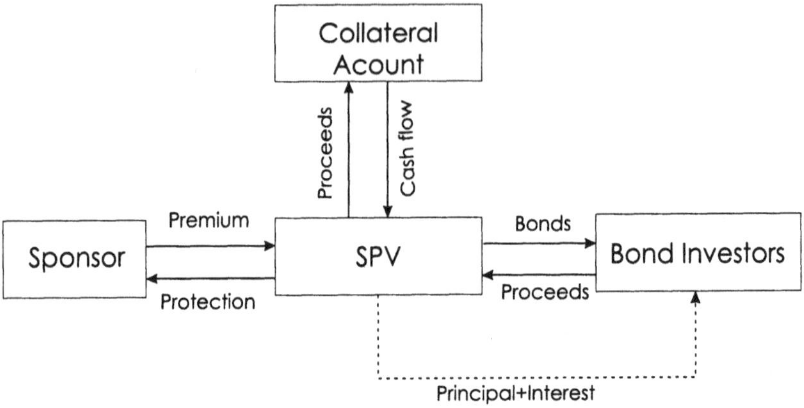

Figure 5.10: Cat-bond structure. Source: Deutsche Bank (in Miller and Keipi 2005: 19), Lane 2004: 3.

est upon the triggering of a defined event (Banks 2005: 113). Hence, one of the most important parameters of a cat-bond is the definition of the trigger event.

Three different trigger events of cat-bonds can be distinguished: indemnity, index and parametric triggers. Regardless of the trigger type, most bonds are structured with initial deductibles and caps (Banks 2005). An **indemnity trigger** involves the actual losses of the issuer. E.g. the event may be the losses from an earthquake in a certain area of a given country over the period of the bond. As a result, the issuer eliminates any instance of basis risk, e.g. the risk of a mismatch between a firm's book of business and the index to which the transaction is linked. They can be compared with a XL-reinsurance contract. **Industry index triggers** are based on recognized industry loss indexes, e.g. in the USA an index is created from property claim service (PCS) loss estimates. The issuer would recover a percentage of industry losses in excess of a predetermined attachment point, subject to the available limit. However, an industry index trigger exposes the ceding company to basis risk to the extent that its actual losses may differ significantly from those of the industry as a whole. **Parametric triggers** are based on one or more physical parameters associated with a peril, e.g. the Richter scale readings of the magnitude of an earthquake at specified data stations. If an event that meets the criteria defined by the parametric trigger occurs and generates losses, principal and or interest payments are suspended. Over the last three or four years cat-bonds with this sort of trigger have become the dominant type (Guy Carpenter 2005: 21).

To allow investors to select their preferred level or risk and return participation, cat-bonds are often issued with at least two tranches. Tranches can be structured in combinations that reflect different levels of interest and/or principal delay or forfeiture. Some tranches result only in a delay of principal other tranches result in a permanent loss of principal and interest (Banks 2005: 118). Hence, principal-at-risk tranches and principal-protected tranches in various degrees can be chosen (see table 5.5).

Tranche	Economic impact of trigger
Tranche A (enhanced)	No loss of principal/interest
Tranche B	Loss of interest
Tranche C	Delay in principal
Tranche D	Partial loss of principal
Tranche E	Total loss of principal
Residual	Total loss of principal and interest

Table 5.5: Catastrophe bond tranches. Source: Banks 2005: 118.

Principal-at-risk bonds typically carry sub-investment grade ratings similar to that of a BB corporate bond (e.g. 1-2 percent probability of loss per year) whereas tranches with A/AA ratings are typically structured with multiple trigger events since the probability of loss under such event is very small (Banks 2005: 118).

Single peril bonds in contrast to multi peril bonds are linked with a specific type of event, e.g. hurricanes in Florida. Cat-bonds mainly protect against windstorms and earthquakes in the USA. New sponsors tapped the cat-bond market in 2003 for perils outside of the USA, e.g. in Japan, Europe and Taiwan (Swiss Re 2004b). With the exception of 2001, there was always a greater amount of risk capital dedicated to single peril than multiple peril transactions in 2004 (see table 5.6).

Year	Single Peril mill. USD	Multiple Peril mill. USD
1997	603.0	30.0
1998	656.1	190.0
1999	730.0	254.8
2000	656.5	482.5
2001	415.0	551.9
2002	961.5	258.0
2003	1 093.8	636.0
2004	662.0	480.8
Total	5 777.9	2 884.0

Table 5.6: Risk capital by number of perils. Source: Guy Carpenter 2005.

The outer boundaries for the tenor of cat-bonds are between one and 5 years. Between 1997 and 2004 20 cat-bonds with a one year tenor, 7 cat-bonds with a 2 year tenor, 19 cat-bonds with a three year tenor, 5 cat-bonds with a 4 year tenor and 8 cat-bonds with a 5 year tenor were issued. Only one cat-bond, started in 1997, had a 10 year tenor. Today, usually cat-bonds with a three-year tenor are preferred. This is due to the fact that sponsors are able to lock in capacity at fixed costs over a multiyear period while still having a manageable time period to foresee risk management and portfolio changes.

Also a multiyear term allows fixed transaction costs to be amortized over a number of years. From an investors side, three years is not a overly long term in light of the market's liquidity (Guy Carpenter 2005).

As with the other ex-ante instruments cat-bonds have advantages as well as disadvantages. Compared to reinsurance, cat-bonds have no credit risk because the capital which is used for loss financing after a trigger event is already there. Reinsurance companies usually do not have enough capital for all their catastrophe exposure. Furthermore, the average price in damage coverage in the reinsurance business is not static but follows a price cycle (see figure 5.11). In the case of cat-bonds such price cycles do not exist. On the other hand, because of the high transaction costs and high sunk costs cat-bonds are more expensive than reinsurance.

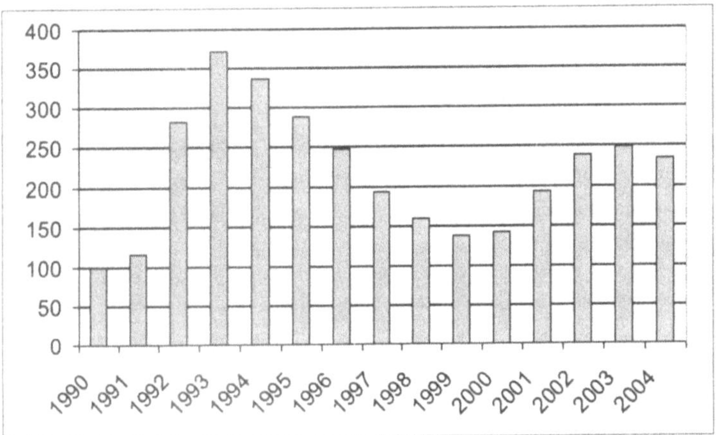

Figure 5.11: World Rate On Line Index. Source: Guy Carpenter 2004: 1.

Sunk costs include legal fees, costs of setting up a SPV, financial entity fees, rating agency fees, as well as fees for the catastrophe modeling agency, verifying agency and indenture trustee. As an example, for a transferring transaction of USD 250 million, the fixed costs lie between 3 and 4.7 million USD, depending on the complexity of the transaction. For bigger sizes of transactions costs may increase (Cardenas, Hochrainer, Mechler, and Pflug 2005)

5.2.6 Summary

A government has two options for loss financing and reconstruction after a disaster: It can rely on ex-post financing measures or it can behave proactive by establishing ex-ante instruments before the disaster. Ex-post financing can be constrained due to a variety of reasons. Ex-ante financing comes with a price: Less government funds are available for important investment decisions and planning objectives. As a consequence economic growth is lower, yet at the same time it is also more stable. Different ex-ante instruments as well as ex-post instruments have different costs, benefits and risks (see table 5.7). To assess the costs, benefits and risks of these measures as well to compare the trade-off between stability and growth on the macroeconomic level, a comprehensive integrated risk management model is needed. Motivated by chapter 3, and based on sections 2.4 and 4.3 as well as chapter 5 the modeling issues are discussed and presented next.

Table 5.7: Costs, benefits and risks of ex-ante instruments. Source: Extended, based on Freeman et al. 2002b and Mechler 2004a.

	Mitigation	**Reserve fund**	**Reinsurance**	**Contingent Credit**	**Catastrophe bond**
Cost before event	Mitigation investment each year times number of years before event	Payment into fund times number of years before event	Premium times number of years before event	Holding fee times number of years before event	At the beginning high transaction costs, then premium times number of years before event
Benefit after event	No disaster event at all or no mitigation effect	Reserve funds and interest available. Funds will not be lost in case of no event	Loss indemnification for elements insured. Increased capital inflows from abroad to affected economy	Funds available immediately. Increased capital inflows from abroad to affected economy	Funds are available immediately
Cost after event	None	None	None	Additional debt service, reduction in ability to take out future debt	None
Risks	Risk that mitigation efforts are not effective or even worsen the impact of the event. Depreciation over time	Risk of depletion before a disaster event. Risk of insufficient funds.	Credit risk	Risk of insufficient funds. Theoretically risk of financial entity going bankrupt	None

Chapter 6

Catastrophe modeling and simulation

Catastrophe modeling is used to assess catastrophic risk and to improve risk management strategies (Grossi, Kunreuther and Windeler 2005: 27). The modeling of catastrophe risk is a complex process that depends on subjective and objective inputs related to the natural hazard. After the catastrophe model is built usually it is too complex to be evaluated analytically, especially if long term economic consequences are considered. In a *simulation* a computer is used to evaluate a model numerically, and data are gathered in order to estimate the characteristics of the model (Law and Kelton 1991: 1). Usually catastrophe modeling implicitly incorporates simulations due to the sheer complexity of the system to be analyzed. Catastrophe modeling and simulation have advantages as well as limitations. Some of them are presented below.

At least four advantages of simulation can be given: (i) Most complex, real world systems with stochastic elements cannot be evaluated analytically; thus, a simulation is sometimes the only type of investigation which is possible, (ii) a simulation allows to estimate the performance of an existing system under some projected set of operating conditions. Hence, alternative system designs or operating policies can be compared, (iii) in a simulation one has much better control over experimental conditions than would generally be possible when experimenting with the system (e.g. real world) itself, (iv) a simulation allows to study a system with a long time frame. While simulation has its advantages, it is not without its drawbacks. For example, a stochastic simulation model produces only estimates of a model's true characteristics for a particular set of input parameters. In addition, simulations models are often expensive and time-consuming to develop (Law and Kelton 1991: 114).

As previously mentioned, catastrophe models use simulation as a tool to assess catastrophic risk. Usually one sets the following goals: Catastrophe models should be able to (i) estimate the probability of occurrence of a catastrophic event, (ii) estimate the upper intensity limits of a particular occurrence, (iii) estimate the financial loss that will result for a particular event, (iv) evaluate the costs of managing an exposure, (v) price each incremental exposure and (vi) gauge accumulations/concentrations of risk. However, a catastrophe model cannot be expected to predict when, where, and with what precise intensity a catastrophic event will occur. Catastrophe models are also not able to provide an exact assessment of the financial losses that may occur, nor can catastrophe models be applied universally to all perils, regions, and locations (Banks 2005: 51).

The next section (6.1) introduces the current risk assessment approach for catastrophe models. These models are used for calculating direct risk (see figure 2.2). Direct risk is defined as a combination of three factors, the hazard, the exposed elements and the vulnerability. The output of such catastrophe models are generally in the form of probability distributions. These probability distributions are needed for the **Catastrophe Simulation model (CatSim)**, which is presented in section 6.3

6.1 Introduction

The modeling of catastrophes is rooted in two fields: Property Insurance and Science. These two separated fields, "mapping risk and measuring hazard" (Grossi, Kunreuther and Windeler 2005: 24) came together in the late 1980s and 1990s because of the rapid development of geographic information systems (GIS), the scientific understanding of natural hazards (e.g. through historical observations), and a high computation power of a new computer generation. In this time period insurers and reinsurers recognized the increasing need of catastrophe models due to a series of large disasters (e.g. Hurricane Andrew, Northridge earthquake, Hanshin Earthquake, Typhoon Mireille). Also at this time several modeling firms developed computer software for the estimation process. In addition, an important open source model to assess losses from natural hazards called HAZUS (Hazards in the U.S.) was developed (see figure 6.1).

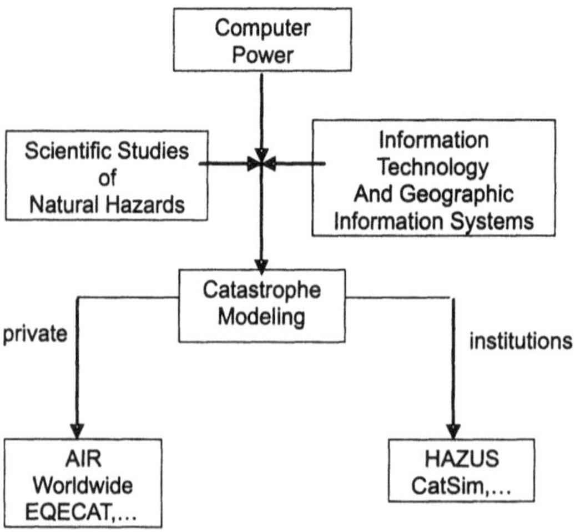

Figure 6.1: Development of catastrophe modeling. Extended on basis of Grossi, Kunreuther and Windeler 2005: 25.

The structure of catastrophe models is influenced by the modeling approach:

- There is the possibility to use only historical loss data for a peril and an assumption of static vulnerabilities. Extreme value theory (EVT) is considered to provide the basis for the statistical modeling of such extreme events (Embrechts, Klüppelberg and Mikosch 1997). EVT seeks to answer the question: "If things go wrong, how wrong can they go?". The main problem here is that one is interested in rare phenomenas that lie outside the range of available observations. In such situations it is essential to rely on a well founded methodology with which statistical models can be built to describe such extreme events. In many fields of modern science, i.e. insurance, extreme value theory is well established (Reiss and Thomas 1997). Due to recent increases in data availability, more applied research has been undertaken to analyze the extreme variations of financial markets (Gilli and Këllezi 2005, McNeil and Frey 2000). However, the lack of historical loss data for natural disasters is a major problem of such approaches. Future losses also might be underestimated because of the static vulnerability assumptions, particularly in fast growing regions. However, it is possible to overlay historical catastrophe events over current vulnerability data to see the effects of such events on the currently exposed elements.
- It is also possible to create models of the physical process of a hazard and connect this with vulnerability data to obtain loss estimates (Baranov et al. 2002). While this is a very complex process, the estimates are more reliable. The models use historical data on natural events but also combine it with engineering knowledge. Some authors therefore distinguish here between the 'Science Module', the 'Engineering Module' and the 'Insurance Coverage Module' of catastrophe models (Kozlowski and Mathewson 1997).

While both approaches can be found in practice, this research focuses on the second one because it is more sophisticated and has more promising connections to other fields for the future, e.g. dasymetric mapping for detailed spatial analysis of the exposed elements (Chen et al. 2004, Thieken et al. 2006), due to its integrated approach of the risk assessment process. The basic components of a catastrophe model consists of at least three respectively: hazard, elements at risk[1], (physical) vulnerability and loss (Kozlowski and Mathewson 1997, Banks 2005: 51, Gurenko and Lester 2005: 243). In principle, the hazard and elements at risk modules enable the calculation of the vulnerability of the structures at risk. From the measure of vulnerability the loss to the inventory is then evaluated. The different catastrophe model components shown in figure 6.2 can be viewed as the starting point for analyzing the impacts of catastrophic events on several variables in a rational manner.

In principle, the hazard and elements at risk modules enable the calculation of the vulnerability of the structures at risk. From the measure of vulnerability the loss to the

[1]Sometimes also called Inventory

Figure 6.2: Structure of catastrophe models. Source: Grossi, Kunreuther and Windeler 2005: 26.

inventory is then evaluated. The different catastrophe model components shown in figure 6.2 can be viewed as the starting point for analyzing the impacts of catastrophic events on several variables in a rational manner.

- **Hazard Module**: The hazard module must incorporate at least three variables regarding the source parameters of the hazard: the locations of future events, their frequency of occurrence and their severity (Mahdyiar and Porter 2005: 47). It is important to distinguish between different hazards (e.g. earthquakes, hurricanes, floods) because each hazard has unique characteristics which require different methodologies to define each probability distribution. Generally this information is based on historical and/or engineering information. At the beginning, the model domain or the region of interest must be defined. Then all relevant sources of hazards must be collected. Next, the probability of occurrence of the event must be calculated. This is generally the most critical and uncertain aspect of the hazard module because damage and loss probabilities are directly related to this value (Mahdyiar and Porter 2005: 52). Another potential problem is the possibility that the frequencies and severities of a hazard are changing over time from global effects such as global warming. Afterwards, the physical parameters that describe the hazard at a specific site are quantified by the model. To estimate the damage potential of the hazard also the intensity changes over the location given a specific site where the event happened has to be calculated.

  Two conceptual examples are considered for illustration: earthquake and hurricane hazards. To determine the frequency and local intensity of an earthquake various parameters are needed, e.g. depth, rupture length, seismic wave amplitude, dip angle, rupture mechanism, location, and magnitude. The spatial distribution of past earthquakes within the region are used to estimate the spatial distribution for future earthquakes. Historical data on earthquake magnitudes are usually fitted to an exponential distribution. The Gutenberg-Richter relationship is used to model the occurrence rate of (characteristic) earthquakes and their magnitude. The Gutenberg-Richter relationship states that the log of cumulative annual frequency of an earthquake declines as the magnitude increases (see figure 6.3).

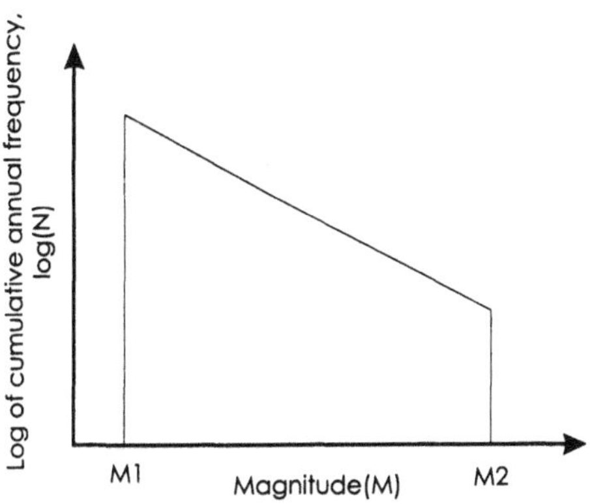

Figure 6.3: Frequency-magnitude relationship of a seismic zone. Source: Mahdyiar and Porter 2005: 53.

In the case of hurricanes, observations of past storm tracks in a given area are used to quantify the geographical distribution of storms. Also, national weather modeling techniques that can estimate storm evolution through making small changes in the atmospheric conditions, which are used to create simulated storm catalogs. The frequency of hurricanes varies with the regional climate conditions and thus should also be accounted for in the model. To estimate the intensity of hurricanes, the differences in the surface terrain and wind durations also have to be taken into account. For example, the relation between wind speed at location z and determining quantities could have the following form (Kozlowski and Mathewson 1997: 329):

$$W_z = f(dp, r, s, l, a, t)$$

where W_z = Wind speed at location z
dp =Ambient pressure minus central pressure
r =Radius of maximum winds
s =Forward speed of the storm
l =Landfall location (longitude, latitude)
a =Angle of incidence at landfall
t =Terrain or roughness coefficient at location z

It is clear that the wind speed is dependent on several variables. Furthermore, the function which connect these variables to the wind speed must be determined, which is usually an engineering task.

- **Elements at Risk Module**: The building inventory is important to estimate the potential future losses to structures and assets of elements at risk. Also the spatial distribution should be captured, e.g. for earthquake damage estimation, engineered buildings in the inventory should also reflect regional differences in construction practice and building codes. To compare different hazard types on a consistent basis, a uniform database and financial assessment of the elements at risk is essential (Grünthal et al. 2006). Furthermore, for the assessment also different resolutions are needed, e.g. hailstorm risk assessments are more sensitive to the resolution of the elements at risk data than earthquake risk assessment (Chen et al. 2004). For insurance companies the required spatial resolution of the exposure data increases in the following order: storm, earthquake, flooding, man-made hazards (Munich Re 2004). The process of inventory development can be a tedious, expensive and time-consuming task. Satellite images and tier classifications can be used beneficial in making the process more affordable (Bendimerad 2001). Also, a rather new and promising approach used to estimate the spatial distribution of assets, e.g. residential buildings at the municipal level, is dasymetric mapping which uses land use information data to disaggregate census data (Thieken et al. 2006).

- **Physical Vulnerability Module**: Here, the model quantifies the physical impact of the hazard on the elements at risk. For example, in the case of financial analysis of building damage due to flooding, damage functions are used which give a relationship between the intensity (e.g. water level) and the damage ratio. Because the intensity and the level of damage are uncertain, the damage itself is an uncertain quantity as well (see figure 6.4).

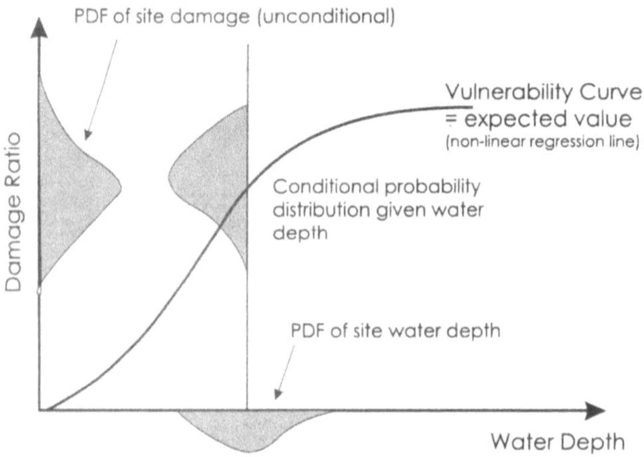

Figure 6.4: Flood vulnerability curve for a specific structure type.

Underlying each damage function is a frequency component and a severity component. The frequency component determines the probability that an exposed element is damaged and the severity component determines the percentage of property that is damaged, assuming damage has occurred. Figure 6.4 is a simplified version of a damage function because most of the time various factors determine the physical vulnerability. For example, the relationship between damage and wind speed for hurricanes is dependent on the construction of the building, the age of the building, and so on. Such relationships can be expressed as follows (Kozlowski and Mathewson 1997: 330):

$$P_{W_z,c,a,s,v} = f(W_z, c, a, s, v)$$

where $P_{W_z,c,a,s,v}$ =	Percent damage at location z for risk characterized by wind speed, c, a, s and v where
c =	Construction of building
a =	Age of building
s =	Number of stories
v =	Coverage (e.g. building, contents, time element)

However, damages can vary by more than just the above variables, and may include regional construction practices, building code and building code enforcement, etc.

- **Loss Module**: The physical losses calculated by the vulnerability module can be translated to monetary losses, such as replacement or repair costs. Various other parameters can also be investigated here; including hazard maps, Value at Risk (VaR), exceedance probability curves, probable maximum loss and loss distribution functions. Again, a simple example about hurricane losses is used for illustration. The total damage in monetary terms caused by a hurricane is calculated according to the following formula (Kozlowski and Mathewson 1997: 331):

$$D_{W_z,c,a,s,v} = E_{z,c,a,s,v} \text{ x } P_{W_z,c,a,s,v}$$

where $D_{W_z,c,a,s,v}$ =	\$ damage at location z for risk characterized by wind speed, c,a,s,v
$E_{z,c,a,s,v}$ =	\$ exposure at location z characterized by c,a,s,v

Because the physical impact on the environment of a given event is uncertain, the losses are also uncertain. Furthermore, each event happens with a different probability which usually has associated uncertainties. Therefore, if all events are considered by simulation one will get probability distributions, which have some degree of uncertainty. This uncertainty can be quantified by confidence regions (see for example figure 6.5).

For illustration, the AIR catastrophe model framework from the private sector is presented below. This approach was developed 1987 and its principle components are illustrated in figure 6.6. The catastrophe model includes the 'Event Generation', the 'Local Intensity', the 'Damage' and the 'Insured Loss' module. In this approach the hazard itself is generated by two modules. The event generation module specifies the frequency,

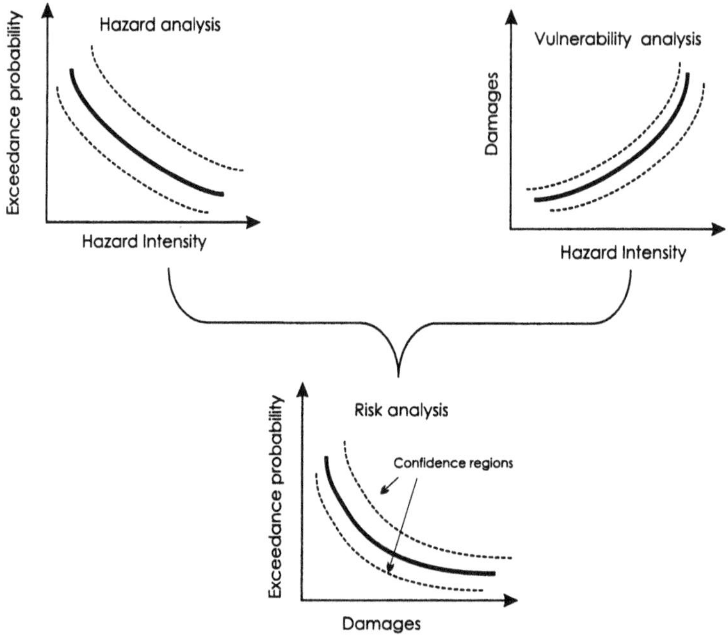

Figure 6.5: Framework for catastrophe modeling results. Source: Adapted from Mechler 2005b: 37.

magnitude and other characteristics of the hazard by geographic location. After the analysis of historical data, probability distributions are developed and used to produce a large catalog of simulated events. The model generates simulated "years" of event activity, which can range from zero to multiple events in one year. Thousands of scenarios are often necessary to produce a complete and stable range of potential annual experiences of catastrophe event activities, to ensure that the extreme tail events are included, as well as provide full spatial coverage. The local intensity module then propagates the event across the affected area for every simulated scenario. For each location within the affected area, local intensity is estimated afterwards. This requires knowledge of the geologic and topographic features of the region. The intensity at each site is a function of the magnitude of the event, the distance from the source of the event (e.g. intensity of earthquakes can be much higher as in the epicenter), and a variety of other local conditions. The functions normally are found by empirical observations and theoretical relationships between these variables.

The damage module of AIRs' scientists and engineers consists mainly of so called damageability relationships, which describe the interaction between buildings, their structural and non structural components, their contents, and the local intensity to which they are exposed. The AIR module estimates a distribution around the mean level of damage for

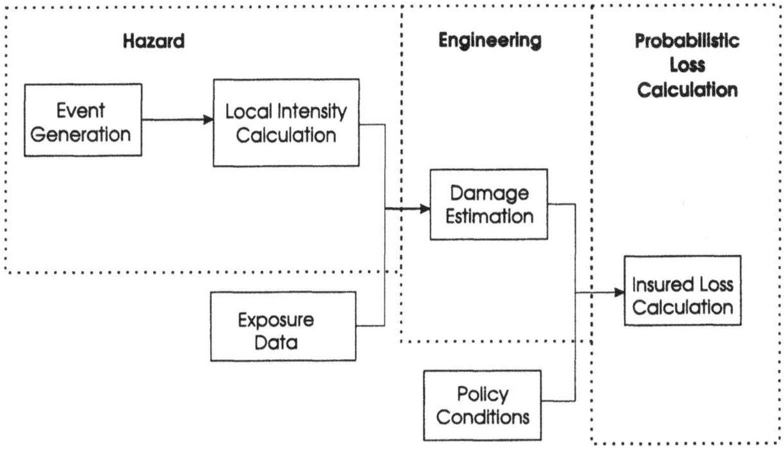

Figure 6.6: AIR catastrophe model approach. Adapted from Grace, Klein, Kleindorfer and Murray 2003: 132.

each local intensity and each structural type, and then constructs a family of probability distributions.

In the insured loss module, the insured losses are calculated by applying the policy conditions (e.g. deductibles, loss triggers, attachment points and exit points) to the total damage estimates. Through the use of the local intensity module the AIR catastrophe model can also handle multiple location policies. This is done by performing a full convolution of the damage distribution of the different locations rather than combining the distributions using the mean and variance.

The losses can be analyzed in various ways. Most prominent today are loss frequency distributions also called damage distribution function, exceedance probability curves (EP) which can also be used to determine the probable maximum loss (PML) and loss return period curves.The probability distributions of gross and net losses for annual aggregate and/or annual occurrence losses can also be expressed as return periods. All these curves are essentially the same but are presented in different ways, which is described below.

As stated above *loss frequency distributions* or *damage distribution functions* are essentially the same as *loss return period curves* and *exceedance probability curves* but are presented differently. Loss distribution functions are ordinary cumulative distribution functions where the horizontal axis represents the range of annual losses, such as the percentage of capital stock destroyed, and the vertical axis represents the probability that losses do not exceed a given level of damage: $x \mapsto F(x)$ (see figure 6.7). The vertical axes can be called the *event axis.* This can be seen most easily by an example: A value of 0.98 on the vertical axis means that with a probability of 98 percent, the losses do not exceed

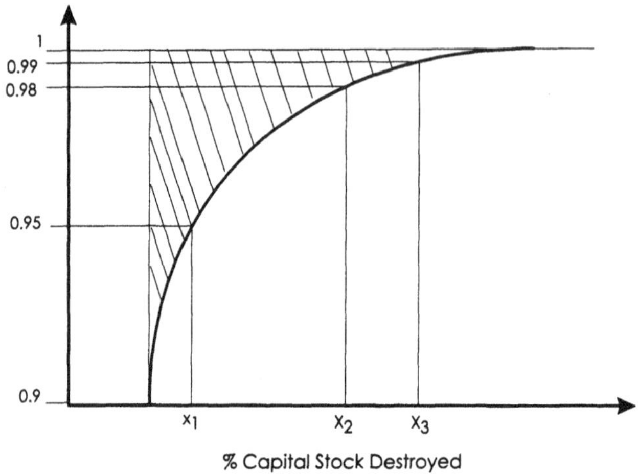

Figure 6.7: Loss frequency distribution.

a given level of damage, say x_2 (see figure 6.7). This means that with a probability of 2 percent, losses will exceed this level of damage x_2. Because the loss distribution function represents annual losses, this 2 percent probability also can be interpreted as a (1/0.02=) "50 year event" or "50 year loss recurrent period". Therefore, the term "50 year event" means that on average one would expect an event of at least this severity once every 50 years[2] . This principle can also be used for all other events (see figure 6.7).

$$\begin{array}{ll} \mathrm{P}(X \leq 0) = 0.9 & \text{(10 year event)} \\ \mathrm{P}(X \leq x_1) = 0.95 & \text{(20-year event)} \\ \mathrm{P}(X \leq x_2) = 0.98 & \text{(50-year event)} \\ \mathrm{P}(X \leq x_3) = 0.99 & \text{(100-year event)} \end{array}$$

Most of the time such probability distributions only consider events with return periods larger than 10 years. It is assumed that events which occur more frequently did not cause any significant damages (probability of first loss). Note, that the annual expected loss is represented by the area above the cumulative distribution curve. These loss distribution functions can be found either by catastrophe simulation experiments explained above, or they can be estimated by a distribution function if some points of the curve are given. For example, one can look at table 6.1 as a starting point for estimating a damage distribution function. These points represent estimations done by reinsurance companies like Swiss Re. Subsequently an extreme value distribution can be estimated through maximum likelihood or other methods.

[2]Stated differently, if X is Bernoulli distributed with success probability p, than the random time between consecutive events has a geometric distribution with mean $1/p$

	% of capital stock destroyed
10-year event loss	0.10 %
100-year event loss	0.45 %
1000-year event loss	0.60%

Table 6.1: Loss return periods. Source: Freeman et al. 2002a: 13.

Loss return period curves are the same as loss frequency distributions but they are presented differently: The vertical line represents the losses while the horizontal line represents the return period (year event axis): $\frac{1}{1-F(x)} \mapsto x$. Figure 6.8 shows a typical loss return period curve.

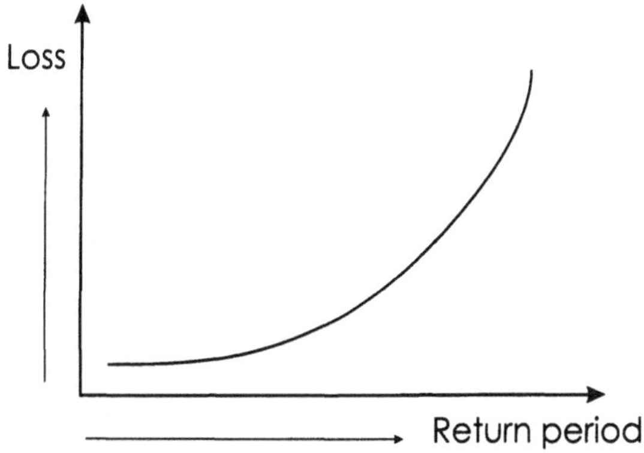

Figure 6.8: Loss return period curve. Source: Banks 2005: 59.

Also *exceedance probability curves* (EP) are an equivalent representation of a loss frequency distributions. They only differ in their presentation, e.g. an EP curve is a graphical representation of the probability that a certain level of loss will be surpassed in a given time period, $x \mapsto 1 - F(x)$. If an annual time period is chosen, this means that the exceedance probability curve contains the same information as the loss frequency function. But while in the loss distribution the vertical axis represents $P(X \leq x_1) = p_1$, the loss exceedance curves vertical axis represents $P(X > x_1) = 1 - p_1$. Figure 6.9 shows the exceedance curve of the loss frequency distribution of figure 6.7.

The Probable maximum loss (PML) is a subjective risk metric and is associated with a given probability of exceedance. It can be easily found using exceedance probability curves. Usually, in the context of catastrophe risk for natural disasters the PML limits are in terms of return periods. For example, assume that an insurer wants to determine its probable maximum loss for a 100 year event with the help of the EP curve in figure 6.9. Because a 100 year event has an annual probability of occurrence of 0.01, the PML is x_3. As one can see the probable maximum loss is a quantile measure. Hence, it is essentially the same as Value at Risk (VaR), which is extensively used in financial markets as a risk

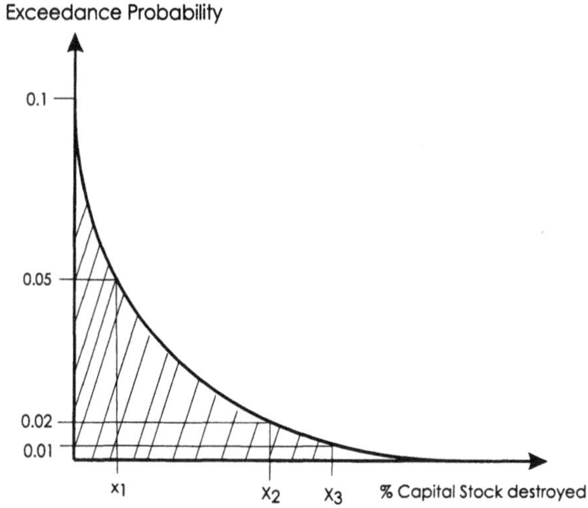

Figure 6.9: Exceedance probability curve.

measure[3]. This can be easily seen through the definition of VaR: Value at Risk is defined as $VaR_p = F^{-1}(1-p)$, where F^{-1} is the quantile function defined as the inverse of the distribution function F. For PML it is the inverse of the exceedance probability curve (for events with probability of occurrence p).

Catastrophe models are essentially risk assessment models. After the risk assessment process the next step is risk management. In this context CatSim, while using the information from the catastrophe models, is seen as a risk management tool against macroeconomic risk (see figure 6.10).

6.2 Objectives

Most of the current risk assessment and risk management models against catastrophe risk today are built to assess direct risks of the private sector. The main actors in this field include insurers, reinsurers as well as brokers and analysts in the financial markets. In the context of natural disaster risk management usually reinsurers are those with the most widespread interest in catastrophe models. Most of the current risk management models do not incorporate long term analysis of economic effects due to natural disasters on the country level. Exceptions are Mechler (2004a) and Freeman et al. (2002a,b).

In the last few years more and more interest on public sector economic vulnerability

[3]In financial markets for internal risk control purposes, most of the financial firms compute a 5% VaR over a one-day holding period. The Basle accord proposed that VaR for the next 10 days and p=1% (100 year event), based on at least 220 days observation period of data, should be computed and then multiplied by the "safety factor" 3, because the normal hypothesis for the profit and loss distribution is widely recognized as unrealistic.

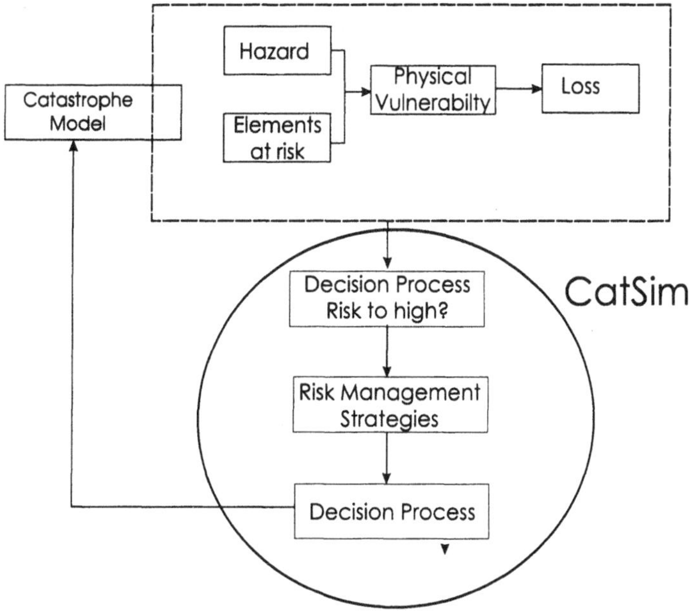

Figure 6.10: CatSim as a risk management tool. Adapted from Grossi, Kunreuther and Windeler 2005: 40.

emerged due to the high losses caused by natural disasters. The repair of damaged public infrastructure can represent a serious drain on public budgets, especially in developing and transition countries. If the government lacks sufficient funds to meet their obligations, it can have serious effects on the economy and livelihood of the population due to at least four reasons: first, public infrastructure is one important factor for economic development (Briceño-Garmendia, Estache, Shafik 2004, Calderón and Servén 2004a,b), second, the need of the public sector for infrastructure development in developing countries is still high. For example, a recent World Bank report about infrastructure in Latin America and the Caribbean states that governments remain at the heart of infrastructure service delivery (Fay and Morrison 2005). Third, though it is not disputed that physical geography can also influence poverty directly, the World Development Report 2006 (World Bank 2005c: 42) states that "*[...]the association between geographic variation in poverty and geographic variation in infrastructure access is typically strong.*" As a consequence, for many people in developing countries the lack of access to infrastructure services means living in isolation from markets and services and having intermittent or no supply of power or water for productive activities and daily existence. This in turn results in a significant curtailment of economic opportunities which increases poverty. Fourth, the public sector is also important in order to improve market functioning and as a result private sector activity (Meier and Rauch 2005). Therefore, especially for developing countries where natural hazards represents a serious threat to long term development goals (e.g. poverty reduction, economic development[4]), pro-active risk management strategies for the public sector should be considered and the trade-off between stability and growth.

Summarizing, (i) a risk management approach is needed which can be operationalized so that (ii) a catastrophe simulation model can be built with, (iii) the consequences of the risk management strategies can be assessed by using risk measures which can be used for cross-country comparisons, and (iv) to bridge the gap between scientific analysis and applied science by the use of user interfaces in a stand alone application, e.g. for workshops. The proposed model (CatSim) which is presented in the next sections should fill these gaps. Including the above summary and the observations made in chapter 3 and 4 the model was built (i) to study the long term macroeconomic effects of natural disaster risks in developing countries (ii) to look at possibilities to lessen their financial vulnerability and macroeconomic risks, (iii) to incorporate and study the trade-offs on macroeconomic variables when proactive instruments are used (iv) to use it as a scientific tool for integrated disaster risk management, e.g. ex-ante portfolio investigations and optimization (v) to reach and help key policy makers in the real world in understanding the complex interrelationship between long term economic development and natural disasters.

Furthermore, the following objectives for the model were set.

- Keep the model flexible. Because different country analysis should be performed with this model the parameter and equation settings could be quite different. The modular structure allows for each module to be changed quickly and easily according to specific needs, e.g. private sector, climate change.
- Build an interactive user interface for training workshops and decision making so that key policy makers can exchange insights and practice loss-mitigation and pre-disaster financial strategies for reducing the financial vulnerability of the public and private sector to the economic losses of disasters. It is important to note that the model is not a decision support tool in the manner that it provides one optimal answer. This is due to the fact that there can be objectives other than financial ones which should be incorporated in the decision making process. However, the model can quickly output financial strategies and their consequences on long term economic development. Hence, it can increase the awareness of decision makers to natural disaster risk and raise a discussion about these problems in their country which in turn can lead to a better assessment of the risks.

6.3 Modeling approach

The model is based on analysis done for developing countries by Freeman et al. (2002a,b)[5]. It is probability based in the sense that the losses due to a natural disaster are determined

[4]Also empirically shown in chapter 3

[5]In detail the author used the model approach based on original versions of G. Pflug and R. Mechler.

by loss distribution functions. The losses in turn have to be financed by the government with already available ex-ante and/or ex-post measures. The ability of the government to finance the losses influences the economic performance of the public sector over the time horizon being considered.

Figure 6.11 shows the modular structure of the model.[6] The user specifies the needed variables in the graphical user interface, called the input module. These variables include the annual loss distribution function (specified by a finite number of points which are afterwards connected by straight lines or by an extreme value distribution), and various economic parameters which describe the elements at risk and the financial resilience. For the scenario module and the sampling module the loss distribution is needed. The impacts of the disaster are generated by a sampling algorithm (e.g. Monte Carlo) specified in the sampling module. Based on the given loss distribution, 1000-5000 scenarios of size and timing of disasters within the time period are generated in the sampling module using an importance sampling technique. The scenarios are stratified samples as we are mainly interested in those scenarios where a catastrophe happens. Given a mix of ex-ante measures, the simulation program calculates estimated economic time series for each of the simulated scenarios and summarizes over the scenarios by taking means, variances, etc. of these output variables. The user may change the mix of ex-ante measures and look at the new results in an interactive manner. Confidence intervals of the response variables are also shown. Therefore "input uncertainty" is given through the loss distribution function, "output uncertainty" is calculated through the model. In the experiment module, different ex-ante portfolio strategies can be analyzed and compared, for example, the user can chose between single or multi-portfolio as well as optimization and vulnerability analysis. The portfolio module summarizes the outcomes of the scenarios and calculates the response variables. This module was separated from the experiment module due to computational issues. The economic module specifies the macroeconomic structure of a country's economy. Through the module structure the economic model can be changed and improved for specific country analysis. In the ex-ante and ex-post module, the instruments' model equations and constraints are kept. Again, the module structure allows changes for specific analysis (see Cardenas et al. 2005 where XL-insurance and catastrophe bonds are compared). In the premium module, the premiums for XL-insurance contracts and other instruments can be calculated. The output is again presented in the user interface so that various analysis can be performed interactively.

Consistent with other models the modeling approach presented in this thesis have advantages and limitations:

- **Advantages:** Integrated modeling approach to assess financial risk management strategies against natural disaster on the country level. Includes ex-ante and ex-post measures from an inter-correlated perspective. Furthermore, decisions in each year

[6]The model itself is written in MATLAB and C++ , the user interfaces were created with the GUI editor in MATLAB.

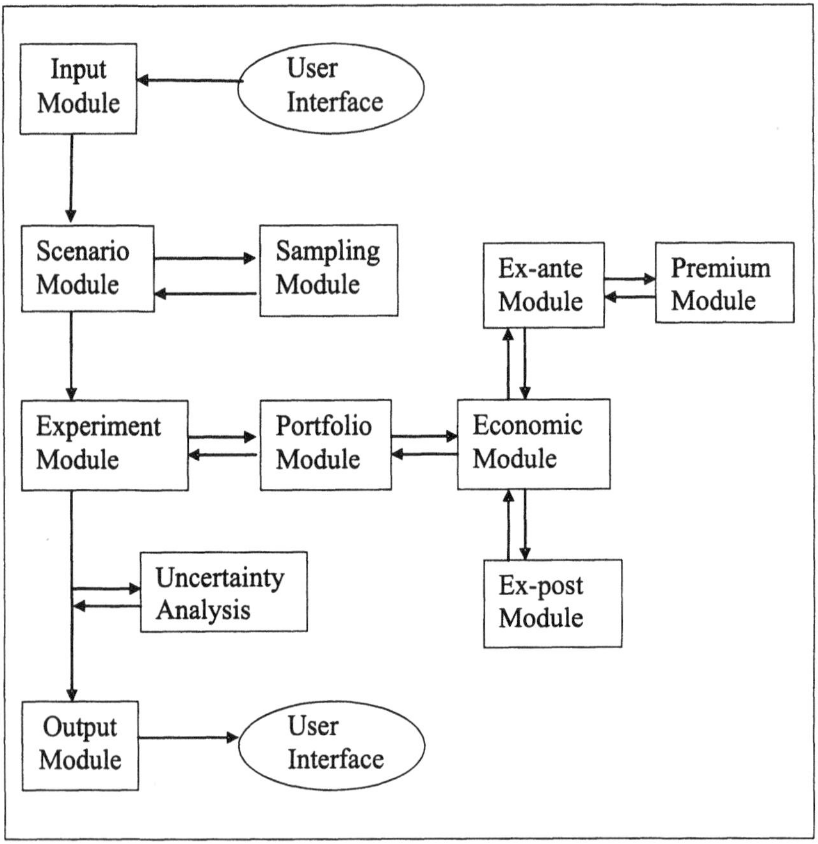

Figure 6.11: CatSim module approach.

influence dynamically the future economic development, for example, an increase in the indebtedness level due to a disaster can limit the possibility of the government to use ex-post and ex-ante instruments in the future. The user can change various parameters for sensitivity analysis and assess their consequences directly. Probability based approach and dynamic modeling of economic effects. The modular structure allows for more precise and thorough country specific analysis. Also upgrading in a systematic manner is possible (e.g. climate change) and new instruments are easy to implement.

- **Disadvantages:** Only parametric representation of direct losses possible through loss distribution functions. While output uncertainty can be handled, input uncertainty cannot be evaluated. No spatial distribution of the losses is considered because of difficulties in estimation processes yet; however, the model itself already has the structure to use the information if available.

Because of the flexibility of this module approach it is important to show the structure of the model equations. Therefore, this study presents a thorough description of the model in standard mode according to the topics outlined in figure 6.11.

6.3.1 Scenario module and sampling module

The scenario and sampling modules need the loss frequency distribution as input. The scenarios are generated through an important sampling algorithm from this distribution.

In standard mode, only one event can happen each year and only scenarios where one or two natural disasters occur in the same time horizon are investigated. However, these assumptions can be relaxed. For example, scenarios with three natural disasters in the time horizon can be chosen; however, the probability of such an scenario is very small and simulations (up to the 10 years) have shown that incorporating such extremely unlikely scenarios do not significant effect the calculation results. The assumption of only one type of hazard event per year can be relaxed, e.g. by performing a convolution of the loss distribution function of the different natural hazards in the sampling module.

Assume now that a T year time horizon (e.g. 10 years) is chosen and the probability of first loss is abbreviated as pfl (e.g. if the first loss starts at the 10 year event the probability of first loss would be 0.1). Furthermore, assume that events happen independently from each other. In standard mode, only scenarios where at most two events happen in the time horizon are generated. This will result in three different disaster scenario groups: the first group comprises the no event scenario, the second group comprises scenarios with only one event within the time horizon, and the third group comprises scenarios with two events within the time horizon. Let N be the random variable representing the number of events within the time horizon T. Probabilities of each scenario and group have to be calculated:

- Group 1: This is the baseline. In this scenario no catastrophic event happens. The probability of a no event scenario is therefore

$$P(N=0) = p_0 = (1 - pfl)^T$$

  The result follows from the fact that $(1 - pfl)$ is the probability that in a given year no catastrophic event occurs and the assumption of independent catastrophic events over the time period.

- Group 2: In this group one catastrophic event within the time horizon occurs. However, one does not know in which year; thus patterns are generated in the following way. For simplicity let us start with the assumption that the catastrophic event happens in the first year. One does not know the impact of such an event, so the impact is taken from the distribution function via monte carlo algorithms in the sampling module. However, one scenario would not be enough because one wants to have scenarios representing impacts across the possible range. Therefore, assume that we create $N1$ scenarios where the catastrophic event will occur in the first year. Notice that each of these scenarios will have different values in the first year for the catastrophe impact. In the next step, $N1$ scenarios where the catastrophic event will occur in the second year are generated and so on, ... At the end $N1$ scenarios are created where the catastrophe happens in the last year (year T). With this method $T * N1$ scenarios are generated for Group 2. The probability of each scenario must be the same for all scenarios in this group because of the independence assumption of the events. Hence, the probability of each scenario is

$$\frac{P(N=1)}{N1} = \frac{p_1}{N1} = \frac{pfl(1-pfl)^{T-1}}{N1}$$

because with probability pfl one disaster will happen and with probability $(1-pfl)$ no disaster will happen each year. The result follows from the independence assumptions.

- Group 3: Because here two events can happen in the time horizon, combinatorial results have to be used to calculate all possible groupings. For illustration, assume a time horizon of 3 years, therefore 3 different scenarios are possible:

Scenario	Year 1	Year 2	Year 3
1	Event	Event	-
2	Event	-	Event
3	-	Event	Event

Through induction one gets the basic combinatorial result that for T years, $T*(T-1)/2$ possible scenarios with two events exist. Following the argumentat in group 2 for every possible scenario $N2$ scenarios are created so that the total amount of scenarios in group 3 is $(T*(T-1)/2)*N2$. Every scenario has a probability of $\frac{p_2}{N2}$ where $p_2 = P(N=2) \approx 1-P(N \leq 1)$ or $p_2 = P(N=2) \approx 1-(P(N=0)+P(N=1))$ because, as previously stated, the probability of higher events is so small that they can usually be neglected. Therefore, each scenario has a probability of $\frac{p_2}{N2}$ with

$$p_2 = \frac{1-[(1-pfl)^T + T*pfl(1-pfl)^{T-1}]}{\frac{T(T-1)}{2}} = \frac{1-p_0-Tp_1}{\frac{T(T-1)}{2}}.$$

To prove that the probabilities sum up to 1, one has to sum up each probability of one scenario times the number of all scenarios for the specific group:

$$p_0 + \frac{p_1}{N1}[N1*T] + \frac{p_2}{N2}[\frac{T(T-1)}{2}N2] = p_0 + p_1*T + \frac{(1-p_0-T*p_1)}{\frac{T(T-1)}{2}}\frac{T(T-1)}{2} = 1.$$

Each scenario can be seen as a vector of length T (the time horizon). In standard mode there is one scenario with no catastrophic event, $N1 * T$ scenarios with one catastrophic event and $N2 * T(T-1)/2$ scenarios with exactly two catastrophic events within the time horizon. Therefore, the total number of scenarios (TNS) is $1 + N1 * T + N2 * T(T-1)/2 = TNS$.

The scenarios are generated in the following way. First, a T times TNS matrix is created, the rows can be seen as the years and the columns can be seen as the specific scenarios. The first column is group one, the baseline scenario, where no event occurs. The second till $N1 + 1$ column are the scenarios where the disaster event occurs in year one, the $N1 + 2$ till the $2 * N1 + 2$ columns are the scenarios where the disaster event occurs in year two, and so on. The same procedure is used for the two event scenarios.

The impacts of the disasters are generated by a sampling algorithm specified in the sampling module. There are two possibilities implemented for the monte carlo sampling, both types are based on the well known inverse transformation method:

Proposition: Let U be a uniformly distributed (0,1) random variable. Define a random variable $X = F^{-1}(U)$ where F is a continuous cumulative distribution function. Then F is the cumulative distribution function of X.

Thus, because all extreme value distributions are continuous and the inverse of these are well known (see for example Reiss 1997: 28), it is easy to draw random variables from them. If no distribution function is estimated but some points (as in table 6.1) are given, these points are connected linearly and a discrete type of the transformation method is used. The later is especially useful to change hazard impacts with all other things being equal in order to look at the effects on the response variables.

6.3.2 Experiment module and portfolio module

The scenario matrix generated by the scenario and sample module is forwarded to the experiment module. In the experiment module different portfolio strategies can be analyzed. Specific experiments also can be chosen from the user interface. Before starting, it is necessary to present the decision variables and some response variables of the model.

The **decision variables** are the ex-ante measures: mitigation, reserve fund, XL-insurance and contingent credit arrangements. While a catastrophe bond could be implemented, it is not presented here because in standard mode the cat-bond is inferior to XL-insurance due to the additional high fix costs.[7] In standard mode, a vector $\vec{V}$ of length n where n is the number of ex-ante measures, is created where each entry represents the percentage of the variable budget the government wants to use for the specific measure

[7]However, this does not mean that this is true in general, for a comparison of XL-insurance and catastrophe bonds using this model, see Cardenas et al. 2005

(see the next section for a detailed description of the variable budget). For convenience this vector is called the **portfolio vector**.

There are several **response variables** that can be calculated: (a) the **probability of a financing gap**[8] (b) the **discounted expected return** for the time period, (c) the **discounted expected shortfall** for the time period, this is the total lack of funds needed to repair all damage, such as the net loss if a financing gap has occurred (d) the **expected reduction of the credit buffer** at the end of the time period. The credit buffer is defined as 150% of the typical export value of the country minus the present value of existing loans (HIPC 2002). A decrease in the credit buffer indicates the country's inability to get new credits for other purposes than repair. (e) The **trajectories** of interesting variables over the time horizon for each scenario. They will be used for the uncertainty module and for the user interface where the trajectories should show intuitively the effects of the ex-ante measures on the response variables.

The generation of the portfolio vector is dependent on the experiment. In standard mode, at least three different experiments can be tested.

- **Experiment 1:** This experiment looks at one specific portfolio which was defined by the user in the user interface. The effects and the visualization of the decision variables on the response variables are shown afterwards. To illustrate the effects of ex-ante instruments assume that the government wants to analyze and compare the macroeconomic effects[9] for a 10 year time horizon with only two alternatives. The first alternative is the baseline case where no ex-ante instruments are used. In the second alternative 30 percent of the available variable budget is used each year with the following portfolio structure: 10 percent for mitigation, 5 percent for reserve funds, 10 percent for insurance and 5 percent for a contingent credit arrangement. The other part of the available budget is used for investments in new infrastructure. Figure 6.12 shows the results of such a portfolio compared to the baseline case. As one can see, with the probability of a financing gap the expected shortfall and the credit buffer drop goes down and therefore stability increases. Also the discounted expected return decreases which means less growth. Therefore, there is a trade-off between stability and growth. With such an approach it is also possible to start more in depth cost-benefit analysis[10].

- **Experiment 2:** The different ex-ante measures are analyzed separately but are compared simultaneously. Specifically, in the beginning the portfolio vector is zero and for each instrument the effects of a small increase in the budget are analyzed up

[8] A financing gap occurs if there is a year in which there are insufficient funds to repair all damage
[9] The parameters for Honduras were used for this example
[10] For a general introduction see for example Moore 1983, Ray 1984 or Hanley and Spash 1993; in the context of government programs see Gramlich 1981 and especially for developing countries Little and Mirrlees 1976; Brent 1998; in the context of natural disaster risk see for example Britton and Oliver 1997 or Mechler 2004a

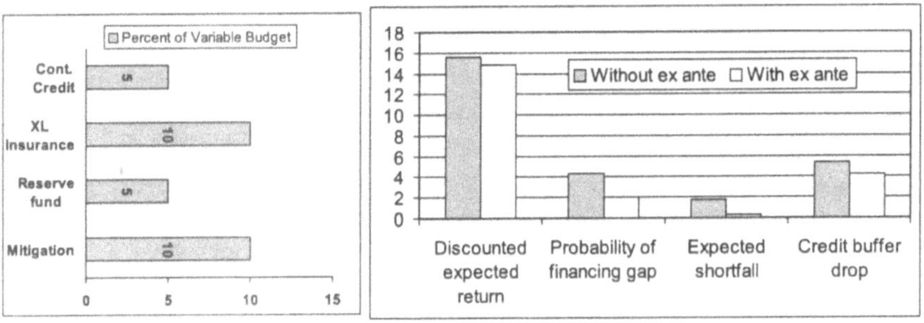

Figure 6.12: Comparison of response variables for different strategies.

to an upper limit. For example, the portfolio vector $\vec{V} = (0, 0, ..., 0, 0)$ is analyzed, then instrument $i(i = 1, ..., n)$ is taken and the budget for $\vec{V}(i)$ is increased by some small amount. This portfolio vector is analyzed and the results are saved. Next, the budget for instrument i is increased again by some small amount, until a limit specified by the user is reached (e.g. use at most 70 percent of the variable budget for instrument i). This is done for each instrument separately and the outcomes are shown in the user interface simultaneously so that the user can compare the different effects of the ex-ante instruments on the response variables. Figure 6.13 shows an example where four ex-ante measures are compared. The vertical axis represents the probability of a financing gap for a 10 year time horizon, the horizontal axis represents the percentage of variable budget used for the ex-ante measures.

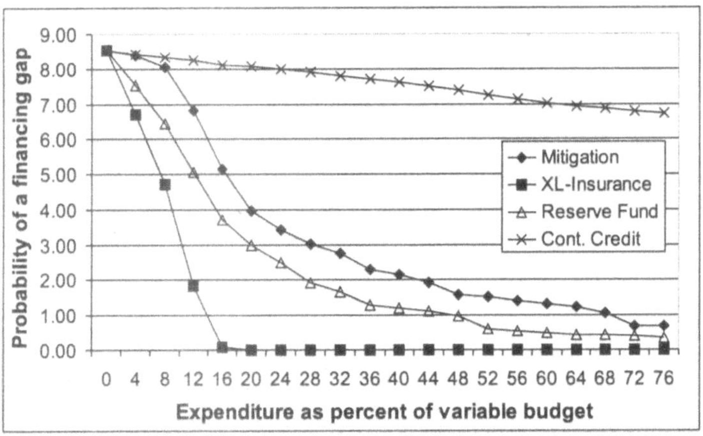

Figure 6.13: Decreasing probability of a financing gap due to higher investments in ex-ante measures.

- **Experiment 3:** A typical experiment would aim at minimizing the probability of a financing gap with a given budget while keeping the discounted expected return above some predefined threshold level. Matlab has some good optimization packages but they are slow. Therefore, a simple algorithm for a fast search for a (local) optimum was written. For the sake of simplicity we consider only three ex-ante measures: mitigation, reserve fund and insurance. Since the expenditures for the three measures add up to a given budget, all admissible portfolios can be shown in a triangle (see figure 6.14).

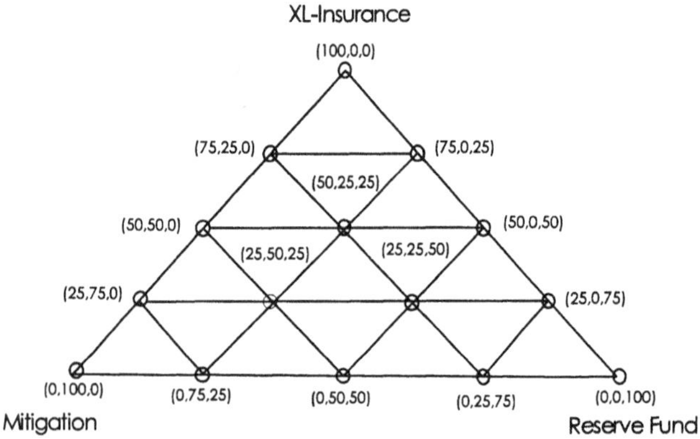

Figure 6.14: Different portfolio structures for three ex-ante measures.

To find the optimal portfolio mix, a simple search algorithm is used which works without any knowledge of the shape or the derivatives of the objective function or the constraint function. Within the triangle, 15 search points (as in figure 6.14) representing 15 portfolios are determined. For all of them the objective function (in our case the probability of a financing gap) and the constraint function (in our case the expected return over the planning horizon) are calculated. The portfolio is selected as the incumbent solution for which the probability of a financing gap is minimal and the discounted expected return is acceptable, i.e. above some given threshold level. For instance, the threshold level can be set at 2 percent under the discounted expected return in the baseline case. In the next step a (smaller) triangle is created surrounding the incumbent solution and the procedure is iterated until the actual triangle is sufficiently small or no better point is found in the surrounding (figure 6.15). It is not guarantied that the solution is the global optimum, but it does provide a local optimum result. Extensions of this algorithm allow larger jumps, search-paths in infeasible areas and adaptive Monte-Carlo optimization techniques (Ermoliev et al. 2000).

The portfolio module summarizes the outcomes of each scenario and calculates the response variables. The module was separated from the experiment module because of

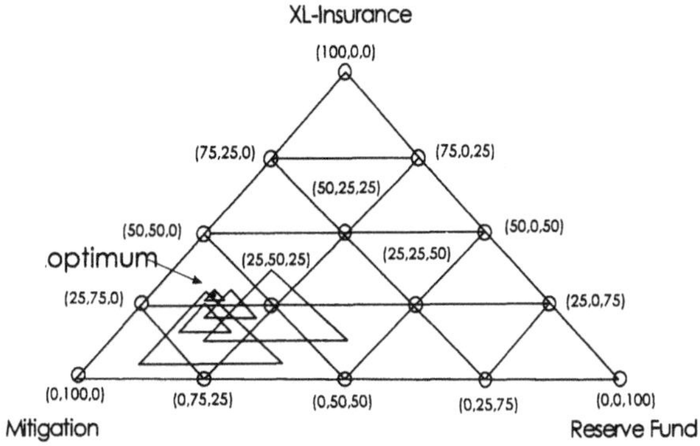

Figure 6.15: Search in a triangular close to one point.

computational and calculating issues. Figure 6.16 shows the principle linkage between the scenario and economic module. The figure shows the disaster events in a two event scenario for a time horizon of 10 years. The bottom figure shows the effects on the growth path, which is calculated within the economic module. As one can see, dependent on the financial resilience of the government the direct loss impacts caused by the disaster can have different effects. While the first event's direct losses are higher than in the second event, government's financial resilience in the second event is lower, causing a larger decrease of GDP.

As explained above (see section 6.3.1) each scenario has a given probability and calculated response variables. The expected value of the return variables is the sum of the values of the response variables of a given scenario times the probability of the scenario, or:

$$\sum_{s=0}^{NTS} ResponseVariable(s) * Prob(s)$$

6.3.3 Economic module

The economic module calculates the response variables for each scenario. The ex-ante strategy represented in the portfolio vector is kept the same for the entire time period. Because percentage values for the investments are used, the actual investments in dollar terms are different over the years, dependent on the amount of variable budget for each year.

The economic module specifies the macroeconomic structure of the country's economy. In standard mode they are not very complicated because the interpretation gets quickly more difficult when more complex modeling equations are used like the 'Revised Minimum Standard Model' of the World Bank. Furthermore, in standard mode only overall effects

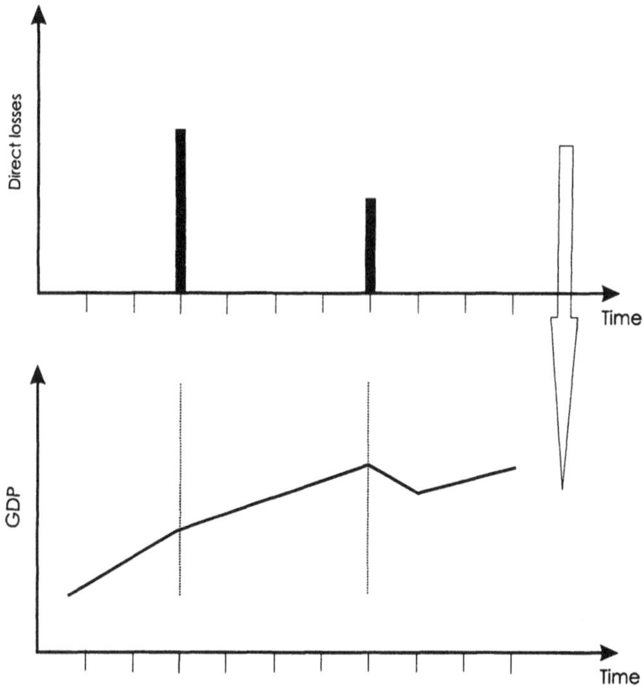

Figure 6.16: The link between disaster events and macroeconomic risk.

are studied, for illustration purposes mainly. For simplicity, some of the input variables for the economic module are listed below. They are needed for the modeling equations:

Variable name	Description
Cap0	Initial capital
roi	Return on investment
Bfx	Fixed budget
dep	Depreciation rate
damage_ratio	Ratio of the loss for the public and private sector
dis	Discount rate for future returns

Table 6.2: Some input variables for the economic module.

Loss frequency functions usually describe the total losses. However, here we are only interested in those losses for which the government is held responsible. The damage ratio therefore describes how many of the total losses the government is responsible for as well as how many of the total losses come from the private sector (see also chapter 4).

1	Cap(0)	← Cap0
2	Lab(0)	← Lab0
3	GDP(t)	← f(Cap(t),Lab(t))
4	Rev(t)	← roi*GDP(t)
5	VBudget(t)	← Rev(t)-Bfx
6	**If** VBudget	≤ 0 **then**
7		$\vec{V}(i) = 0$ $(i = 1, ..., n)$
8	**else**	
9		$\vec{V}(i)$=Vbudget*$X(i)$ $(i = 1, ..., n)$
10	**end if**	
11	Inv(t)	←Rev(t)-Bfx-$\vec{V}(1)$...-$\vec{V}(n)$-add(t)
12	Cap0(t)	←Cap(t-1)*(1-dep)+Inv(t)
13	Loss_full	←Cap0(t)*Cat(t)
14	Loss_gov	←Cap0(t)*Cat(t)*damage_ratio
15	Cap(t)	←Cap0(t)-Loss_gov_gap
16	DiscRet	←DiscRet+roi*Cap(t)*(1+dis)^(-(t-1))
17	DiscGap	←DiscGap+Loss_gov_gap*(1+dis)^(-(t-1))
18	dCB	←CBO-CB(T+1)

Table 6.3: Economic module equations.

We refer to table 6.3 in the following explanations. First, the capital stock (private and public) and labor are initialized (1)(2). GDP is produced with the inputs labor and capital[11] (3) (in standard mode only the return is calculated, however one can see that it is possible to have a connection with the private sector). The government revenue is a function of GDP (4). The variable budget is the revenue minus the fixed budget (5). Therefore the variable budget can be seen as the budget the government can use for new projects. If no variable budget is feasible, no ex-ante measures can be used (6)(7). Otherwise, the percentage amount specified in the experiment model is taken from the variable budget (9). Therefore, the amount used for ex-ante measures is now in dollar terms. Government investment adding to capital stock is the residual in the government budget (the revenue) after spending for fixed budget, the ex-ante measures and additional costs due to the ex-post options undertaken in the previous period's, e.g. debt service payments, ex-post loans (11). Investment may also become negative which is considered as a selling of public assets. The capital stock before the disaster is determined by the last periods' depreciated capital stock plus investment (12). The full direct loss due to the disaster is determined by the relative catastrophe loss of capital stock in period t (13). However, if only the public sector loss is needed, the physical loss is only a percentage of the total loss (see also chapter 4)(14). After these calculations Loss_gov is first sent to the ex-ante module and then to the ex-post module. If all instruments are used and Loss_gov is still positive (let this loss be called Loss_gov_gap), a financing gap occurred and part of the lost capital stock will remain unreplaced, affecting GDP and revenues

[11]Using production functions like Cobb-Douglas or CES (constant-elasticity-of-substitution).

(15). The discounted return as well as the discounted financing shortfall are calculated with equations (16)(17). The credit buffer reduction is calculated at the end of the time horizon T (18).

6.3.4 *Ex-ante instruments module*

The two most important input parameters of the ex-ante module are the total loss of capital stock and the losses to the government (Loss_full and Loss_gov). Also other input parameters are used, some of which are shown in table 6.4:

Variable name	Description
fmi	Factor for mitigation
dep	Depreciation rate
att	Attachment point
exi	Exit point
Ref0	Initial reserve fund
irf	Interest rate for reserve fund
icc	Interest rate for contingent credit
fcc	Fee for contingent credit

Table 6.4: Some input variables for the ex-ante module.

Four different ex-ante measures and their modeling approach are explained in the following. The principle advantages and disadvantages of these measures were already discussed in section 5.2. Here the specific modeling parts of these instruments in standard mode are presented. It should be noted that if more than one ex-ante measure is used, there must be an order specifying which one is taken first. This should be not to difficult to determine, thus if all four ex-ante measures are used the following order should be: mitigation, reinsurance, reserve fund and last contingent credit.

Mitigation

Mitigation (e.g. retrofitting of houses) is somewhat different than the other measures presented below. Not only because it is not a financial instrument, but also because mitigation can save lives while the others cannot and it can have effects on other measures, like a decrease in insurance premiums because of lower expected losses. Unfortunately, the studying of mitigation on a macro level is quite difficult and is not yet fully understood, but there is no doubt that this measure has the potential to become very important (and sometimes already is). Also, if someone wants to study different dimensions of ex-ante measures, such as reducing the probability of a financing gap and the loss of lives caused by disasters, mitigation seems to be the most important one due to the link with other financial measures like insurance (Kunreuther 1996, Kunreuther 1997).

The discussion in the literature suggests that mitigation should be modeled in a case-specific way. As already discussed in section 5.2, in a stylized way mitigation effects can be seen as step functions[12]. Section 5.2 provided a detailed explanation, thus here only the model equations are presented.

We refer in the following to table 6.5. The mitigation efforts (for convenience let *xmit* be the expenses for mitigation each year) are accumulated over the years where no disaster happens, or where a disaster happens but with such a small impact that no damages occur (1). As already stated, mitigation will prevent damages up to some magnitude of the hazard. If the magnitude is higher, there will be two losses: the loss of mitigation efforts and the loss of the property. In this scenario, the impacts of the event would be at least the same as without mitigation efforts (potentially even worse). The factor fmi describes the efficiency of the mitigation investments. Hence, the impact of a natural hazard which is measured according to the losses is compared with the mitigation efforts (2). No losses occur if mitigation efforts withstand the impact (3), otherwise the full loss occurs (5).

1	Mitigation(t)	←Mitigation(t-1)*(1-dep)+ xmit
2	**If** Loss_gov	< Mitigation(t)*fmi **then**
3		Loss_gov← 0
4	**else**	
5		Mitigation(t)← 0
6	**end if**	

Table 6.5: Mitigation modeling.

XL Insurance

The XL-insurance contract is explained in section 6.3.6. Assume that the premium is already calculated and therefore also the attachment point and the exit point are determined. Since attachment and exit point are in percentages (of capital stock insured), they must be multiplied with the capital stock at risk in the given year (let us call the result attp and exitp). Afterwards it must be determined if the losses are higher than the attachment point (1). If yes, the government gets a claim determined by the losses and the attachment point (2), if the losses are higher than the exit point (3), the government receives the highest claim which is possible in this contract (4). The residual losses are the losses minus the claim (6).

[12]It should be clear that the mitigation effects can and should be modeled in more detail. The problem is that currently no damage ratios curves for aggregate levels exists. However, there are efforts in this field and these results could also be used here.

If ((Loss_gov > attp)	& (Loss_gov <= exitp)**then**
	Claim← Loss_gov-attp
elseif	(Loss_gov > exitp)
	Claim← exitp-attp
end if	
Loss_gov	←Loss_gov-Claim

Table 6.6: XL-insurance modeling.

Reserve fund

At the first year the reserve fund is initialized (1). The reserve fund accumulation is described by the interest rate irf on the reserve fund of the last period plus the new payments (lets call it *xref*) into the fund (2). If Loss_gov is not zero, the reserve fund is depleted to the extent necessary (3).

1	Ref(0)	←Ref0
2	Ref(t)	←Ref(t-1)*(1+irf)+xref
3	Takeout	←min(Ref,Loss_gov)
4	Loss_gov	←Loss_gov-Takeout
5	Ref(t)	←Ref(t)-Takeout

Table 6.7: Reserve fund modeling.

Contingent credit

A contingent credit (CC) is available upon the occurrence of a pre-defined disaster event. The contingent credit is triggered to the extent necessary and reserved in advance due to the annual payments (lets call it *xcc*). However, afterwards large debt payments are necessary. A contingent credit is limited by the credit buffer (2). Using a contingent credit will necessitate debt service payments for interest and amortization of the loan, which will be contained in the add(t) vector (4). Also, the credit buffer is decreased for all years until the end of the duration period of the credit (5).

This completes the ex-ante stage. If the losses cannot be covered by these measures, ex-post resources are used, if available.

6.3.5 Ex-post instruments module

The ex-post instruments were already discussed in section 5.1. Therefore, only the modeling of these measures are presented here. As before, the user can choose the ordering

1	CCmin	←(Loss_gov,xcc/fcc)
2	CC	←min(CC,CB(t))
3	Loss_gov	←Loss_gov-CC
4	add(s)	←add(s)+annuity(CC,icc)
5	CB(s)	←CB(s)-NPV(CC,icc,s)

Table 6.8: Contingent credit modeling.

of the ex-post measures available. Let Loss_gov again represent the losses for the government which cannot be covered by the ex-ante instruments with. The ex-post instruments include budget diversion, assistance, taxation, domestic credit, MFI credits and bond credits. Each ex-post measure is used only if the losses are not covered yet. The following table shows some of the input variables needed for the ex-post module:

Variable name	Description
dir	Diversion to revenue
Aid	Assistance
dor	Ratio of maximal diversion to revenue
ido	Interest rate for domestic credit
CBO	Credit buffer determined by the external debt limit
imf	Interest rate for MFI loan
ibd	Interest rate for international bond

Table 6.9: Input variables for the ex-post module.

Assistance

Assistance is assumed to be 10.4 percent of the total losses of capital stock (1). This value is taken from a rough regression analysis of historical data (see Freeman et al 2002b: 34) for developing countries and can be changed in the user interface for sensitivity analysis. The number will be quite lower in developed countries. For example, looking at the member states of the European Union, in the case of a major natural disaster aid up to 6 percent of direct damages can be requested from the European Union Solidarity Fund. However, some conditions for this form of assistance have to be fulfilled. Only financial aid is provided for emergency measures in the event of a natural disaster causing direct damages above 3 billion Euros (at 2002 prices) or 0.6 percent of GNI. The fund can be mobilized even if the threshold is not met, e.g. for a neighboring State that is affected by the same major natural disaster or for extraordinary regional disasters which affects the majority of the population of a region and have serious effects on its economic stability and living conditions. The payments are limited to finance operations undertaken by the public authorities alleviating non insurable damages[13]. A member country affected by

[13]Council Regulation (2002) No 2012/2002 of 11 November 2002 establishing the European Union Solidarity Fund.

a disaster receives a lower rate of aid of 2.5 percent for the part of total direct damage below the "major disaster" threshold and a higher share of aid of 6 percent for the part of the damage exceeding the threshold (European Commission 2005). **Budget diversion**

1	Maxaid	←Aid*Loss_full
2	Aid	←min(Loss_gov,Maxaid)
3	Loss_gov	←Loss_gov-Aid

Table 6.10: Assistance modeling.

The maximal budget diversion is a percentage of the revenue(1). However, the diversion process reduces the next years' budget(4).

1	Maxdiv	←dir*Rev
2	Div	←min(Loss_gov,Maxdiv)
3	Loss_gov	←Loss_gov-Div
4	add(t+1)	←add(t+1)+Div

Table 6.11: Budget diversion modeling.

Domestic credit

If Loss_gov is not zero, loss financing through a domestic credit is also possible. It is assumed that the maximal domestic credit available is a fixed fraction of the revenue (1) and it can only be used once in the time horizon. The additional costs are updated (4) and the credit buffer is adjusted accordingly (5), using the net present value (NPV) of the credit (for s within the duration of the credit):

MFI and bond credits

Foreign credit to cover the losses of the disaster is constrained by the external debt sustainability indicator, the credit buffer (1). In principal the government can choose

1	Maxdom	←Rev*dor
2	Dom	←min(Maxdom,Loss_gov)
3	Loss_gov	←Loss_gov-Dom
4	add(s)	←add(s)+annuity(Dom,ido)
5	CB(s)	←CB(s)-NPV(Dom,ido,s)

Table 6.12: Domestic credit modeling.

1	Maxmfi	←ratioMI*CB(t)
2	Mfi	←min(Maxmfi,ratioMI*Loss_gov)
3	MaxBnd	←CB0*(1-ratioMI)
4	Bnd	←min(MaxBnd,(1-ratioMI)*Loss_gov)
5	Loss_gov	←Loss_gov-Mfi-Bnd
6	add(s)	←add(s)+annuity(MFI,imf)
7	add(s)	←add(s)+annuity(Bnd,imf)
8	CBS(s)	←CB(s)-NPV(Mfi,imf,s)
9	CBS(s)	←CB(s)-NPV(Bnd,ibd,s)

Table 6.13: MFI and bond credit modeling.

between MFI and bond credits or a combination of the two, determined by ratioMI (2)-(5). Again the additional costs are updated and the credit buffer is adjusted accordingly, using the NPV of the credit (6)-(9).

6.3.6 Premium module: The pricing of XL-insurance contracts

Excess of loss (re-)insurance is a more typical insurance strategy for catastrophic risk allowing to insure against certain "layers" of risk, e.g. insuring against events in excess of the 100 year up to the 200 year hurricane event. The rationale behind insuring layers is that losses up to a certain limit can likely be borne without major difficulties; whereas for the rarer but more catastrophic events, risk transfer needs to be undertaken. XL-insurance is usually purchased from reinsurers by insurers or reinsurers in order to protect their portfolios. As governments already act as quasi-insurers by bundling and paying for the reconstruction of their own assets (infrastructure, buildings etc.), it is assumed that they protect their portfolio of assets by purchasing XL-insurance. Another option for even higher risks is the purchase of catastrophe bonds, but is not discussed here.

The excess of loss layer is determined by two points: The attachment point (A) and the exit point (E). The claim payment depends on the size of the damage y (see figure 6.17). In other words, the insurance pays:

$$C(y) = \begin{cases} 0 & \text{if y} \leq \text{A} \\ y - A & \text{if A} < \text{y} < \text{E} \\ E - A & \text{if y} \geq \text{E} \end{cases}$$

To calculate the premium for a given attachment and exit point, one has to know the loss distribution function[14] (figure 6.7). If the loss distribution function is denoted by $F(y)$ then the par-price can be calculated by integration:

[14]If the damage is expressed in terms of the fraction relative to the total stock at risk the integration limits are between $[0, 1]$

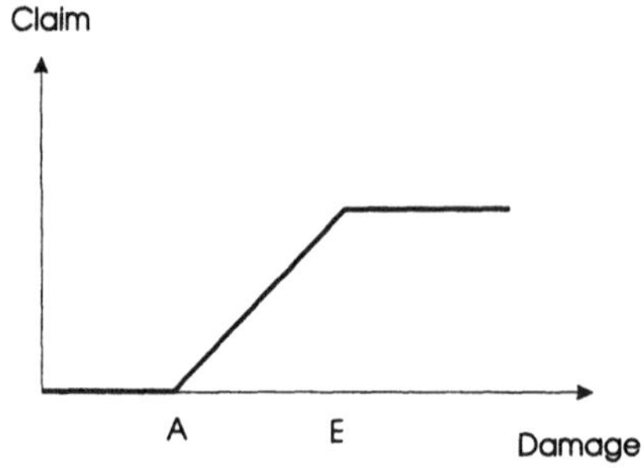

Figure 6.17: Structure of XL-insurance.

$$\pi_p(C,F) = \int_0^\infty C(y)dF(y)$$

However, the insurance company asks for an additional loading factor to be added to the par-price. This loading factor must always be greater (or equal) to 1 (no risk premium is smaller than the par-price), and it must be increasing for higher layers. To calculate the new price, a function $h(p)$, $0 \leq p \leq 1$, is considered, which have the properties stated above, namely:

- $h(p) \geq 1$
- $h(p)$ is increasing and continuous from the right

A practical example for a function h can be seen in figure 6.20.
The risk-adjusted price of the contract is then:

$$\begin{aligned}\pi_h(C,F) &= \int_0^\infty C(y)h(F(y))dF(y) = \\ &= \int_0^\infty C(F^{-1}(p))h(p)dp\end{aligned}$$

because y is the p-th quantile of the loss distribution. If F has a density f, one can rewrite the integral so the adjusted price is:

$$\begin{aligned}\pi_h(C,F) &= \int_0^\infty C(y)h(F(y))f(y)dy = \\ &= \int_0^\infty C(y)g(y)dy\end{aligned}$$

The function $g(y) = h(F(y))f(y)$ can be seen as a kind of weighting function. The weight function g may be calculated for every interval of constancy of the density f.

Mathematical expectations have to be calculated using the density, but premiums have to be calculated using the weight function (the weight function g is the basis for the calculation of premiums for layered insurance contracts). Figure 6.18 shows the weight function g as a solid line and the density as a dotted line.

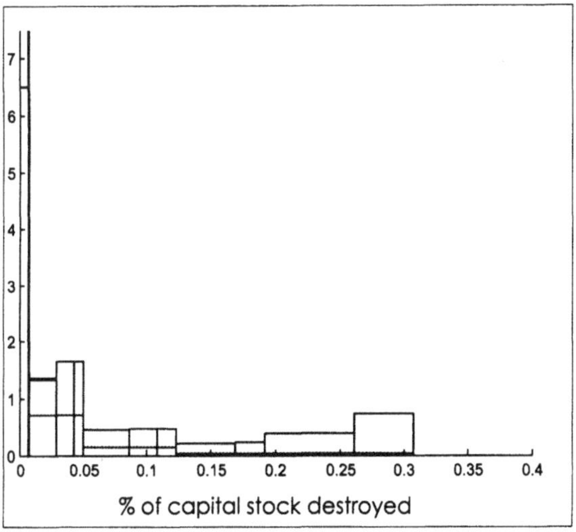

Figure 6.18: Weight function and density for XL-insurance.

The premiums are calculated for the layered insurance as a function of the attachment point and the exit point (this means for different layers one gets different premiums); however, an algorithm was written[15] so that for a given attachment point and a given budget the exit point can be calculated. As mentioned above, the weight function g is the basis for the calculation of premiums for layered insurance contracts: For instance, suppose that the attachment level of a contract is 0.00 and 0.05 respectively. The following graph (figure 6.19) shows the premium (upper curves) and the expected loss (lower curves) of such contracts as a function of the limit.

As one can see, the higher the layers the higher the premiums are away from the expected losses. This can be partly explained by the larger uncertainty inherent in the loss calculations from catastrophe models which is reflected in the loading factors. Typical loading factors used in reinsurance companies for the specific layers are shown in figure 6.20.

As figure 6.17 is showing, the claim function is bounded by E. Hence, the maximum claim payment would be $m = E - A$. However, the XL-insurance contract also pays m

[15]The modeling and software programs are written with G. Pflug

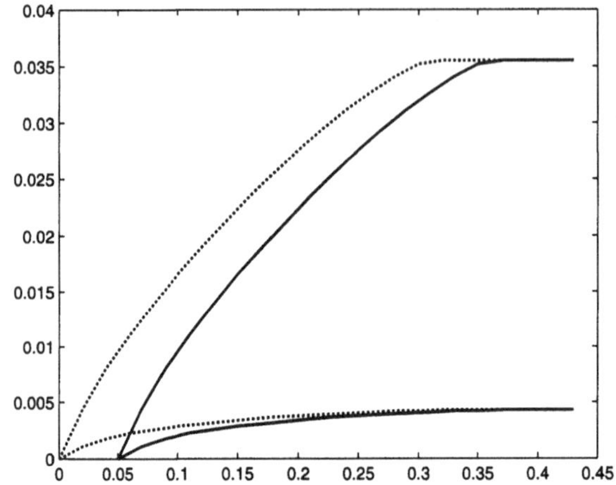

Figure 6.19: Premiums vs. expected losses.

if the losses are above the exit point E. For the adjusted price calculation one can also consider the loading factors above the exit point to be equal to the exit point loading factors. In other words, consider the following adjusted loading function:

$$p^* = P(C(Y) < m) = \int_{[0,E)} dF(y) = F(E-)$$

and set

$$h_E(p) = min(h(p), h(p^*)).$$

Layer (Quantile)	Loading factors
[0.000 0.850)	1.13
[0.850 0.947)	1.57
[0.947 0.965)	1.89
[0.965 0.975)	2.32
[0.975 0.985)	3.27
[0.985 0.988)	3.50
[0.988 0.992)	4.88
[0.992 0.993)	5.43
[0.993 0.996)	8.75
[0.996 0.998)	17.00
[0.998 1.000)	20.00

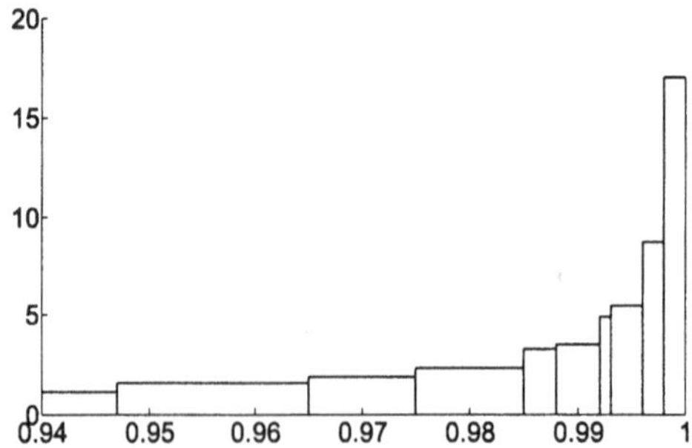

Figure 6.20: Loading factors and quantiles. Based and extended on Pollner et al. 2001: 21, Mechler 2004a: 102.

Then, the adjusted premium is

$$\begin{aligned}\pi_{h_E}(C,F) &= \int_0^\infty C(y)min(h(F(y)),h(F(E-)))dF(y) = \\ &= \int_0^1 C(F^{-1}(p))min(h(p),h(p^*))dp\end{aligned}$$

6.3.7 Uncertainty module

There are different types of uncertainty one can refer to. A widely recognized distinction is between aleatory and epistemic uncertainty (Oberkampf et al. 2004). Aleatory uncertainty is the uncertainty that arise because of unpredictable variation in the performance or the inherent randomness of the system under study. Aleatory uncertainty can not be reduced; however, more knowledge of the system can result in a better quantification of this type of uncertainty. Aleatory uncertainty is inherent in a nondeterministic (stochastic) phenomenon. Thus, one way to represent it is via probability distributions. Epistemic uncertainty is the uncertainty attributable to incomplete knowledge about the system. Hence, it is possible to reduce it over time as more data is collected and more research is completed (National Research Council 1997). If all epistemic uncertainty is eliminated only aleatory uncertainty remain.

The distinction between aleatory and epistemic uncertainty is somewhat arbitrary. Aleatory uncertainty in the present time maybe cast into epistemic uncertainty at a later time (Hanks and Cornell 1994). This raises the question if there is only one kind of uncertainty; namely that which stems from the lack of knowledge. Be as it may, usually the system under study is not fully understood or has to be simulated for other purposes and therefore needs to be analyzed, whereas the distinction between the two types of uncertainty is helpful, e.g. reduction of epistemic uncertainty first. In this process there is the possibility that new knowledge will change the view on the system so that some of the uncertainty first viewed as aleatory becomes epistemic. Hence, even if there is conceptually no difference between aleatory and epistemic uncertainty the advantage to differentiate between them is clear: concentrate on the epistemic uncertainty first.

For an particular system of interest that is mathematically modeled, one can distinguish between parametric uncertainty and model form uncertainty. Parametric uncertainty can be entirely aleatoric in nature, whereas model form uncertainty is fundamentally epistemic in nature (Oberkampf et al. 2004). In CatSim aleatory uncertainty is represented with distribution functions or exceedance curves, like the probability that a given direct loss is not exceeded. It is possible to use confidence intervals around these exceedance curves to reflect the epistemic uncertainty in it (Kunreuther 2002); however, if only historical data of natural disaster events are used usually only few data points exist and therefore such estimates are not very reliable. As already mentioned the calculated response variables are expected values and therefore it is important to measure the variability around these values. In the uncertainty module confidence regions around these estimates can be calculated. For example, in standard mode the variances of each response variable and the 95 percent confidence region is calculated under the (simplistic) assumption of normal distributed random variables. Because of the user interface and the modular structure it is easy to due sensitivity analyses afterwards, or, if new information is at hand update the model.

Epistemic uncertainty is harder to be mathematically represented than aleatory uncertainty. Usually, the mathematical treatment of epistemic uncertainties requires the encoding, and aggregation of expert opinions. Different methods exist to aggregate them; however, various problems arise due to the social component in the weighting process (Paté-Cornell 1996).

6.3.8 Measuring financial vulnerability

In the following section, an approach is presented demonstrating how to measure the current financial vulnerability of the government against a catastrophic event if only the current available ex-post and/or already committed ex-ante measures are used. For the sake of simplicity we assume that only ex-post instruments are available, but extending the approach to also incorporate ex-ante measures is straightforward. The following assumptions are made:

- A one year time horizon is chosen, e.g. the current situation is examined, not a situation in the future. The disaster happens at the beginning of the year and the financial situation of the government at the end of the year is calculated.
- A loss distribution function $F(y)$ is given. The distribution is assumed to be continuous. This is not a restriction because in the case of catastrophe risks, extreme value distributions are used.
- There are k different ex-post financial instruments the government can or may use. It is assumed that these measures come into play immediately after the disaster happens and are available without any time delay.

One way of estimating how vulnerable a government is against losses due to a natural disaster event, is by calculating the critical year event or critical return period. The **critical year event** is defined as the year event which causes a financing gap for the *first* time. The return period is called **critical return period**. It can be calculated in the following way: The maximum amount of ex-post measures available to finance losses due to a catastrophic event is calculated first by the economic model, e.g. a vector $\vec{b}_p = (b_1, ..., b_k)'$ is obtained where $b_i (i = 1, ..., k)$ is the maximum percentage of capital stock that can be used to finance the losses using ex-post instrument i. Using the loss distribution which is also defined in terms of percent of capital stock destroyed, the critical return period is calculated by the following formula:

$$\frac{1}{1 - F(\sum_{i=1}^{k} b_i)}$$

Furthermore, it is also possible to calculate the loss financing scheme for specific year events (up to the critical event). They can be used to assess the current financial resilience in more detail. The loss financing scheme is dependent on the advantages and disadvantages of each ex-post instrument, hence the question is, which ex-post measure should be used first, which one second, and so on, to finance the losses? Instead of a more detailed optimization problem with given prices reflecting the advantages and disadvantages of the ex-post measures (which are difficult or impossible to determine), it is assumed that there is a (strict) order between those instruments represented (lexicographical) in the vector $\vec{x}_p = (x_{p1}, ..., x_{pk})'$, so that the first entry (instrument) would be preferred until depletion before the other instruments are used and so on. Let again $\vec{b}_p = (b_1, ..., b_k)'$ be the maximal amount for each ex-post instrument (in percent of capital stock) for a given event which is calculated with the economic model. To obtain the financing scheme $\vec{x}_p = (x_{p1}, ..., x_{pk})'$ for a given event with return period $1/y$ one has to solve:

$$\begin{aligned}
x_{p1} + ... + x_{pk} &= F^{-1}(y) \qquad \text{with } 0 \leq y \leq 1 \\
&\text{s.t } \vec{x}_p \leq \vec{b}_p \\
\text{where} & \\
& x_p = \begin{pmatrix} x_{p1} \\ \vdots \\ x_{pk} \end{pmatrix}, b_p = \begin{pmatrix} b_1 \\ \vdots \\ b_k \end{pmatrix}, \\
& x_{p2}(b_1 - x_{p1}) = 0 \\
& \vdots \\
& x_{pk}(b_{k-1} - x_{pk-1}) = 0 \\
& x_{pi} \geq 0 \qquad i = 1, ..., k.
\end{aligned}$$

Notice that if $1/y$ is the critical return period, all ex-post measures are used up to the maximum amount available, therefore $\vec{x}_p = \vec{b}_p$. Since $\vec{b}_p$ is (nonlinearly) dependent on the return period, the relative composition of $\vec{x}_p$ is different for every event size. A user interface was created to compare the different loss financing schemes for all events until the critical event (see the figure 7.3). These mixes could be used as guidelines for specific, more detailed sensitivity analysis.

6.3.9 User interfaces, implementation and policy issues

The involvement of stakeholders, e.g. responsible authorities, in disaster research has not been explicitly mandated yet. While it is difficult to anticipate everything that such stakeholders might need to make informed, holistic, and state-of-the-art decisions, at a minimum they certainly need computer-generated decision aids and holistic government policies (Mileti 1999). One possibility to bridge the gap between the scientific assessment of risk and implementation and policy issues could be with the help of user interfaces where the information is presented in such a way, so that also non-scientific people can understand it easily. On the same time, it is important that they recognize the complex relationship of the variables under consideration, the assumptions of the model, and the future consequences of their decisions they make today. From such approaches this can lead to synergies among researchers, stakeholders, and the private industry (e.g. development of marketable products).

For example, the cluster "Forest fire simulation system" of the German Research Network for Natural Disasters (DFNK) created an enabling atmosphere of multidisciplinary forest fire research in Germany through an integrative multi-disciplinary approach (Merz et al. 2006). However, one of the problems they encountered was the heterogeneity of the user community which made it difficult to identify adequate users and their specific needs; on the other hand such integrated concepts allow developing comprehensive solutions that are not possible with disciplinary approaches (Merz et al. 2006). CatSim, which uses a top-down approach and therefore addresses key policy makers on the national level, e.g. finance ministers, try to bridge the gap between scientific analysis and policy and implementation issues in the real world by the use of user interfaces. The need of such graphical interfaces stems from the fact, that risk reduction and funding remains a relatively low priority in development plans, processes and practical implementation. One of the main reasons is that risk reduction is not mainstreamed into development work. Other explanations include the lack of knowledge and understanding of the nature or risk and the competition of risk reduction with other pressing development needs (Trobe and Venton 2003). As a consequence, it is important to show the costs and benefits of proactive risk management strategies in a way so that it is easily understood and seen. Therefore, the user interface around CatSim was built to visualize these costs and benefits of proactive strategies. While the results of such a top down approach usually can not be used for a concrete decision which can be implemented right afterwards, it can serve as a first step to built a proactive risk management strategy against public sector risk. As already mentioned, because of the modular structure of the model, it is possible to make a detailed country analysis afterwards. However, at the beginning the objective should be to increase the awareness of key policy makers on the federal level to catastrophe risk due to natural disasters and possible risk management strategies.

Risk awareness often evolves through four major phases (Cullen and Small 2004): Discovery, Amplification, Management Decision and Implementation. Governments both in developed and developing countries already anticipated the rising economic and human losses due to natural disasters (Benson and Clay 2004, Newkirk 2001, Fairbairn 1998). Now, management decisions to decrease the risk of such losses have to be analyzed and afterwards implemented. In this context the government has two proactive management options: they can reduce the risk or they can spread the risk. Improved government action to reduce the impacts of natural disasters include regulations, e.g. for constructing new buildings, code enforcement, upgrading existing buildings as well as land-use planning and policies to prevent that exposure is increasing in hazard prone areas. Especially in developing countries the improvement of application and enforcement of codes are key measures for risk reduction (Spence 2004). In the case of land use planning the government can establish links with the (re-)insurance industry to initiate collaborations for the creation of hazard maps which are beneficial for both sides. The government can restrict or limit the immigration of people in hazard prone areas; the (re-)insurance company can implement products which are coupled with risk reduction measures regulated by the government, so that it can decrease their risk premiums to affordable rates; the government can give hazard maps to the local levels to initiate and enhance initiatives for local mitigation projects (however, this would require a decentralization of the decision making process to the sub-national level which is rather an exception than the rule in developing countries, see for example El-Masri and Tipple 2002). Such collaboration is currently underway in Austria between the ministry of life and the insurance industry (Project name: HORA) to produce hazard maps for the whole country which can be used by the population to assess their risk due to natural hazards in their specific region. Hazard maps can and should also be used by local governments to pay attention to policies that limit vulnerability against hazards; however, this is often not the case even in developed countries. For example, Burby (2006) analyzed the economic impacts of Hurricane Katrina and explained the unprecedented losses from the disaster by two paradoxes, one called the "local government paradox" which he stated as follows "while [...] citizens bear the brunt of human suffering and financial loss in disasters, local officials pay insufficient attention to policies to limit vulnerability" (Burby 2006: 171). Hence, even when hazardous areas are known local authorities allow intensive development. While this could be prevented, e.g. by states regulations for local governments, the other paradox is more striking in nature. The "safe development paradox" describes the increased potential for catastrophic property damages and economic losses by the government effort to make hazardous areas safer. In the case of failure, e.g. breaking of a levee, due to the high exposure in the area more damages occur than if restricted land use policies were set. Therefore, when development or mitigation is improperly assessed long term vulnerability due to extreme events can thereby increase (Etkin 1999).

There is also the possibility to insure for the more extreme events and use mitigation options for the more frequent events. For example, in CatSim mitigation measures are modeled ideally as step functions, where the full loss occur if the impact of the hazard is higher than the structure is built for. In the simulations usually mitigation has to be above some investment level to be effective, however, there are increasing marginal costs for mitigation and therefore at some point the increase of the robustness of structures is outweighed by the costs and other measures, e.g. financial ones, are from an benefit cost analysis point of view more efficient investments. In CatSim only the economic benefits are assessed and therefore, optimal portfolios of different ex-ante measures, e.g. mitigation, reserve fund, insurance may not be optimal if other variables come into play, e.g. reduction of loss of life. Again, to overcome such problems, user interfaces and multidisciplinary discussions can lead to some overall conclusions, which can stimulate further research.

Summarizing, user interfaces are proposed for catastrophe models to bridge the gap between scientific analysis and policy and implementation issues. Furthermore, such user interfaces can increase the awareness of natural disaster risks and can serve as a communication point between various disciplines which can lead to fruitful discussions to decrease vulnerability in various dimensions. Furthermore, such models can also help to mainstream disaster risk management strategies in development planning processes.

Chapter 7

Case Studies

In this chapter the risk management framework presented in section 2.4 is used to examine the financial vulnerability and macroeconomic risk of three different governments in developing countries against natural hazards. Furthermore, ex-ante instruments which increase their financial resilience, explained in section 5.2, are examined and compared with their costs for the government.

The case studies were examined according to figure 2.2: (i) First, the direct risk and the current financial resilience are examined for each of the cases. The direct risk is described through a (annual) loss distribution, explained in section 6.1. The financial resilience is determined by the amount of ex-post instruments the government can use to finance its losses, see section 5.1. Then, (ii) the financial vulnerability is calculated via the method proposed in section 6.3.8, e.g. the maximum amount of loss financing is calculated through the economic module and transformed into the corresponding return period, called the critical year event, through the given loss distribution. It should be noted here that loss financing schemes for year events lower than the critical one can also be examined using this proposed methodology. Until now, the investigation is rather a static one, because the consequences of a financing gap were not analyzed for the future; the time horizon of the planning and investigation period was set as the next year. In the following (iii), future consequences, e.g. macroeconomic risks, and possible risk management strategies are investigated, based on a 10 year time horizon. One important risk measure here is the probability that a financing gap will occur. This can be lowered by ex-ante instruments, including mitigation measures, a reserve fund, XL-Insurance or a contingent credit arrangement. However, such instruments come with a price of forgone investments in other projects, e.g. infrastructure development. As a consequence maximum growth can not be achieved when ex-ante instruments are used. Therefore, there is always a trade-off between growth and stability. After the macroeconomic risk assessment and risk management investigations, the process (iv) can be started again from the beginning, e.g. to study the effects of different parameters settings or to examine more extreme situations, e.g no ex-post measures available. As already mentioned, user interfaces were built which can be used as a guideline through the risk management process (see the appendix). The user interfaces present the results so that important implications can be seen easily. Because too much space would be needed to present the results of the case studies in this user interfaces a general description and presentation of them can be found in the appendix.

It should be noted, that the results of the case studies should not be interpreted as a thorough risk analysis of the public sector for the specific country because the economic models are set to standard mode and therefore the equations are rather rudimentary. However, the analysis can give overall insights to possible risk management strategies which could be feasible in each particular case. These studies should demonstrate the flexible and coherent approach presented in this thesis. The input data was taken from various publications. For example, some of the loss frequency distributions which constitute the direct risk for each country are taken from Freeman et al. (2002a,b). The parameters for the simulation were taken from estimations done in the Risk and Vulnerability group in IIASA and are again taken from Freeman et al. 2002a,b. These parameters have some uncertainty in it and are rather rough estimates. However, as said before, for a thorough analysis specific economic model approaches for each country are needed. The purpose here is to show an overall approach to macroeconomic risk management for governments which can be used for arbitrary country case studies.

The countries were chosen under the following three considerations. First, each of the selected countries has interest in risk management strategies for public sector risk (Charvériat 2000, Freeman et. al 2002b, Mechler 2004a, Mechler 2005a). Second, they differ in their size and their economic situation: while Honduras and El Salvador are rather small countries with a land area of 111.890 sq km and 20.720 sq km respectively, Colombia is a big country with approximately 1 mill sq km land area (World Bank 2004). However, Colombia is highly indebted while for Honduras and El Salvador in comparison the debt situation is critical but less severe (Freeman et al. 2002b). Furthermore, the primary natural hazards differ in each country: while the main risk in Honduras is due to Hurricane hazard causing flooding, mudslides and wind damage, El Salvador primary hazard are Earthquakes, and Colombia main risks are Earthquakes and Floods (Munich Re 2006 NATHAN). Detailed presentations of the socioeconomic situation and loss statistics both in human and economic terms in the past of the selected countries can be found numerously in the literature (Freeman et al. 2002 a,b, Mechler 2004a, EM-DAT 2006, Munich Re 2006 NATHAN) and are omitted here.

7.1 Honduras

Honduras is subjected to earthquakes and hurricanes whereas the later also causes flooding, mudslides and wind damage. Annual expected direct losses due to earthquake and storm/flood hazard are 0.06 percent and 0.42 percent of total capital stock respectively. The numbers represent the area above the loss distribution (see figure 6.7). The distributions can be found in Freeman et al. (2002a: 47) and were estimated by least squares methods from data points given by Swiss Reinsurance Company. Here, using the expected direct annual loss as an overall risk measure, the biggest economic threat to Honduras represents storm/flood hazard, hence, only this one is investigated further. There is also the possibility to convolute both loss distributions and get one overall loss distribution, because storm/flood hazards are independent from earthquake hazards. However, for the risk management stage this would create some ambiguity how the ex-ante instruments should be priced, e.g. for multi-peril XL-insurance different loading factors would be needed. Table 7.1 shows the loss return periods for storm/flood hazard. It is here assumed that no significant losses occur for events with a return period less than 10 years, e.g. the probability of first loss is 0.1.

	% capital stock destroyed
20- year event loss	0.77
50- year event loss	5.00
100- year event loss	12.31
500- year event loss	30.77
1000- year event loss	30.78
Expected loss	0.43

Table 7.1: Loss return periods for Honduras. Flood and storm hazard. Source: Based and extended from Freeman et al. 2002a: 17.

The loss frequency distribution was estimated as a Gamma distribution with parameter $\alpha = 0.0187$ and $\beta = 21.401$ and a shift of -0.0435 (see figure 7.1). However, it is also possible to connect the loss return data points by straight lines, which fastens up the calculation procedures and do not change the results significantly.

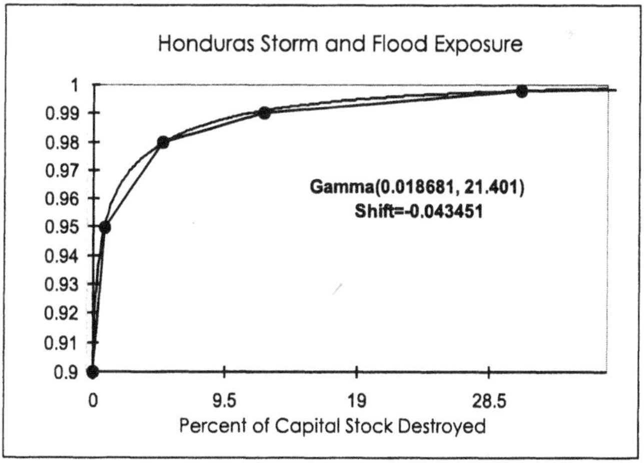

Figure 7.1: Loss distribution for Honduras.

As already mentioned, the economic module is set to a standard mode. Table 7.2 shows the parameter settings used for the simulation. Furthermore, in table 7.3 the parameter settings for the available ex-post measures are shown, which determine the financial resilience of Honduras government.

initial capital (Cap0)	13.9 (billion USD)
fixed budget (Bfx)	2.083 (billion USD)
return on investment (roi)	20 %
discount rate for future returns (dis)	12 %
depreciation rate (dep)	2 %
credit buffer	1.1 (billion USD)

Table 7.2: Economic parameters for Honduras.

ratio of maximal diversion to revenue (dir)	7.3 %
ratio of maximal domestic credit to revenue	3.0 %
interest rate for domestic credit (ido)	10.2 %
interest rate for MFI loan (imf)	0.75 %
interest rate for international bond (ibd)	10.2 %
Assistance (Aid)	10.4 %

Table 7.3: Ex-post parameters for Honduras.

For the ex-ante measures the factor for mitigation, interest rate of the reserve fund and contingent credit are needed. The factor for mitigation which describes the efficiency of the mitigation investments is set to 4.5 (see section 6.3.4). For the reserve fund an interest rate of 5.72 percent and for the contingent credit an interest rate of 6 percent is chosen. The above parameters are used for the simulations in the following sections. First, some specific events and their loss financing schema are analyzed. Then the critical return period is calculated, e.g. the year event when the financing gap starts. Second, the macroeconomic risk for the public sector for a time horizon of 10 years is analyzed and risk management strategies are assessed afterwards.

7.1.1 Financial vulnerability

To assess the financial vulnerability of the government, one can, to catch a glimpse at the problem, start by looking at different year events and the ability of the government to finance the corresponding losses. Here, the 20-, 50-, 100-, and 500 year event are chosen because these points were the basis for the estimation of the loss distribution. Note, that only 50 percent of the total direct losses the government is responsible for, see section 4.3.1. Figure 7.2 shows the loss financing of the government for the different year events.[1]

As one can see, the higher the year event, the higher the losses and therefore, more dollar amount of the available ex-post financing instruments have to be used. For example, a 50 year event would cause losses of about 407 million USD to the government.

[1]It is assumed, that the event happens next year, therefore the initial values are changed according to the economic model.

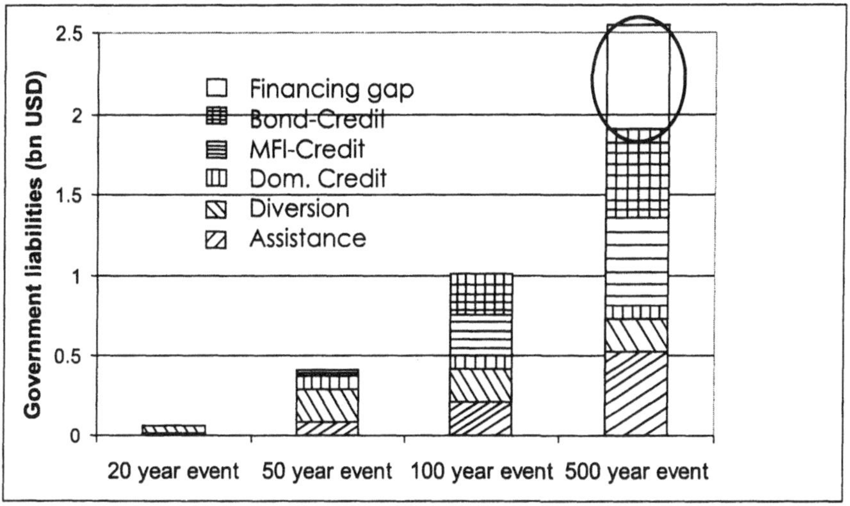

Figure 7.2: Loss financing for specific events (Honduras).

However, no financing gap would occur because the losses could be financed through aid from the outside worth 85 million USD, diversion worth 202 million USD, a domestic credit worth 30 million USD and equal amounts of MFI and bond credits each worth of 45 million USD. Also, no financing gap occur for the 100 year event. However, the 500 year event would be quite devastating. It would result in losses up to 2.51 billion USD and even if the government would use their ex-post measures to their maximum amount, a financing gap of 661 million USD would occur.

While this first examination of the financial vulnerability gives a first impression of the financing mechanism, it is also interesting to see at which specific year event the financing gap starts, e.g. the critical return period. Based on the assumptions in section 6.3.8 and recognizing that all ex-post measures are used to the maximum amount available, for Honduras the financing gap would start at a return period higher than a 156 year event, e.g. a 157- year event would cause a depletion of all ex-post measures available for the government to finance the losses caused by the event. Therefore the critical return period is a 157 year event. This event would destroy 20.6 percent of the total capital stock at risk and cause losses of about 1.68 billion USD to the government. Observe, all events with higher return periods would increase the financing gap and therefore the possibility of negative long term economic effects due to the disaster event. Furthermore, because the ex-post instruments are already used to the maximum, lower amounts are available in the future, which in turn decrease its financial resilience for future events. As a consequence, a critical year event could be much lower than the 157 year event.

The financing schema for the government is not only different for events with different impacts but it also depends on the order in which the ex-post measures is used first. However, this is not important for those events with a return period higher than the critical one because in that case all ex-post measures are used. In figure 7.3 possible financing schemes for events with lower return periods than the critical one are shown and compared.

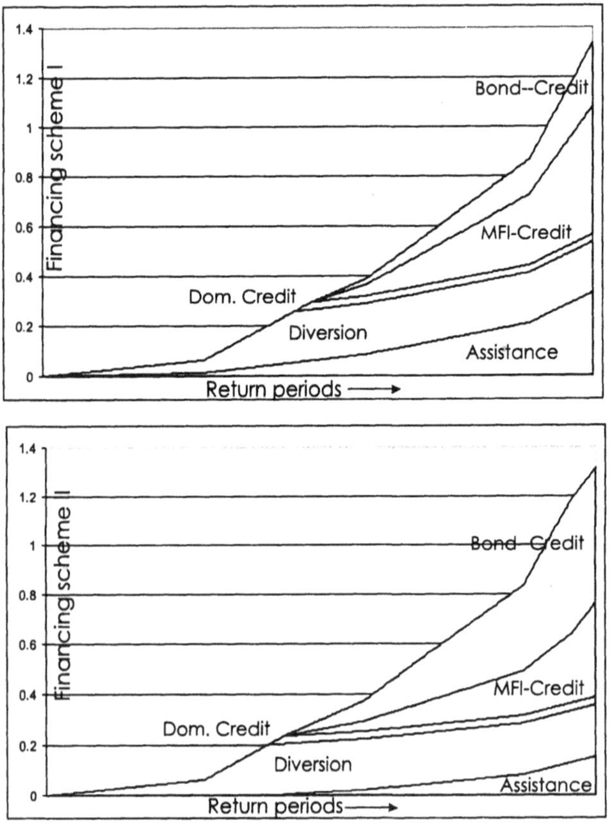

Figure 7.3: Financing schemes dependent on ex-post ordering.

In the first picture in figure 7.3 the following ordering was chosen: aid, diversion, domestic credit, MFI credit and bond credit. For the second picture a more realistic ordering was assumed: diversion, domestic credit, aid, MFI and bond credit. While the pictures look quite different, all losses in both cases can be financed through the ex-post measures. In the user interface different orderings can be tested. For the macroeconomic risk management approach this ordering is not important because only those events which are causing a financing gap are of interest.

7.1.2 *Macroeconomic risk management strategies*

While the knowledge of the critical year event is valuable for its own reasons the consequences for the future of such inability to refinance the losses are far more important and interesting to the government. As proposed, one important risk measure here is the probability that a financing gap occur in the next years. Here, a time horizon of 10 years was chosen for the investigation. As one result from the simulation run (more than 3600 scenarios were generated), the probability that a financing gap will occur in the next 10 years if only the available (ex-post) resources are used was calculated to be around 8.4 percent. In other words, there is nearly a 1 out of 12 chance of having a financing gap in the next 10 years due to storms and flooding. The expected financing gap is around 35 million USD, which means that the government of Honduras can expect a financing gap in the next 10 years of around 35 million USD on average, if a financing gap would occur.

Ex-ante measures like mitigation, XL-insurance, a reserve fund or a contingent credit arrangement can be used to increase the financial resilience which in turn will decrease the macroeconomic risk (e.g. the probability of a financing gap). However, ex-ante measures come with a price. The mean return on capital stock decreases with budget funds spent on ex-ante measures as these funds cannot be used for other investments.

Looking at figure 7.4 one can see that the possible growth paths (measured here in billion USD) with and without ex-ante measures (here XL-insurance) are different: while the growth paths without any ex-ante measures can be very high but also very low, the growth paths with ex-ante measures cannot be as high as in the case without ex-ante measures but on the other hand they cannot be as low as in the case without ex-ante measures. Hence, there is a trade-off between stability and growth.

The simulation study above revealed that the probability of a financing gap for a 10 year time horizon is around 8.4 percent, and the expected financing gap is around 35 million USD. The decision maker, e.g. finance minister or key policy maker in this field, has to answer the question how much risk he wants to take. If the risk is seen as too high, the question is then how to lower it. Figure 7.5 shows the reduction of the probability of a financing gap by investments in ex-ante measures, e.g. mitigation, XL-insurance, reserve fund and contingent credit. As one can see, the more money that is spent on these measures the lower the probability of a financing gap is. Furthermore, some of these measures are reducing the financing gap probability faster than other ones, given the same money spent on each of them (figure 7.5). For example if 8 percent of the variable budget is spent on mitigation a reduction from 8.5 to 8 percent can be achieved. If 8 percent of the variable budget is spent on a reserve fund a reduction of the probability from 8.5 to 6.4 percent can be achieved. If the same amount is spent on a contingent credit arrangement only a short reduction to 8.3 percent is achieved[2]. The best ex-ante instrument in terms of the reduction of the financing gap probability is the XL-insurance. A reduction from

[2]The amount of contingent credit is not only determined by the expenditure for the instrument but also on the credit buffer (see section 6.3.4). Because Honduras is highly indebted, it is not always possible

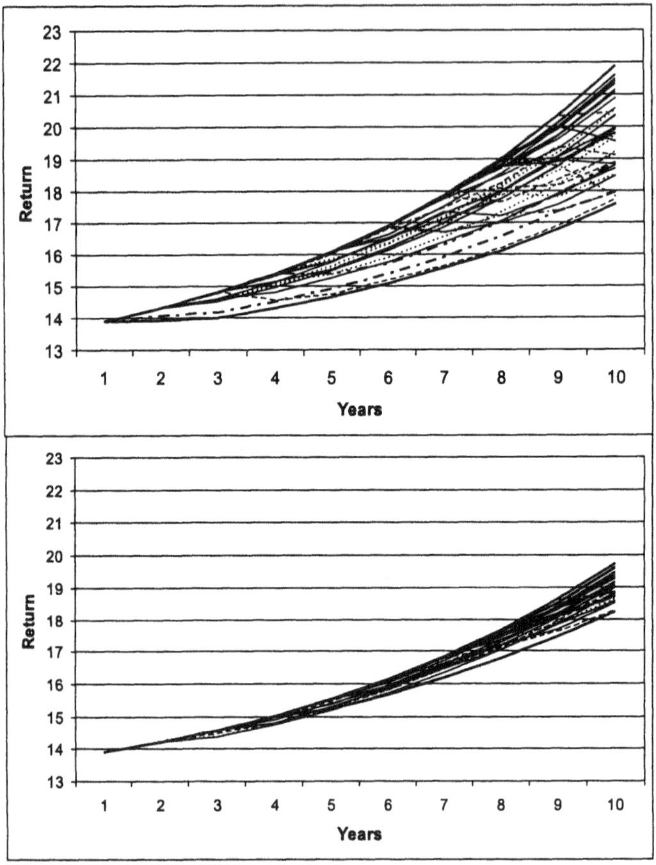

Figure 7.4: Return growth paths with and without insurance.

8.5 to 4.7 is possible if the attachment point was chosen to be 0.77 percent (20 year event). Therefore, if only the reduction of the probability is seen as important for the decision, XL-insurance is superior to a reserve fund, a reserve fund is superior to mitigation and mitigation is superior to a contingent credit.

Another interesting question which is also connected with the financing gap probability is how much the discounted expected gap is reduced by the ex-ante measures. The picture is quite similar to figure 7.5. XL-insurance is superior to a reserve fund, a reserve fund is superior to mitigation and mitigation is superior to a contingent credit. For example, if again 8 percent of the variable budget is used for XL-insurance the mean financing

for them to use the contingent credit to its full extent. However, if such restrictions are not made, contingent credits would be always preferable in terms of reduction of the financing gap probability.

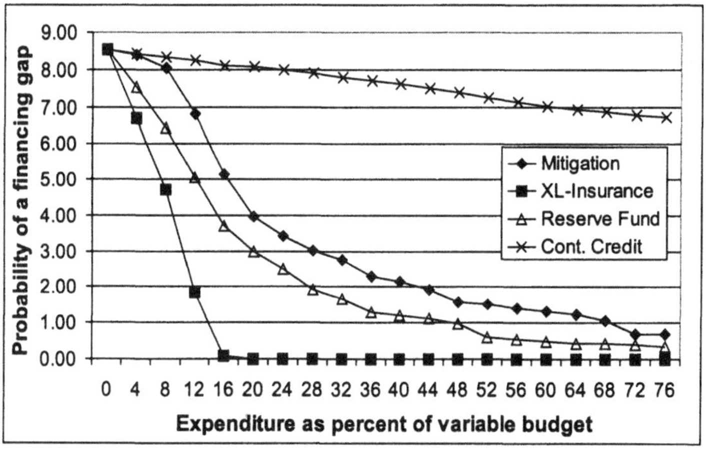

Figure 7.5: Risk reduction due to ex-ante measures (Honduras).

gap is reduced from 35 million USD to 7 million USD, if the money is used for a reserve fund the mean reduces to 18 million USD, for mitigation a reduction to 32 million USD and for a contingent credit only a reduction to 33 million USD is achieved.

While the occurrence of a financing gap is decreased by investments in ex-ante measures also the return on capital stock is decreased. Figure 7.6 shows the reduction of the discounted expected return when ex-ante measures are used. For a given amount of budget, the expected returns are nearly the same for all of the instruments. For example, if 8 percent of the variable budget is used the discounted expected return is 22.70 bn USD for mitigation, 22.76 bn USD for XL-insurance, 22.71 bn USD for the reserve fund and 22.68 bn USD for the contingent credit. Interestingly, the variance of the return goes down as the investments increase due to the higher stable growth paths which are achieved. Especially for the XL-insurance the variance decreases faster than the other ex-ante measures. This can be explained by the fact that insurance contracts need no accumulation time like in the case of mitigation and reserve fund. As an example, suppose again that 8 percent of the variable budget is used for the instruments. Then, the variance of the return is 0.19 bn USD for mitigation, 0.06 bn USD for XL-insurance, 0.15 bn USD for the reserve fund and 0.20 bn USD for the contingent credit arrangement.

Figure 7.7 shows the credit buffer drop for different investments in ex-ante measures. A big decrease in the credit buffer indicates the inability of the country to get new credits for other purposes than repair in the future. As one can see the credit buffer drop is very high if no ex-ante instruments are used, because money has to be borrowed to finance losses. For investments in mitigation, XL-insurance and a reserve fund, the drop is reduced because the amount of borrowed money for loss financing decreases. In the case of the

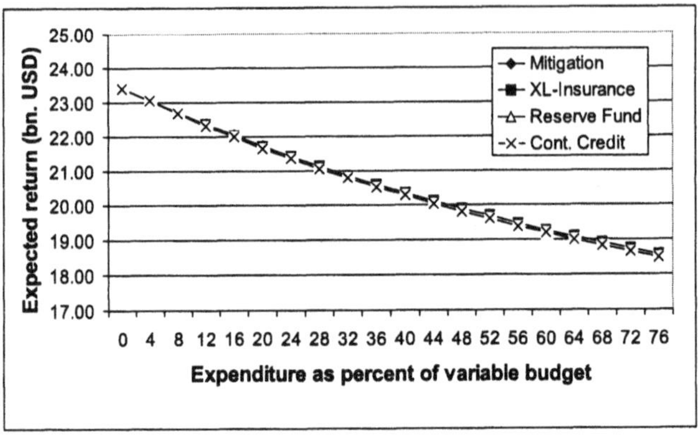

Figure 7.6: Decreasing returns due to investments in ex-ante instruments (Honduras).

contingent credit the graph first goes up, and then it reduces due to higher amounts spent on contingent credit. The reason for the latter is that a contingent credit increases the debt stock and has to be repaid in the future (intertemporal risk spreading).

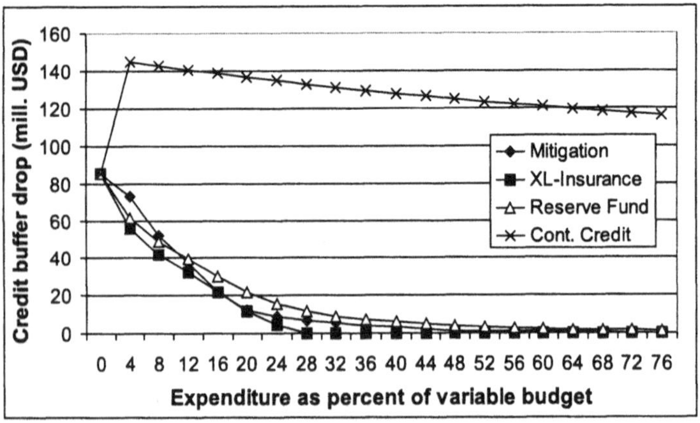

Figure 7.7: Credit buffer drop reduction due to investments in ex-ante instruments (Honduras).

7.1.3 Summary

Honduras is severely exposed to storm and flood hazards. The analysis has shown that proactive risk management approaches could significantly decrease their financial vulnerability and macroeconomic risk. However, a proactive approach comes with a price in terms of lesser (possible) growth. This trade-off between stability and growth is shown in figure 7.8. Higher investments in ex-ante measures lead to lower returns but higher stability. Because the XL-insurance is superior over the other three instruments, a local optimum search (see section 6.3.2) always gives a portfolio selection were all money is invested in insurance. However, there are also other important dimensions which are not considered in the model either because it is not possible to quantify them or because of lack of information, e.g. mitigation would also reduce the loss of life.

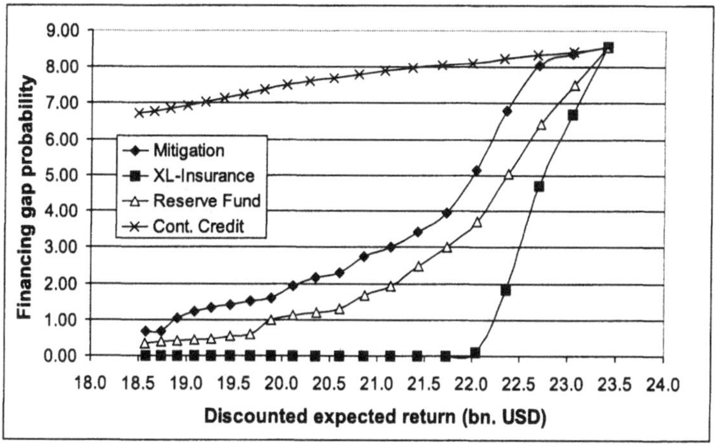

Figure 7.8: Trade-off: Stability (financing gap) vs. Growth (return).

Because the contingent credit arrangement was tied to the credit buffer, due to the high indebtedness level of Honduras the probability of a financing gap in the 10 year time period could not be reduced very well with this instrument. If such restriction would not exist a contingent credit would be very effective for loss financing in the short run, however, the indebtedness level would increase very much in the near future and as a consequence would only worsen the already critical indebtedness situation, which is certainly not the goal of the government.

From an economic point of view mitigation and reserve fund are second-best options. While mitigation is less effective than a reserve fund it has additional advantages, e.g. physical protection. It is also interesting that mitigation investments have to be above some level, so that the capital stock is effectively protected. This can be seen by figure 7.5 were the slope of the curve goes down after an investment of more than 8 percent of the variable budget. Furthermore, mitigation reduces the credit buffer drop more effectively than a reserve fund for higher investments (see figure 7.7) which can be explained by the modeling approach of mitigation as a step function: no losses occur for smaller events and therefore no mitigation efforts are lost. However, the discounted expected financing gap is always higher for mitigation than for the reserve fund. This can be explained by the fact that events with high impacts are destroying mitigation efforts in two ways, the money used for mitigation is lost and no protection was achieved.

7.2 El Salvador

El Salvador is highly subjected to earthquake hazard. In the last hundred years it has been affected by at least 14 major earthquakes, including those of Jucuapa-Chinameca in 1951, San Salvador in 1965, 1986 and 2001. Especially recent earthquakes caused greater destruction and higher damages due to landslides caused by the earthquake (Fernández et al. 2001). Using the EM-DAT database (2006) between 1902 and 2005 to calculate some loss statistics for different natural disaster types, earthquake hazard represents the most serious thread to the country: on average, more than 400 people were killed, more than 3.000 are injured and more than 270.000 people were affected per earthquake event. But not only are the damages in human terms, due to earthquake events in El Salvador, devastating, also the economic impacts and consequences are overwhelming. For example, the two earthquakes of 2001 severely disrupted the country's economic and social progress. While the losses were approximately at 12 percent of 2000 GDP, it was estimated that its development was put back by several years (ECLAC 2003(4): 89)

Furthermore, flooding mainly due to the El Niño affect occur. However, due to the special nature of El Niño, e.g. recurrence interval can be predicted to be between 3 and 8 years, in the following, the focus is on earthquake risk. The loss return periods are shown in table 7.4 and are based on estimation results from Freeman et al. 2002b.

	% of capital stock destroyed
20- year event loss	2
50- year event loss	8
100- year event loss	25
500- year event loss	30
1000- year event loss	31
Expected loss	0.6465

Table 7.4: Loss return periods for El Salvador. Earthquake hazard. Source: Based and extended from Freeman et al. 2002b.

Unfortunately, these values are very vague and should be interpreted with caution; they are not estimations from insurance companies but rather extrapolations from historical losses. A Weibull loss distribution with parameter $\alpha = 0.261$ and $\beta = 0.048$ and a shift of -1.17 was estimated (see figure 7.9).

The annual expected loss is calculated as 0.64 percent of the total capital stock. Therefore, the expected direct risk for El Salvador is higher than for Honduras. However, this does not mean that it is more financially more vulnerable because this depends on its financial resilience which is assessed in the next section. Furthermore, also the tail behav-

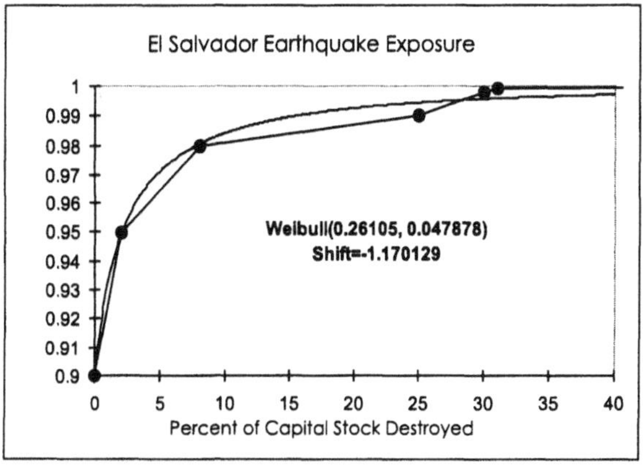

Figure 7.9: Loss distribution for El Salvador.

ior, e.g. thickness, is important. The economic parameters for the simulation are shown in table 7.5.

initial capital (Cap0)	12 (billion USD)
fixed budget (Bfx)	1.87 (billion USD)
return on investment (roi)	20 %
discount rate for future returns (dis)	12 %
depreciation rate (dep)	7 %
credit buffer	1.0 (billion USD)

Table 7.5: Economic parameters for El Salvador.

Again, also the following parameter of the ex-post measures is needed for the simulation (table 7.6). The factor for mitigation is set again to 4.5 (see section 6.3.4) and the interest rates for the reserve fund and for the contingent credit are set to 5.72 and 6 percent respectively.

ratio of maximal diversion to revenue (dir)	17.2 %
ratio of maximal domestic credit to revenue	0.0 %
interest rate for domestic credit (ido)	15.9 %
interest rate for MFI loan (imf)	7.5 %
interest rate for international bond (ibd)	7.6 %
Assistance (Aid)	10.4 %

Table 7.6: Ex-post parameters for El Salvador.

7.2.1 Financial vulnerability

As with Honduras, different year events are examined first. Figure 7.10 shows the loss financing schemes of the government for the 20-, 50-, 100- and 500 year event. Again, it is assumed that the government has to finance 50 percent of the total losses. As one can see, no financing gap occurs if a 20-, 50-, or 100 year event would happen. For example, in the case of a 50 year event, the losses to the government would be around 537 million USD which could be financed through assistance worth 107 million USD, diversion worth 413 million USD and credits from abroad (MFI and international bonds) worth 17 million USD. While loss financing for the 100 year event is possible, the 500 year event would case a financing gap of about 198 million US$. As one can see by figure 7.10 the maximum feasible amount of ex-post resources is nearly reached for the 100 year event, which means that the financing gap will be near this value.

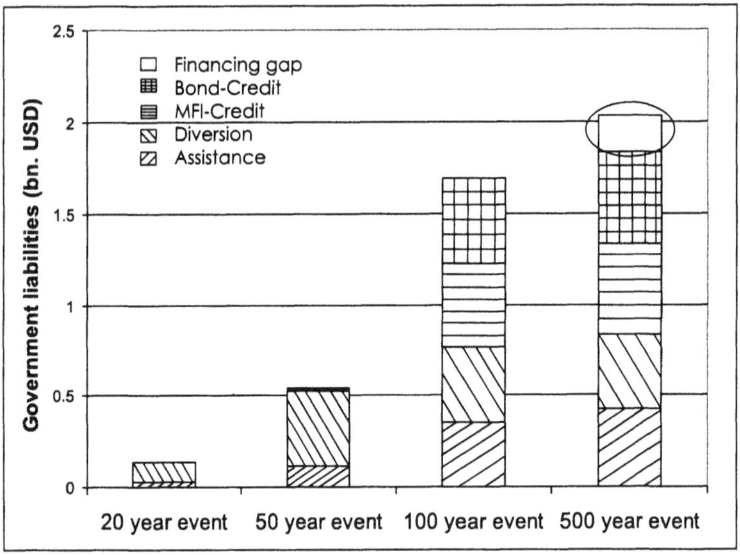

Figure 7.10: Loss financing for specific events (El Salvador).

While this first discrete (only 4 different loss return periods are used) examination gives some overall insight into governments loss financing ability, in the next step the whole loss distribution will be used to determine the exact year event when the financing gap will start. Therefore, the maximum amount the government is able to raise has to be determined and transformed into the (critical) return period using the (continuous) loss distribution. The 128 year event is found to be the first event where a financing gap would start, e.g. a 128 year event would cause the depletion of all ex-post measures available for the government. This also means that year events with higher return periods, e.g. a 150 year event, are also causing a financing gap. Such events with higher return periods than the critical one are also causing larger financing gaps because, as the losses increase the loss financing ability of the government already reached its maximum amount. How rapid the increase of the financing gap after the critical return period is, is dependent on the tail of the distribution. The thicker they are the higher the losses for lower year events. In this case the critical year event would destroy 26.3 percent of the total capital stock and would cause losses to the government of about 1.784 billion USD. Compared to the case of Honduras, El Salvador is more financial vulnerable because the critical return period is smaller than for Honduras (157 year event). However, nothing is said yet about the macroeconomic risk El Salvador is exposed to.

7.2.2 Macroeconomic risk management strategies

As in the case of Honduras, for comparison reasons a time horizon of 10 years was chosen. Here, the probability of a financing gap using only ex-post measures is around 4.6 percent, which means that there is a 1/20 chance of a financing gap in the next 10 years due to an earthquake event. Compared to Honduras, where the probability is 8.4 percent, the government in El Salvador has a lower risk that a financing gap will occur in the future. This can be seen as a direct comparison of the risk situation using a flow measure which is possible through the methodology presented here. Furthermore, the expected financing gap for the government in El Salvador is around 4.9 million USD which is much lower than for Honduras (35 million USD), mainly because the direct risk is higher for the later.

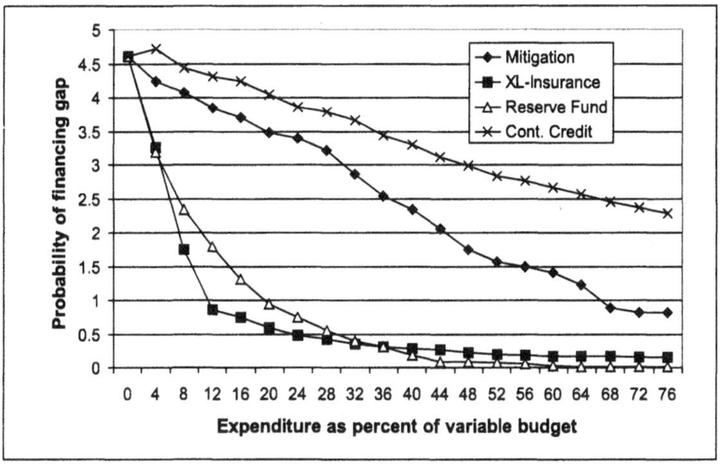

Figure 7.11: Risk reduction through ex-ante investment (El Salvador).

The decision maker has to decide if he wants to take the risk or else invest in risk reduction measures. Again, four different ex-ante measures can be used. Mitigation, e.g. building earthquake resistant houses, XL-insurance, e.g. insuring some layers of the loss portfolio, a reserve fund, e.g. annual capital accumulation, or a contingent credit. This will increase government's financial resilience and therefore decrease its macroeconomic risk. In figure 7.11 the relationship between the investments in ex-ante measures and the reduction of the probability of a financing gap is shown. As one can see, XL-insurance and a reserve fund are the best options here. Interestingly, if more than 36 percent of the variable budget is used, the reserve fund is superior to the XL-insurance. This can be explained by the fact that the attachment point was set here to cover also the first loss, which means that mainly those events are insured which already can be financed by ex-post measures. The reserve funds accumulation is very efficient for risk reduction if enough funds are spent each year. Mitigation is the second-best option and the contingent credit is less efficient. Especially at low level expenditures, the contingent credit arrangements worsen the situation by the reduction of the credit buffer which in turn limits the ex-post capabilities of the government. This effect can also be seen on the discounted expected financing gap graph (figure 7.12) is looked at. Here small investments into the contingent credit arrangement increase first the expected gap. Investments have to be over 16 percent of the variable budget so that a decrease of the expected gap compared to the no investment scenario can be observed. However, the other ex-ante instruments are more efficient by reducing the expected gap. For example, using 16 percent of the variable budget for mitigation would decrease the gap to 3.8 million. Using a reserve fund would decrease the gap to 1.2 million and using XL-insurance would reduce the expected financing gap to 0.8 million USD.

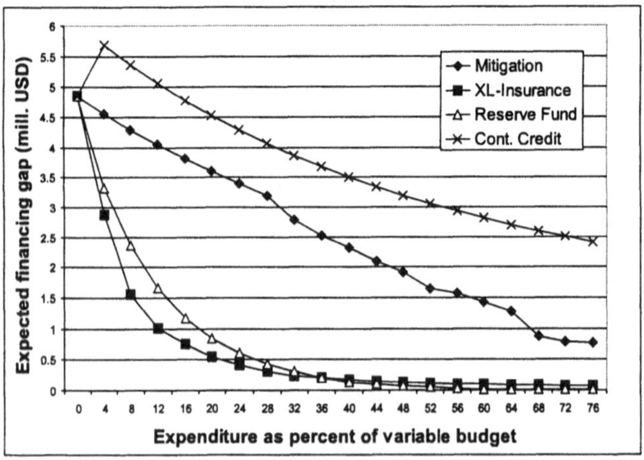

Figure 7.12: Reduction of the expected financing gap through investments in ex-ante measures (El Salvador).

In figure 7.13 the reduction of the credit buffer drop due to the different ex-ante investments is shown. As in the case of Honduras the contingent credit arrangement behaves worst if the credit buffer drop wants to be reduced effectively. This can be explained by the large debt payments for the government after the disaster. The increase in its debt situation also decrease its credit buffer. Because of the decrease of the credit buffer the availability of ex-post credits from abroad is also decreased. Given that El Salvador is very much dependent on such credits (see figure 7.10) a contingent credit only worsen the situation. While the contingent credit behaves worst, the reserve fund is superior over the other measures. After some investment level also mitigation seems to be very effective. For example, using 35 percent of the variable budget for the ex-ante instruments, the credit buffer drop decrease from 66 million USD to 46 million USD for XL-insurance, to 11 million USD for the reserve fund and to 10 million USD for mitigation. As one can see, the XL-insurance in this case does not behave the most favorable. At least one reason for this result can be given. Because the XL-insurance attachment point was the 20 year event, higher losses were not insured due to the high costs. This in turn makes the insurance contract not very effective for loss financing. For higher losses credits from abroad are needed, and therefore insurance has no or little positive effects on the credit buffer. As the investments for XL-Insurance gets higher, the higher the exit level can be chosen, which in turn lessen the impacts on the credit buffer by disencumbering the ex-post measures. However, as a general statement, XL-insurance should be used for higher risk layers.

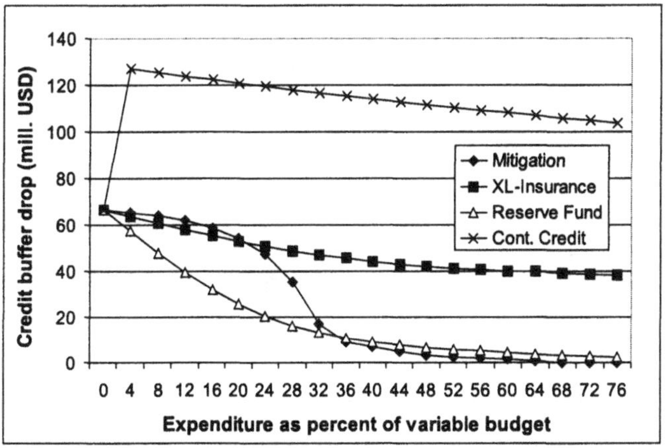

Figure 7.13: Credit buffer drop due to ex-ante investments (El Salvador).

7.2.3 Summary

While the macroeconomic risk, e.g. indebtedness, is reduced, the return on capital stock also decreases. For example, while the discounted expected return without ex-ante measures is around 14.53 billion USD for the 10 year time horizon it would be reduced to 13.9 billion USD if 20 percent of the variable budget is spent for the ex-ante instruments. Therefore, average drops of 5 percent of return on capital investments in 10 years are the costs of such investments. However, the variance of the return is also reduced by the ex-ante measures, which means that the stability of the returns is increased, however, on lower levels. This effect is the same as figure 7.4 is showing. Especially, XL-insurance and the reserve fund behave very efficiently, e.g. the variance is reduced very fast the higher the investments in these instruments are. Figure 7.14 is showing one aspect of the trade-off between stability and growth. While a contingent credit is least efficient and mitigation is also not very good, XL-insurance and reserve fund behave quite good. Especially for higher investments in ex-ante measures a reserve fund is superior to all the other instruments. This can be explained by the already efficient ex-post instruments available.

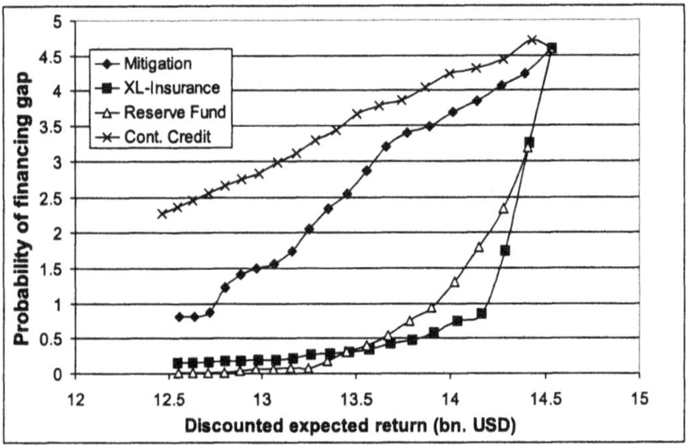

Figure 7.14: Trade-off between stability and growth (El Salvador).

However, as figure 7.11 was showing, the reduction of the probability (of a financing gap) to zero is not possible for the reserve fund. A small risk remains but is negligible (below 0.01 percent). Therefore, a proactive approach with a reserve fund with sufficient annual payments would be a better option because first, the money is not lost as in the case with insurance and second, the reserve fund is as efficient in risk reduction as insurance while keeping in addition the credit buffer drop very low. One could ask if insurance would behave better if higher attachment points are taken. The answer is twofold: while the probability of a financing gap goes down faster than the reserve fund, the credit buffer drop is always higher compared to a reserve fund. There is also the possibility to find a (local) optimal mix between insurance and a reserve fund. For example, if 40 percent of the variable budget is used to minimize the probability of a financing gap while keeping the expected return drop (compared to the no ex-ante scenario) above 5 percent than 10 percent should be used for a reserve fund and the other 30 percent for a XL-insurance. However, with such a portfolio the credit buffer drop and the expected financing gap are higher than in the case where everything is invested in the reserve fund. A multi-objective optimization is not feasible yet and therefore the overall suggestion is that a reserve fund arrangement is superior to the other ex-ante measures.

7.3 Colombia

Colombia is mainly exposed to volcanic eruption, earthquakes and floods. Between 1906 and 2005 EM-DAT (2006) recorded 6 volcanic eruptions, 21 earthquakes and 51 flood events. While the average death toll per event is highest for volcanic eruption (3.802), mainly due to the exceptionally high death toll in 1985 (21.800 people killed), it is lower (but still high) for earthquakes (157) and floods (48). The average damages (in current mill. USD) are also highest for volcanic eruptions (166 mill. USD), again due the high damages in 1985 (1.000 mill. USD), and are lower for earthquakes (109 mill USD) and floods (10 mill USD) (EM-DAT 2006). As in the case of El Salvador, a multi-hazard analysis could (and actually should) be done, however, due to data limitations and the problem of interpreting the results only earthquake hazard is looked at.

	percent of capital stock destroyed
20- year event loss	1.5
50- year event loss	3.8
100- year event loss	6.2
500- year event loss	11
1000- year event loss	15
Expected loss	0.2638

Table 7.7: Loss return periods for Colombia. Earthquake hazard. Source: Based and extended from Freeman et al. 2002b.

In table 7.7 the loss return periods for earthquake hazard is shown. Furthermore, figure 7.15 presents the estimated loss distribution.

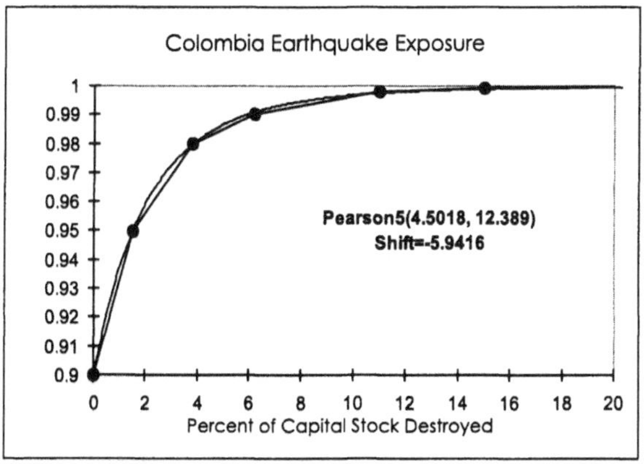

Figure 7.15: Loss distribution for Colombia.

As one can see, a Pearson5- distribution (also known as Inverse Gamma distribution) with parameters $\alpha = 4.501$ and $\beta = 12.389$ with a shift of -5.942 was estimated. By calculating the area above the curve the annual expected direct losses are 0.26 percent of the total capital stock at risk. Compared to Honduras and El Salvador, Colombia has the lowest expected annual loss. Also, when the tails of the three different loss distributions are examined one can see that the tails for Colombia are thinner, compared to Honduras and El Salvador.

Again, like in the case with El Salvador, these estimates are rather rough. Table 7.8 shows the parameters used for the economic module. Note, that the credit buffer is set to zero indicating that Colombia is not able to borrow money from the outside.

initial capital (Cap0)	130 (billion USD)
fixed budget (Bfx)	12.43 (billion USD)
return on investment (roi)	15 %
discount rate for future returns (dis)	12 %
depreciation rate (dep)	7 %
credit buffer	0.0 (billion USD)

Table 7.8: Economic parameters for Colombia.

The financial resilience of Colombia is determined by the amount of ex-post measures they can use. The following estimates are taken for the simulation (table 7.9).

ratio of maximal diversion to revenue (dir)	19.7 %
ratio of maximal domestic credit to revenue	0.0 %
interest rate for domestic credit (ido)	12.10 %
interest rate for MFI loan (imf)	7.5 %
interest rate for international bond (ibd)	10.8 %
Assistance (Aid)	10.4 %

Table 7.9: Ex-post parameters for Colombia.

Again, for the ex-ante measures the factor for mitigation, interest rate of the reserve fund and contingent credit are needed. The factor for mitigation is set to 4.5. For the reserve fund an interest rate of 5.72 percent and for the contingent credit a interest rate of 6 percent is used in the simulation.

7.3.1 Financial vulnerability

As shown in figure 7.16 the Colombian government is very dependent on assistance and his ability to divert its budget in times of need. Due to its indebtedness, e.g. the credit buffer was set to zero, for the government cannot raise any funds from the outside by MFI or international bond credits. However, this does not seem to be a problem at least up to the 100 year event, as figure 7.16 indicates. For example, a 100 year event would cause losses to the government of about 4.3 billion USD, which could be financed through assistance (0.9 billion USD) and diversion (2.4 billion USD). Note that assistance is also dependent on the media coverage of the event, which could increase or decrease the amount of assistance it can get from the outside. Also the ability to divert the budget can be lower than estimated here for various reasons. In the user interface of the model, these parameters can be changed interactively so that sensitivity analysis can be performed quite quickly. As one can see, the 20-, 50- and 100 year event did not start a financing gap. However, the 500 year event cause approximately 7.7 bn USD losses to the government, whereas 5.5 bn US$ of these losses can be financed. Hence, the resulting financing gap for a 500 year event is around 2.2 bn USD.

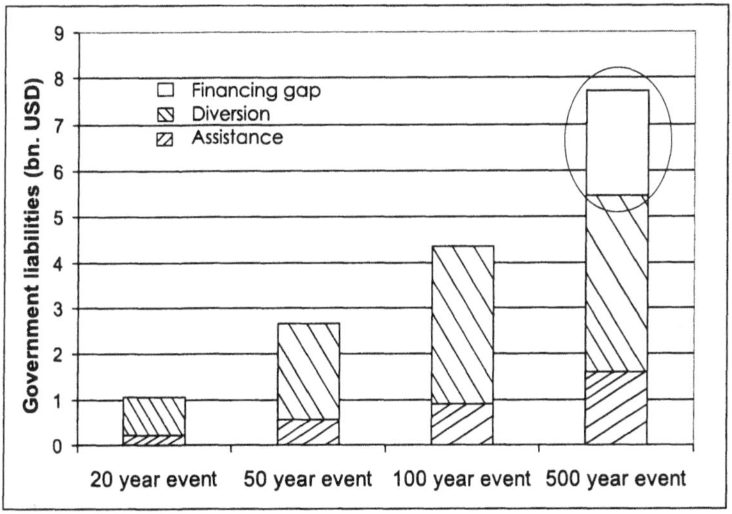

Figure 7.16: Loss financing for specific events (Colombia).

The loss distribution enables the calculation of the critical return period. It is estimated as the 114 year event which destroys 6.52 percent of the total capital stock. The losses for the government amount to 4.85 bn USD. In other words, the maximum amount of capital the government can raise is 4.8 bn USD. Observe, that in figure 7.16 for the 500 year event more than this amount of money was available. This is due the modeling of assistance as a function of the total losses, which means that for higher losses, also more assistance from the outside is available. However, after the critical year event, the increase in marginal increase of assistance is always smaller than the marginal increase of the financing gap.

7.3.2 Macroeconomic risk management strategies

The time horizon for the simulation was set again to 10 years. The probability of a financing gap is around 11 percent for the Colombian government. Using this probability as a risk measure, compared to Honduras and El Salvador, Colombia has the highest risk of not being able to finance the losses due to a catastrophic event. The chance of such an situation in the next 10 years is 1:10. The expected financing gap is around 109.6 million USD. Therefore, Colombia can expect a financing gap in the next 10 years of around 110 million US$ on average, if a financing gap occurs. The expected financing gap is higher here because the capital stock at risk is higher than in the case of the smaller countries Honduras and El Salvador. Therefore, a direct comparison of the gap should not be done. However, for the decision maker, the expected gap is important. If he decides that the risk should be reduced, proactive measures have to be used.

In figure 7.17 one can see the reduction of the probability of a financing gap through the investments in the four ex-ante measures mitigation, XL-insurance, reserve fund and contingent credit. While the reserve fund is more effective for risk reduction than mitigation and XL-insurance (attachment point was set to the 20 year event) in decreasing the probability of a financing gap, the XL-insurance shows some interesting behavior.

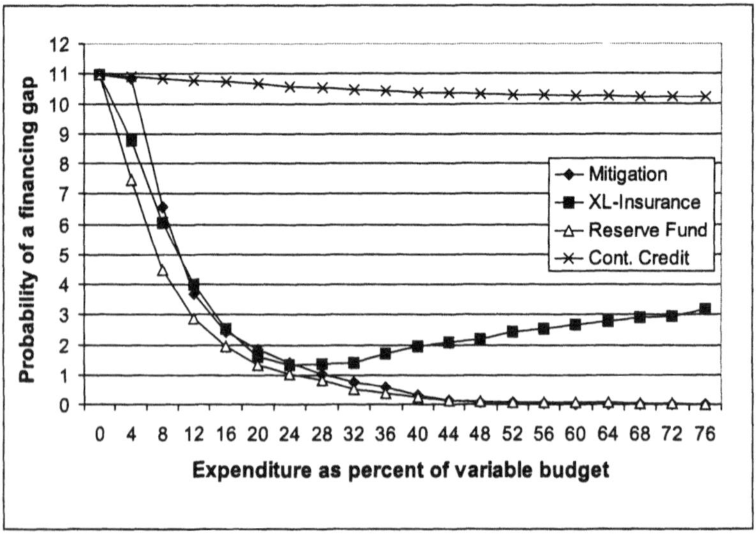

Figure 7.17: Risk reduction through ex-ante instruments (Colombia).

The XL-insurance reduces the probability of a financing gap very fast if the investments in this measure are below 24 percent of the variable budget. Afterwards, the XL-insurance seems to be less efficient even when more money is spent for this instrument. This effect can be explained at least by two arguments which are also interrelated to each other: correlation between ex-ante and ex-post measures and efficiency.

First, because the Colombian government only can use diversion as an active ex-post instrument this measure is critical for its loss financing. The investment in XL-insurance has opportunity costs, e.g. less investment in new projects. While to a certain extent the investment in the XL-insurance gives higher protection, it also reduces the returns for the government which in turn reduces the capacity of the government to diversify money. *Second*, because the attachment point was set for small events (attachment point is the 20 year event) the XL-insurance is, compared to the other measures less efficient here, because these events also can be financed by other ex-ante or ex-post measures. With ex-post measures the critical return period is 114 years. This number changes in the 10 years for each scenario according to the financial resilience of the government. For example, if two 114 year events happen in two subsequent years, the second event will be more devastating than the first one, because less money for the ex-post instruments is available. One can imagine a situation where an event which caused high losses can be compensated quite easily but a second smaller event afterwards has devastating effects. Therefore, if XL-insurance is used, smaller events should be financed through ex-post measures and larger events should be financed with XL-insurance arrangements. If a higher attachment point is used (e.g. 50 year event) the XL-insurance is superior to the other ex-ante instruments, but the observed effect still happens. Therefore, the relationships between ex-ante and ex-post measures have to be considered, because there is the possibility that at some point of ex-ante investments the efficiency and availability of ex-post investments can be influenced in such a negative way so that macroeconomic risks will increase again (see also figure 7.18).

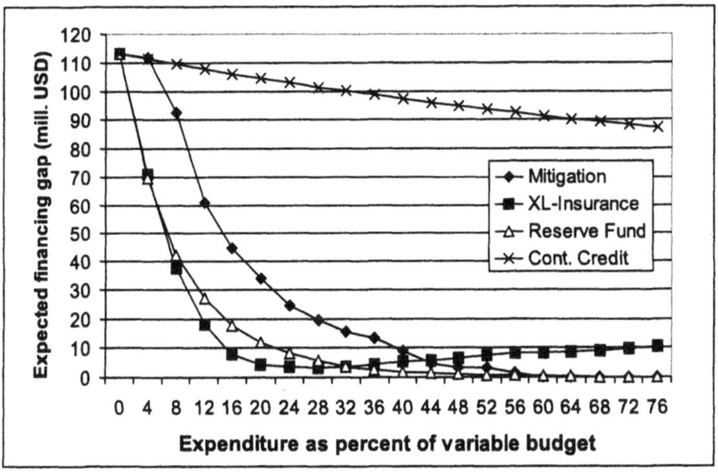

Figure 7.18: Expected financing gap and investments in ex-ante measures (Colombia).

Because of the investments in the ex-ante measures the expected return of capital investments is lower than in the no ex-ante instrument scenario. Because the figure looks similar to the ones for Honduras and El Salvador it is omitted here.

7.3.3 Summary

Figure 7.19 is showing the trade-off between stability and growth. The reserve fund seems to be superior to the XL-insurance, however, this pictures flips if higher attachment points are chosen but also in that case the reserve fund seems quite effective.

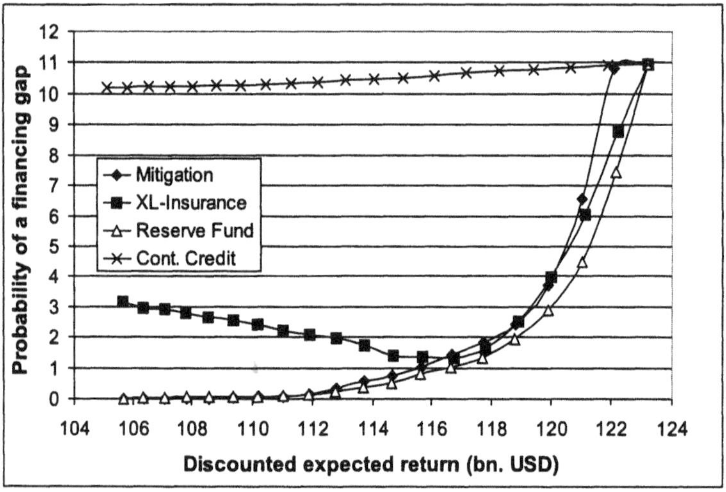

Figure 7.19: Trade-off between stability and growth (Colombia).

Most interesting, a XL-insurance arrangement can worsen the financing gap probability in this case study if the investment level is above some critical line (here, expenditures above 24 percent of the variable budget). This can be explained through the interaction of the ex-ante instruments with the ex-post measures. After the critical expenditure level is reached, further investments in the ex-ante measure decrease the financial resilience of the government. Due to less efficient ex-post performances, e.g. the marginal benefit from investments in XL-insurance is outweighed by the marginal reduction of ex-post loss financing resources due to the ex-ante investment. As a consequence the financial resilience decreases. As already mentioned, XL-insurance arrangements are more effective for higher layers than for lower layers because the lower layers can be handled through ex-post instruments. In practice usually the middle layers, from the 50 year event up to the 200 year event, are looked at. However, negative relationships between proactive investment against natural disaster risk and ex-post resources should be assessed where possible, to avoid unwanted effects.

Chapter 8

Conclusion and future work

As stated in the introduction this thesis focuses on the consequences of sudden-onset natural disasters on the macroeconomic level, especially for the public sector in developing countries. To lessen the impacts of natural disasters proactive risk management strategies were considered and incorporated into an integrated risk management approach to study and assess the costs and benefits of such strategies. The approach was operationalized and built into a catastrophe simulation model called CatSim, which is based on previous work done by G. Pflug and R. Mechler (Freeman et al. 2002a,b). In addition, graphical user interfaces were created to bridge the gap between scientific analysis and policy and implementation issues in the real world. In the following, a summary of the main findings in each chapter including a proposal for future work is presented.

Chapter two introduced the notion of risk as an abstract idea or a cognitive construction of the world which is interrelated with two other concepts, probability and chance. While the perception of risk differs for different people due to psychological, sociological and economic reasons, risk in a mathematical context relates outcomes and their probability of their occurrence in a systematic manner. Furthermore, the perception of risk can be handled there with utility functions. Risk in the context of natural disaster was defined as outcome risk, e.g the risk of a particular outcome is measured through the probability that this outcome occurs. Hence, a probability based approach was needed. At the end of chapter two an integrated risk management approach was presented:

Direct risk is defined as a function of the natural hazard, the exposed elements and the physical vulnerability. The direct risk and the financial resilience are determining the financial vulnerability (stock effects) which in turn influences the long-term macroeconomic risks the country is exposed to (flow effects). Risk management instruments which increase the financial resilience can be used to decrease the financial vulnerability and therefore the macroeconomic risk.

While reserve funds, excess of loss insurance, catastrophe bonds and contingent credit arrangements can be seen as financial risk management instruments, mitigation is viewed here as a structural prevention measure. Mitigation decreases the direct risk by increasing the physical susceptibility of the exposed elements. As a consequence mitigation can also decrease the premiums for insurance. Most important, mitigation can save lives.

Chapter three investigated the economic impacts of natural disasters on the macroeconomic level in more detail. Furthermore, loss statistics were presented. A discrepancy in the insurance density and losses between countries of different income groups was found. Reasons for the increase of natural disaster losses and a literature review about empirical studies of macroeconomic losses were presented. In addition an empirical investigation of a sample of natural disaster events between 1960 and 2000 was created to study the average macroeconomic effects in the long run due to natural disasters. The sample was created under specific controlled conditions to increase the validity of the results. Only those disaster events which had a relatively stable period 4 years before and 4 year after the disaster, e.g. no other disaster events, no economic crises due to other reasons and son on, were used for the study. The sample consisted of 85 disaster events in 45 countries:

One of the main findings of the empirical analysis is the observation of negative short and long term economic development measured by the GDP level and the occurrence of a natural disaster. Especially countries with land area smaller than 100.000 sq km and a loss per GDP ratio higher than 3 percent showed negative long term effects. Two different impacts of natural disasters on the economic development measured by the GDP level for countries with land area smaller than 100.000 sq km in the sample are found: while a disaster event appears to also have some positive impact if it causes direct losses below 3 percent (as a share of GDP), it has increasing negative impacts for long term economic development if losses are higher than 3 and 4 percent. Similar results are obtained also for bigger countries, however, it seems that in this cases other variables becoming increasingly important for the overall economic performance during the post-disaster years. Especially, indirect effects play a vital role, when long term economic developments are explored further.

Two questions emerged: first, why do some countries economies do better after a disaster event than others/? As it was shown, the direct losses (compared to GDP) and the land area have some explanatory power to answer the question, however they did not reflect the complex relationships which constitute the economic vulnerability of a country due to a natural disaster. Furthermore, the results should not be misunderstood by assuming that natural disasters can also be seen as 'good' events, as they can lead to an increase in economic development. It should be stressed that natural disasters per to be seen as 'bad' events. They destroy stocks which must be rebuilt and even if the stock is replaced with better equipment, it is not rational to rely on a natural disaster to get rid of them or to rely on believes of positive effects because of luck. In a macroeconomic context pre-conditions of the country, the impact of the disaster, indirect effects and the financial vulnerability are the overall parameters which influence the economic development in the long run. Therefore, to address this topic a modeling approach was needed. The second question is: why were no negative effects for smaller events found/? This can be due to the fact that only one event in the given length of time was analyzed. For example, small events can seriously hamper the economy if they occur more frequently. Hence, such situations also have to be considered in the modeling. The empirical investigation of the sample also relativize the results of Albala-Bertrand (1993a,b), e.g. here overall negative effects on macroeconomic variables due to natural disasters were found.

Chapter four introduced the three risk bearers on the country level, in the case of a natural disaster event: the government, the domestic private sector and international entities. While in the first section general risk financing instruments were presented, specific risk instruments for the private sector, mainly insurance, were investigated. Afterwards, the government's responsibilities in the case of a disaster event were defined. Repairing damaged infrastructure and providing financial assistance to the business sector and households can be seen as the major (financial) issues the government is responsible for after a disaster. Qualitative conditions when a government should behave risk averse were given, furthermore already introduced governmental programmes in some countries were investigated and overall risk management strategies the government may use presented.

While chapter four was an overall investigation, **chapter five** was examining thoroughly the possible ex-post and ex-ante loss financing instruments the government may use: in principle the government has two options for loss financing. It can rely on *ex-post* financing sources or it can arrange *ex-ante* risk financing strategies before the event occurs. Ex-post measures include diversion from budget, taxation, outside assistance, domestic bonds and credits, as well as multilateral and international borrowing. Ex-ante measures include mitigation, (re)insurance, reserve fund, contingent credit and catastrophe bonds. The pros and cons of these measures were discussed and summarized.

Chapter six introduced the approach now used in catastrophe modeling. In the first section, the state-of-the-art approach for the calculation of the direct risk was presented. Different representations of the direct loss in the literature, e.g. loss distributions, exceedance probability curves, and loss return period curves, were connected together to show that they are essentially the same, e.g. incorporate the same information. Afterwards, the own catastrophe modeling approach is presented. CatSim is probability based and uses important sampling algorithms and stratified scenarios for the simulation of catastrophe events catalogs. The model has a module structure so that it can be easily changed according to specific needs. Furthermore, a method to calculate the price of excess of loss insurance was implemented.

A methodology to measure the financial vulnerability with the financing gap concept through loss distribution functions was presented. As a result critical return periods, e.g. the year event when the financing gap first starts, as well as financing schemes can be calculated. Also a user interface for applied analysis and workshops was created and incorporated into a software program based on the Matlab environment which can be used also as a stand-alone application.

Chapter seven looked at three case studies Honduras, El Salvador and Colombia and demonstrated the flexible and coherent approach presented in this thesis. Some interesting results were found.

For **Honduras**, the XL-insurance is superior over mitigation, reserve fund and contingent credit. Mitigation and reserve fund are in this case the second-best options. While mitigation is less effective than a reserve fund it has additional advantages, e.g. physical protection. It is also interesting that mitigation investments have to be above a certain investment level, so that the capital stock is effectively protected. Furthermore, mitigation reduces the credit buffer drop more effectively than a reserve fund for higher investments which can be explained by the modeling approach of mitigation as a step function: no losses occur for smaller events and no mitigation efforts are then lost. However, the discounted expected financing gap is always higher for mitigation than for the reserve fund. This can be explained by the fact that events with high impacts are destroying mitigation efforts in two ways, the money used for mitigation is lost and no protection was achieved.

For **El Salvador** a contingent credit is least efficient and mitigation is also not effective, while XL-insurance and reserve fund behave quite good. Especially for higher investments in ex-ante measures a reserve fund is superior to all the other instruments. This can be explained by the already efficient ex-post instruments available there. Therefore, a proactive approach with a reserve fund with sufficient annual payments would be a better option. In this case the money is not lost as in the case with insurance and the reserve fund is as efficient in risk reduction as insurance, while keeping the credit buffer drop very low.

In the case of **Colombia** a very interesting effect was observed. A XL-insurance arrangement can worsen the financing gap probability if the investment level is above a critical line (here, expenditures above 24 percent of the variable budget). This can be explained through the interaction of the ex-ante instruments with the ex-post measures. After the critical expenditure level is reached, further investments in the ex-ante measure decrease the financial resilience of the government due to less efficient ex-post loss financing performances. Furthermore, XL-insurance arrangements are more effective for higher layers than for lower layers because for the lower layers the ex-post instruments can efficiently deal with it.

Several areas for future work can be outlined

- Spatial loss distributions would enable the modeling of the economic effects in more detail. While the model already is capable to use such information, the estimation of spatial loss distributions is very difficult; however, it would be very valuable.

According to 6.2 the spatial distribution of the exposed elements and the hazard is needed. Especially for applications in large-scale risk assessment studies, dasymetric mapping approaches are now used to provide realistic estimates of the number of exposed assets, e.g. spatial distribution of residential buildings over the country (Thieken et al. 2006). This maps can then be overlaid with hazard risk maps. Combining this information with vulnerability curves spatial loss distributions could be estimated. There is also the possibility to disaggregate the loss estimates for various sectors, allowing an even more detailed analysis of the possible effects on the countries economy.

- One of the advantages of the simple economic growth framework used for the case studies was the easy interpretation of the consequences of government's financial vulnerability and its macroeconomic risk due to natural disasters. While the main focus here was on the public sector, the private sector modeling was rather rudimentary and has to be improved, especially for developed countries, if macroeconomic variables such as GDP also wanted to be studied. For example, the RMSM-X World Bank model could be used as a possible starting point (see Mechler 2004a).

- The model in its current state assumes that the frequency and severity of hazard events do not increase over time. Looking into the future, e.g. 2050 or 2100, this may not be the case also due to climate change. One way to incorporate such situations into the model is to change the parameters of the loss distribution over time.

The model presented in this thesis is the starting point for various other research of natural disasters and their macroeconomic long run effects, including (i) the combination of the model with bottom up approaches, (ii) the creation of a world map where the financial vulnerability and macroeconomic risk for different countries can be compared, (iii) incorporating other important dimensions in the model, e.g. loss of life, and (iv) workshops for key policy makers to help them building the capacity to evaluate ex-ante financial instruments and compare their benefits with investments in loss reduction.

Literature

Adams, J. (1995). Risk. London, UCL Press.

Adger, W. N. (1999). "Social Vulnerability to Climate Change and Extremes in Coastal Vietnam." World Development 27(2): 249-269.

Albala-Bertrand, J. M. (1993a). The Political Economy of Large Natural Disasters. Oxford, Clarendon Press.

Albala-Bertrand, J. M. (1993b). "Natural Disasters Situations and Growth: A Macroeconomic Model for Sudden Disasters Impacts." World Development 21(9): 1417-1434.

Alexander, D. (1993). Natural Disasters. London, UCL Press.

Alexander, D. (1997). "The Study of Natural Disasters, 1977-1997: Some Reflections on a Changing Field of Knowledge." Disasters 21(4): 284-304.

Alexander, D. (2000). Confronting Catastrophe. Oxford, Oxford University Press.

Altay, G., G. Deodatis, G. Franco, P. Gülkan, H. Kunreuther, H. Lus, E. Mete, N. Seeber, A. W. Smyth and Ö. Yüzügüllü (2002). Benefit-Cost Analysis for Earthquake Mitigation: Evaluating Measures for Apartment Houses in Turkey. Presentation at the second annual IIASA-DPRI meeting. Integrated Disaster Risk Management: Megacity Vulnerability and Resilience. 29-31 July, Laxenburg, Austria.

Andersen, T. J. (2001). Managing Economic Exposures of Natural Disasters: Exploring Alternative Financial Risk Opportunities and Instruments. Washington DC, IDB.

Anderson, M. (1995). Vulnerability to Disaster and Sustainable Development: A General Framework for Assessing Vulnerability. In M. Munasinghe and C. Clarke (eds.). Disaster Prevention for Sustainable Development: Economic and Policy Issues. Washington DC, World Bank: 41-59.

Armendáriz de Aghion, B. and J. Murdoch (2005). The Economics of Microfinance. London, MIT Press.

Arrow, K. J. and R. C. Lind (1970). "Uncertainty and the Evaluation of Public Investment Decisions." The American Economic Review 60(2): 364-378.

Assailly, J.-P. (1994). The Psychogenetic Approach to Risk. In B. Munier and M. J. Machina (eds.). Models and Experiments in Risk and Rationality. Dordrecht, Kluwer Academic Publishers: 3-16.

Auffret, P. (2003). High Consumption Volatility: The Impact of Natural Disasters? Research Working Paper 2962, The World Bank.

Aven, T., E. F. Nilsen and T. Nilsen (2004). "Expressing Economic Risk - A Review and Presentation of a Unifying Approach." Risk Analysis 24(4): 989-1005.

Baird, A., P. O'Keefe, K. Westgate and B. Wisner (1975). Towards an Explanation and Reduction of Disaster Proneness. Disaster Research Unit Occasional Paper 1. London, Bradford University.

Banks, E. (2005). Catastrophic Risk. Analysis and Management. Chichester, Wiley Finance.

Baranov, S., B. Digas, T. Ermolieva, and V. Rozenberg (2002). Earthquake Risk Management: Scenario Generator. IIASA Interim Report 02-025. Laxenburg, Austria, IIASA.

Barone, E. (1908). The Ministry of Production in the Collectivist State. In F. A. von Hayek (eds.). Collectivist Economic Planning. London, George Routledge and Sons.

Beck, U. (1992). Risk Society: Towards a New Modernity. London, Sage Publications.

Belli, P. (1997). The Comparative Advantage of Government. A Review. Research Working Paper 1834. Washington DC, World Bank.

Bendimerad, F. (2001). "Loss Estimation: A Powerful Tool for Risk Assessment and Mitigation." Soil Dynamics and Earthquake Engineering 21(5): 467-472.

Benson, C. (1997a). The Economic Impacts of Natural Disasters in Fiji. ODI Working Paper. London, Overseas Development Institute.

Benson, C. (1997b). The Economic Impacts of Natural Disasters in the Phillipines. ODI Working Paper. London, Overseas Development Insitute.

Benson, C. (1997c). The Economic Impacts of Natural Disasters in Vietnam. ODI Working Paper. London, Overseas Development Institute.

Benson, C. (1998). Drought and the Zimbabwe Economy, 1980-93. In H. ONeill and J. Toye (eds.). A World Without Famine. London, MacMillan.

Benson, C. and E. J. Clay (1998). The Impact of Drought on Sub-Saharan African Economies. Washington DC, World Bank.

Benson, C. and E. J. Clay (2000). Developing Countries and the Economic and Financial Impacts of Natural Disasters. In A. Kreimer and M. Arnold (eds.). Managing Disaster Risk in Emerging Economies. Washington DC, World Bank.

Benson, C. and E. J. Clay (2004). Understanding the Economic and Financial Impacts of Natural Disasters. Disaster Risk Management Series 4. Washington DC, World Bank.

Benson, C. and J. Twigg (2004). Measuring Mitigation: Methodologies for Assessing Natural Hazard Risks and the Net Benefits of Mitigation. A Scoping Study. Geneva, ProVention Consortium.

Berliner, B. (1982). Limits of Insurability of Risks. Englewood Cliffs, Prentice Hall.

Bernstein, L. P. (1996). Against the Gods. New York, John Wiley and Sons.

Blomquist, J., J. P. Cordoba, M. Verhoeven, P. Moser and C. Bouillon (2002). Social Safety Nets in Response to Crises: Lessons and Guidelines from Asia and Latin

America. In OECD (eds.). Towards Asia's Sustainable Development: The Role of Social Protection. Paris: 297-332.

Brent, R. J. (1998). Cost-Benefit Analysis for Developing Countries. Cheltenham, Edward Elgar Publishing.

Briceño-Garmendia, C., A. Estache and N. Shafik (2004). Infrastructure Services in Developing Countries: Access, Quality, Costs and Policy Reform. Research Working Paper 3468. Washington DC, World Bank.

Britton, N. R. and J. Oliver (1997). Financial Risk, Management for Natural Catastrophes. Brisbane, AON Group Australia Limited.

Brooks, N. (2003). Vulnerability, Risk and Adaptation: A Conceptual Framework. Tyndall Centre Working Paper 38. University of East Anglia, Norwich, UK.

Burby, J. R. (1991). Sharing Environmental Risks: How to Control Governments losses in Natural Disasters. Bolder, Westview Press.

Burby, J. R. (2006). Hurricane Katrina and the Paradoxes of Government Disaster Policy: Bringing About Wise Governmental Decisions for Hazardous Areas. ANNALs, AAPSS 604: 171-191.

Calderón, C. and L. Servén (2004a). Trends in Infrastructure in Latin America, 1980-2001. Research Working Paper 3401. Washington DC, World Bank.

Calderón, C. and L. Servén (2004b). The Effects of Infrastructure Development on Growth and Income Distribution. Research Working Paper 3401. Washington DC, World Bank.

Caplan, P. (2000). Risk Revisited. London, Pluto Press.

Cardenas, V., S. Hochrainer, R. Mechler and G. Pflug (2005). Assessing the Financial Management of Public Sector Disaster Risk: The Mexican Case. Fifth annual IIASA-DPRI meeting. "Integrated Disaster Risk Management (IDRiM): Innovations in Science and Policy", 14-18 September 2005, China, Beijing, Beijing Normal University.

Cardona, O. D. (2004). The Need for Rethinking the Concepts of Vulnerability and Risk from a Holistic Perspective: A Necessary Review and Criticism for Effective Risk Management. In G. Bankoff, G. Frerks and D. Hilhorst (eds.). Mapping Vulnerability: Disasters, Developemt and People. London, Earthscan Publishers.

Carr, L. J. (1932). "Disaster and the Sequence-Pattern Concept of Social Change." American Journal of Sociology 38(2): 207-218.

Chapman, D. (1994). Natural Hazards. Melbourne, Oxford University Press.

Charvériat, C. (2000). Natural Disasters in Latin America and the Caribbean: An Overview of Risk. Working Paper 434. Washington DC, IDB.

Chen, K., J. McAneny, R. Blong, R. Leigh, L. Hunter, and C. Magill (2004). Defining area at risk and its effect in catastrophe loss estimation: a dasymetric mapping approach. Applied Geography 24(2):97-117.

Clay, E. J. et al. (1995). Evaluation of ODA's Response to the 1991-92 Southern African Drought. Evaluation Report EV568. London. London, Overseas Development Administration.

Clay, E. J., C. Barrow, C. Benson, J. Dempster, P. Kokelaar, E. Philai and J. Seamans (1999). An Evaluation of HMG's Response to the Montserrat Volcanic Emergency. Evaluation Report EV635. London, Department of International Development.

Coates, D. R. (1981). Environmental Geology. New York, Wiley and Sons.

Courbage, C. and P. M. Liedtke (2003). "On insurability, its limits and extensions." Insurance research & practice 18(2): 44-49.

Crowards, T. (1999). Comparative Susceptibility to Natural Disasters in the Caribbean. Central Bank of Barbados Annual Review Seminar, St. Michael, Caribbean Development Bank.

Cuny, D. F. (1983). Disasters and Prevention. New York, Oxford University Press.

Cullen, A.C. and M.J. Small (2004). Uncertain Risk. The Role and Limits of Quantitative Assessment. In T. McDaniels and M.J. Small (eds.). Risk Analysis and Society. New York, Cambridge University Press.

Dacy, D. C. and H. Kunreuther (1969). The Economics of Natural Disasters: Implications for Federal Policy. New York, The Free Press.

Dilley, M., R. Chen, U. Deichmann, A. Lerner-Lam, and M. Arnold, with J. Agwe, P. Buys, O. Kjekstad, B. Lyon and G. Yetman (2005). Disaster Risk Management Series No. 5: Natural Disaster Hotspots, A Global Risk Analysis. Washington DC, World Bank.

Dischel, R. S. and P. Barrieu (2002). Financial Weather Contracts and their Application in Risk Management. In R. S. Dischel (eds.) Climate Risk and the Weather Market. London, Risk Books.

Doherty, N. A. (2000). Integrated Risk Management: Techniques and Strategies for Reducing Risk. New York, McGraw-Hill.

Dong, W. and P. Grossi (2005). Insurance Portfolio Management. In P. Grossi and H. Kunreuther (eds.). Catastrophe Modeling: A New Approach to Managing Risk. New York, Springer.

Douglas, M. and A. Wildavsky (1982). Risk and Culture. An Essay on the Selection of Technological and Environmental Dangers. Berkeley, University of California Press.

Downing, T. E., R. Butterfield, S. Cohen, S. Huq, R. Moss, A. Rahman, Y. Sokona and L. Stephen (2001). Vulnerability Indices: Climate Change Impacts and Adaptation. Policy Series 3. Nairobi, United Nations Environment Programme.

ECLAC (2003). Handbook for Estimating the Socio-Economic Effects of Natural Disasters. Mexico City, United Nations Economic Commission for Latin America and the Caribbean.

El-Masri, S. and A.G. Tipple (2002). Natural disaster, mitigation and sustainability: a review in developing countries. International Planning Studies 7(2): 157-175.

Embrechts, P., C. Klüppelberg and T. Mikosch (1997). Modelling Extremal Events. Berlin, Springer.

EM-DAT (2006). International Disaster Database. Brussels, Belgium, Centre for Research on the Epidemiology of Disasters, Université Catholique de Louvain.

Erdik, M. and N. Aydinoglu (2003). Earthquake Vulnerability of Buildings in Turkey. Third annual DPRI-IIASA Meeting. "Integrated Disaster Risk Management: Coping with Regional Vulnerability", 3-5 July, Japan, Kyoto.

Ermoliev, Y., T. Ermolieva, GJ. MacDonald, V. Norkin,V. and A. Amendola (2000). A system approach to management of catastrophic risks. European Journal of Operational Research 122(2): 452-460.

Etkin, D. (1999). "Risk Transference and Related Trends: Driving Forces Towards More Mega-Disasters." Environmental Hazards 1(2): 69-75.

European Commision (2005). Bericht der Kommision. Solidaritaetsfonds der Europeaeischen Union. Jahresbericht 2004. KOM(2005)709.

Fairbairn, T.I.J. (1998). "Economic consequences of natural disasters among Pacific island Countries." Pacific Economic Bulletin 13(2): 54-63.

Fay, M. and M. Morrison (2005). Infrastructure in Latin America & the Caribbean. Recent Developments and Key Challenges. Washington DC, World Bank.

Fernández, G., G. Verdejo and L.J. Pérez (2001). "Earthquakes in El Salvador." Epidemiological Bulletion/PAHO 22(1): 1-2.

Ferranti, D., G. E. Perry, I. S. Gill and L. Servén, with F. H. G. Ferreira, N. Ilahi, W. F. Maloney and M. Rama (2000). Securing our Future in a Global Economy. Washington DC, The World Bank.

Fischer, S. and W. Easterly (1990). "The Economics of the Government Budget Constraint." The World Bank Research Observer 5(2): 127-142.

Fournier d'Albe, E. M. (1979). "Objectives of Volcanic Monitoring and Prediction." Journal of the Geological Society 136(3): 321-326.

Freeman, P. K. (2000). Catastrophe Risk: A Model to Evaluate the Decision Process for Developing Countries. PhD Thesis. Vienna, University of Vienna.

Freeman, P. K. (2003). Natural Hazard Risk and Privatization. In A. Kramer, M. Arnold and A. Carlin (eds.). Building Safer Cities. The Future of Disaster Risk. Washington DC, World Bank.

Freeman, P. K., L. Martin, R. Mechler, K. Warner and P. Hausmann (2002a). Catastrophes and Development. Integrating Natural Catastrophes into Development Planning. Working Paper 26279. Washington DC, The World Bank.

Freeman, P. K., A. M. Leslie, J. Linnerooth-Bayer, R. Mechler, S. Saldana, G. Pflug and K. Warner (2002b). National Systems for the Comprehensive Management: Financing Reconstruction. Phase II Background Study for the IDB. Washington DC, IDB.

Freeman, P.K and G. Pflug (2003). Infrastructure in Developing and Transition Countries: Risk and Protection. Risk Analysis 23(3): 601-609.

Freeman, P. K., L. Martin, J. Linnerooth-Bayer, R. Mechler, G. Pflug and K. Warner (2003). Disaster Risk Management: National Systems for the Comprehensive Management of Disaster Risk and Financial Strategies for Natural disaster Reconstruction. Washington DC, IDB.

Freeman, P. K., L. Martin, R. Mechler and K. Warner (2004). "A Methodology for Incorporating Natural Catastrophes into Macroeconomic Projections." Disaster Prevention and Management 13(4): 337-342.

Frischknecht, C., R. Romerio, J. Rossiaud, J. Wagner, S. Bertrand, J. Laporte and T. Harding (2003). Integrated "Natural" Risk Management: The Basic Assessment; an essay. Third annual DPRI-IIASA Meeting."Integrated Disaster Risk Management: Coping with Regional Vulnerability", 3-5 July, Japan, Kyoto.

Fritz, C. E. (1961). Disaster. In R. K. Merton and R. A. Nisbet (eds.). Contemporary Social Problems. New York, Brace and World Inc.

Froot, K. A. (1998). The evolving market for catastrophic event risk. Cambridge, Harvard Business School and Marsh and McLennan Securities.

Froot, K. A. (1999). The Financing Of Catastrophe Risk. Chicago, University of Chicago Press.

Funaro-Curtis, R. (1982). Natural Disasters and the Development Process: A Discussion of Issues. Washington DC, Office of Foreign Disaster Assistance, U.S. Agency for International Development.

Gibbs, T. (1997). Effects of Hurricane Luis on Structures in Antigua. In R. Ahmad (eds.). Natural Hazards and Hazards Management in the Greater Caribbean and Latin America. Jamaica, University of West Indies.: 165-176.

Giddens, A. (1991). Modernity and Self-Identity: Self and Society in the Late Modern Age. Cambridge, Polity Press.

Gilli, M. and E. Këllezi (2005). An Application of Extreme Value Theory of Measuring Financial Risk. Preprint submitted to Elsevier Science, 2 May 2005. 'www.unige.ch/ses/metri/gilli/evtrm/GilliKelleziEVT.pdf'

Goes, A. and R. J. Skees (2003). Financing Natural Disaster Risk Using Charity Contributions and Ex-Ante Index Insurance. American Agricultural Economics Association Annual Meeting, Canada, Montreal.

Gopalakrishnan, C. and N. Okada (2003). Designing New Institutions for Implementing Integrated Disaster Risk Management (IDRM): Key Elements and Future Directions. Third annual DPRI-IIASA Meeting. "Integrated Disaster Risk Management: Coping with Regional Vulnerability", 3-5 July, Japan, Kyoto.

Grace, M. F., R. W. Klein, P. R. Kleindorfer and M. R. Murray (2003). Catastrophe Insurance. Consumer Demand, Markets and Regulation. Boston, Kluwer Academic Publishers.

Gramlich, E. M. (1981). Benefit-Cost Analysis of Government Programs. London, Prentice-Hall.

Grossi, P. and H. Kunreuther (2005). Introduction: Needs, Stakeholders, and Government Initiatives. In P. Grossi and H. Kunreuther (eds.). Catastrophe Modeling: A New Approach to Managing Risk. New York, Springer.

Grossi, P., H. Kunreuther, and D. Windeler (2005). An Introduction to Catastrophe Models and Insurance. In P. Grossi and H. Kunreuther (eds.). Catastrophe Modeling: A New Approach to Managing Risk. New York, Springer.

Grünthal, G., A.H. Thieken, J. Schwarz, K.S. Radtke, A. Smolka and B. Merz (2006). "Comparative risk assessment for the city of Cologne, Germany - storms, floods, earthquakes." Natural Hazards 38(1-2): 21-44.

Gurenko, E. (2004). Catastrophe Risk and Reinsurance: A Country Risk Management Perspective. London, Risk Books.

Gurenko, E. and R. Lester (2005). Rapid Onset Natural Disasters: The Role of Risk Financing in Effective Catastrophe Risk Management. In OECD (eds.). Catastrophe Risks and Insurance. OECD Publishing.

Guy Carpenter (2003). The World Catastrophe Reinsurance Market 2003. New York, Guy Carpenter.

Guy Carpenter (2004). The World Catastrophe Reinsurance Market 2004. New York, Guy Carpenter.

Guy Carpenter (2005). The Growing Appetite for Catastrophe Risk. The Catastrophe Bond Market at Year-End 2004. New York, Guy Carpenter.

Hanley, N. and C. L. Spash (1993). Cost-Benefit Analysis and the Environment. Brookfield, Edward Elgar Publishing.

Hanks, T.C. and C. A. Cornell (1994). Probabilistic Seismic Hazard Analysis: A Beginner's Guide. Proceedings of the Fifth Symposium on Current Issues Related to Nuclear Power Plant Structures, Equipment and Piping, North Carolina State University, Raleigh, N.C.

Harrington, S. E. and G. Niehaus (2001). "Government Insurance, Tax Policy, and the Affordability and Availability of Catastrophe Insurance." Journal of Insurance Regulation 19(4): 591-612.

HIPC (2002). About the HIPC Initiative. Washington DC.

Hiroki, K. (2003). Comprehensive Approach to Management of Flood Risk and Vulnerability - A case stury in the Abukuma River Basin. Third annual DPRI-IIASA Meeting. "Integrated Disaster Risk Management: Coping with Regional Vulnerability", 3-5 July, Japan, Kyoto.

Hochrainer, S. (2005). "Naturkatastrophen: Risikowahrnehmung und Vorsorgestrategien. Eine Empirische Untersuchung zum Hochwasser 2002 in Schwertberg." Sozialwissenschaftliche Rundschau SWSR 45(1): 63-85.

Hogg, V. R. and S. A. Klugman (1984). Loss Distributions. New York, Wiley and Sons.

Hoogeveen, J. G. M. (2000). Risk and Insurance by the Poor in Developing Nations. In A. Kreimer and M. Arnold (eds.). Managing Disaster Risk in Emerging Countries. Washington DC, World Bank: 103-128.

Hornig, S. (1993). "Reading Risk: Public Response to Print Media Accounts of Technological Risk." Public Understanding of Science 2(2): 95-109.

Hotelling, H. (1938). "The General Welfare in Relation to Problems of Taxation and of Railway and Utility Rates." Econometrica 6(3): 242-269.

IDB (2000). Facing the Challenge of Natural Disasters in Latin America and the Caribbean. An IDB Action Plan. Washington DC, Inter-American Development Bank.

IDNDR (1992). Internationally Agreed Glossary of Basic Terms related to Disaster Management. United Nations Department of Humanitarian Affairs, DNA/93/36, Geneva.

IFRC (2004). World Disasters Report. Focus on Community Resilience. International Federation of Red Cross and Red Crescent Societies.

IMF and WB (2001). El Salvador. IMF and World Bank Staff Assessment of the Macroeconomic Effects of the Earthquakes. Washington DC, World Bank.

Ingleton, J. (1999). Natural Disaster Risk Management: A Presentation to Commemorate the International Decade for Natural Disaster Reduction (IDNDR) 1990-2000. Leicester, Tudor Rose.

International Labour Organization (2005). Inventory of Micro-Insurance Schemes in the Philippines. Strategies and Against Social Exclusion and Poverty (STEP) Programme. Switzerland.

Kahn, M. E. (2005). "The Death Toll from Natural Disasters: The Role of Income, Geography, and Institutions." The Review of Economics and Statistics 87(2): 271-284.

Keipi, K. and J. Tyson (2002). Planning and Financial Protection to Survive Disasters. Sustainable Development Department Technical Studies Series. Washington DC, IDB.

Kent, R. (1999). Essential Conceptual Shifts and Policy Perspectives. In J. Ingleton (eds.). Natural Disaster Management: A Presentation to Commemorate the International Decade for Natural Disaster Reduction (IDNDR) 1990-2000. Leicester, Tudor Rose.

Kimaro, T. A., Y. Tachikawa and K. Takara (2003). Assessing the Impact of Land Use Changes on Flood Risk. Third annual DPRI-IIASA Meeting."Integrated Disaster Risk Management: Coping with Regional Vulnerability", 3-5 July, Japan, Kyoto.

Klein, R. J. T., R. J. Nicholls and F. Thomalla (2003). "Resilience to Natural Hazards: How Useful is this Concept?" Environmental Hazards 5(12): 35-45.

Kleist, L., A.H. Thieken, P. Köhler, M. Müller, I. Seifert, D. Borst and U. Werner (2006). "Estimation of the regional stock of residential buildings as a basis for a comparative risk assessment in Germany." Natural Hazards and Earth System Sciences 6(4): 541-552.

Kozlowski, R. T. and S. B. Mathewson (1997). "A Primer on Catastrophe Modeling." Journal of Insurance Regulation 15(3): 322-341.

Kramer, R. A. (1995). Advantages and Limitations of Benefit-Cost Analysis for Evaluating Investments in Natural Disaster Mitigation. In M. Munasinghe and C. Clarke (eds.). Disaster Prevention for Sustainable Development: Economic Policy Issues. Washington DC, World Bank: 61-76.

Kreimer, A. and M. Arnold (2000). "World Bank's role in reducing impacts of disasters." Natural Hazards Review 1(1): 37-42.

Kreimer, A. and M. Arnold, (eds.) (2000). Managing Disaster Risk in Emerging Economies. Disaster Risk Management Series. Washington DC, World Bank.

Kreimer, A., M. Arnold and A. Carlin (2003). Building Safer Cities: The Future of Disaster Risk. Washington DC, World Bank.

Kunreuther, H. (1996). "Mitigating Disaster Losses through Insurance." Journal of Risk and Uncertainty 12(2): 171-187.

Kunreuther, H. (1997). Managing Catastrophe Risks Through Insurance and Mitigation. Fifth Alexander Howden Conference on Financial Risk Management for Natural Catastrophes, August, Australia, Gold Coast.

Kunreuther, H. (1998). Insurability Conditions and the Supply of Coverage. In H. Kunreuther and R. J. Roth (eds.). Paying the Price: The Status and Role of Insurance Against Natural Disasters in the United States. Washington DC, Joseph Henry Press: 17-50.

Kunreuther, H. (1999). "Insurance as an Integrating Policy Tool for Disaster Management: The Role of Public-Private Partnerships." Earthquake Spectra 15(4): 725-745.

Kunreuther, J. (2002). "Risk Analysis and Risk Management in an Uncertain World." Risk Analysis 22(4): 655-664.

Kunreuther, H., R. Hogarth and J. Meszaros (1993). "Insurer Ambiguity and Market Failure." Journal of Risk and Uncertainty 7(1): 71-87.

Kunreuther, H. and J. Linnerooth-Bayer (2003). "The Financial Management of Catastrophic Flood Risks in Emerging Economy Countries." Risk Analysis 23(3): 627-639.

Lane, M. N. (2004). The Viability and Likely Pricing of "CAT-Bonds" for Developing Countries. Lane Financial 2004.

Lane, M. N. and R. G. Beckwith (2001). Current Trends in Risk-Linked Securitizations. Lane Financial 2001.

Lange, O. (1942). "The Foundations of Welfare Economics." Econometrica 10(3): 215-228.

Law, A. M. and W. D. Kelton (1991). Simulation Modeling and Analysis. New York, McGraw-Hill.

Lerner, P. A. (1934). "The Concept of Monopoly and the Measurement of Monopoly Power." Review of Economic Studies 1(3): 157-175.

Lerner, P. A. (1944). The Economics of Control: Principles of Welfare Economics. New York, MacMillan.

Linnerooth-Bayer, J., S. Quijano, R. Loefstedt and S. Elahi (1999). The Uninsured Elements of Natural Catastrophic Losses: Seven Studies of Earthquake and Flood Disasters. Laxenburg, International Institute for Applied System Analysis (IIASA).

Linnerooth-Bayer, J. and H. Kunreuther (2003). "The Financial Management of Catastrophic Flood Risks in Emerging-Economy Countries." Risk Analysis 23(3): 627-639.

Linnerooth-Bayer, J., M. J. Mace and R. Verheyen (2003). Insurance-related Actions and Risk Assessment in the Context of the UNFCCCC. Background paper prepared for the UNFCCC Secretariat, Bonn.

Linnerooth-Bayer, J., R. Mechler and G. Pflug (2005). "Refocusing Disaster Aid." Science 309(5737): 1044-1046.

Little, I. M. D. and J. A. Mirrlees (1976). Project Appraisal and Planning for Developing Countries. London, Heinemann Eductional Books.

Loefstedt, R. and L. Frewer (1998). Risk & Modern Society. London, Earthscan Publications.

Lowrance, W. W. (1976). Of Acceptable Risk. Los Altos, William Kaufmann.

Lupton, D. (1999). Risk and Sociocultural Theory. New Directions and Perspectives. Cambridge, University Press.

Mahdyiar, M. and B. Porter (2005). The Risk Assessment Process: The Role of Catastrophe Modeling in Dealing with Natural. In P. Grossi and H. Kunreuther (eds.). Catastrophe Modeling: A New Approach to Managing Risk. New York, Springer.

Markowitz, H. (1959) Portfolio Selection: Efficient Diversification of Investments. Cowles Foundation Monograph 16. New York, Wiley.

Martelli, A., R. Antonucci, P. Clemente, M. Dolce, A. Dusi, M. Ferrini, M. Forni, M. Indirli and B. Spadoni (2004). Earthquake Protection of Schools in Italy: Present State and needs and Perspectives for Improvement. Fourth annual DPRI-IIASA Meeting. "Integrated Disaster Risk Management: Challenges of Implementation", 3-7 July, Italy, Ravello.

Maskrey, A. (1989). Disaster Mitigation: A Community Based Approach. Oxford, Oxfam.

McIsaac, D. and D. Babbel (1995). The World Bank Primer on Reinsurance. Policy Research Working Paper 1512. Washington DC, World Bank.

McNeil, A. J. and R. Frey (2000). "Estimation of Tail-related Risk Measures for Heteroscedastic Financial Time Series: An Extreme Value Approach." Journal of Empirical Finance 7(3-4): 271-300.

Mechler, R. and J. Weichselgartner (2002). Disaster Loss Financing in Germany - The Case of the Elbe River Floods 2002. Interim Report, IR-03-021. Laxenburg, IIASA.

Mechler, R. (2004a). Natural Disaster Risk Management and Financing Disaster Losses in Developing Countries. Karlsruhe, Verlag Versicherungswirtschaft GmbH.

Mechler, R. (2004b). Macroeconomic Impacts of Natural Disasters. In K. Demeter, N. E. Erkan and A. Guener (eds.). The Role of Local Governments in Reducing the Risk of Disasters. Washington DC, World Bank.

Mechler, R. (2005a). Financing Disaster Risk in Developing and Emerging Economy Countries. In OECD (eds.). Catastrophe Risks and Insurance, OECD.

Mechler, R. (2005b). Cost-Benefit Analysis of Natural Disaster Risk Management in Developing Countries". GTZ Working Paper. Sector Cooperation.

Mechler, R., S. Hochrainer, J. Linnerooth-Bayer and G. Pflug (2006). Public Sector Financial Vulnerability to Disasters. The IIASA-Catsim Model. In J. Birkmann (eds.). Measuring Vulnerability and Coping Capacity to Hazards of Natural Origin. Concepts and Methods. United Nations University Press.

Meier, G. G. and E. Rauch (2005). Leading Issues in Economic Development. Oxford, Oxford University Press.

Merz, B., J. Friedrich, M. Disse, J., Schwarz, J. Goldammer, and J.G. Wächter (2006). "Possibilities and Limitations of Interdisciplinary, User-oriented Research: Experiences from the German Research Network Natural Disasters." Natural Hazards 38(1-2): 3-20.

Meulbroek, L. (2002). "The Promise and Challenge of Integrated Risk Management." Risk Management and Insurance Review 5(1): 55-66.

Meyers Enzyklopädisches Lexikon (1971). Mannheim.

Mileti, D. S. (1999). Disasters by Design. Washington DC, Joseph Henry Press.

Miller, S. and K. Keipi (2005). Strategies and Financial Instruments for Disaster Risk Management in Latin America and the Caribbean. Sustainable development department technical paper series. Washington DC, IDB.

Moore, R. J. (1983). The Business of Risk. London, Cambridge University Press.

Moss, D. A. (2002).When all else fails. Government as the Ultimate Risk Manager. Cambridge, Harvard University Press.

Munich Re (2002). World of Natural Hazards (CD-Rom). Munich, Munich Reinsurance Company.

Munich Re (2004). Geographical Underwriting. TOPICS Geo: Jahresrückblick Naturkatastrophen 2003: 44-49.

Munich Re (2005a). Weather Catastrophes and Climate Change. Is there still Hope for Us. Knowledge Series. Munich, Munich Re Group.

Munich Re (2005b). Topics Geo. Annual Review: Natural Catastrophes 2005. Munich, Munich Reinsurance Company.

Munich Re NatCatSERVICE (2005). Natural Disasters According to Income Groups 1980-2004. Munich, Munich Reinsurance Company.

Munich Re (2006). Nathan: NATural Hazards Assessment Network. Munich, Munich Re Group. http://mrnathan.munichre.com

Murlidharan, T. L. and H. Shah (2003). Economic Consequences of Catastrophes Triggered by Natural Hazards. Stanford University: Department of Civil and Environmental Engineering, Report 143.

National Research Council (1997). Recommendations for Probabilistic Seismic Hazard Analysis: Guidance on Uncertainty and the Use of Experts. Washington DC, National Academy Press.

Nell, M. and A. Richter (2005). Catastrophic Events as Threats to Society: Private and Public Risk Management Strategies. In M. Frenkel, U. Hommel and M. Rodulf (eds.). Risk Management: Challenge and Opportunity. Berlin, Springer.

Newkirk, R.T. (2001). "The Increasing Cost of Disasters in Developed Countries: A Challenge to Local Planning and Government." Journal of Contingencies and Crisis Management 9(3): 159-170.

Oberkampf, W.L., J.C. Helton, C.A. Joslyn, S.F. Wojtkiewicz, and S. Ferson (2004). "Challenge problems: uncertainty in system response given uncertain parameters." Reliability Engineering and System Safety 85(1-3): 11-19.

Otero, R. C. and R. Z. Marti (1995). The Impacts of Natural Disasters on Developing Economies: Implications for the International Development and Disaster Community. In M. Munasinghe and C. Clarke (eds.). Disaster Prevention for Sustainable Development: Economic and Policy Issues. Washington DC, World Bank.

Oxford English Dictionary (1970). London, Oxford University Press.

PAHO/WHO (1994). A World Safe From Natural Disasters. The Journey from Latin America and the Caribbean. Washington DC, Pan American Health Organization.

Pantoja, E. (2002). Microfinance and Disaster Risk Management. Experiences and Lessons Learned. Washington, DC, World Bank, ProVention Consortium.

Pareto, V. (1906). Manual of Political Economy. New York, Augustus M. Kelley.

Pelling, M. and J. I. Uitto (2001). "Small Island Developing States: Natural Disaster Vulnerability and Global Change." Environmental Hazards 3(2): 49-62.

Pelling, M., A. Oezerdem and S. Barakat (2002). "The Macro-Economic Impact of Disasters." Progress in Development Studies 2(4): 283-305.

Petak, W. J. and A. A. Atkisson (1982). Natural Hazard Risk Assessment and Public Policy: Anticipating the Unexpected. New York, Springer.

Peterson, M. (2002). "The Limits of Catastrophe Aversion." Risk Analysis 22(3): 527-538.

Paté-Cornell, M. E. (1996). "Uncertainties in risk analysis: Six levels of treatment." Reliability Engineering ans System Safety 54 (2-3): 95-111.

Piaget, J. and B. Inhelder (1969). The Psychology of the Child. New York, Basic Books.

Pichon, F. and J. Uquillas (1997). "Agricultural Intensification and Poverty Reduction in Latin America's Risk Prone Areas: Opportunities and Challenges." Journal of Developing Areas 31(4): 479-514.

Plate, E. J. and B. Merz (2001). Naturkatastrophen. Ursachen-Auswirkungen-Vorsorge. Stuttgart, E. Schweizenbart'sche Verlagsbuchhandlung (Naegele und Obermiller).

Pollner, J. (2000). Managing catastrophic risks using alternative risk financing & insurance pooling mechanisms. Washington DC, World Bank.

Pollner, J. D. (2001). Catastrophe Risk Management. Using Alternative Risk Financing and Insurance Pooling Mechanisms. Research Working Paper 2560. Washington DC, World Bank.

Pollner, J. D. et al. (2001). Honduras. Catastrophe risk exposure of public assets. An analysis of financing instruments for smoothing fiscal volatility. Washington DC, World Bank.

Quarantelli, E. L. (1991). Disaster Response: Generic or Agent-Specific? In A. Kreimer and M. Munasinghe (eds.). Foundations of Insurance Economics: Readings in Economics and Finance. Boston, Kluwer Academic Publishers: 83-98.

Rahn, P. H. (1986). Engineering Geology: An Environmental Approach. New York, Elsevier.

Rasmussen, T. N. (2004). Macroeconomic Implications of Natural Disasters in the Caribbean. IMF Working Paper 224. Washington DC, IMF

Ray, A. (1984). Cost-Benefit Analysis. Issues and Methodologies. London, John Hopkins University Press.

Reiss, R. D. and M. Thomas (1997). Statistical Analysis of Extreme Values. Basel, Birkhäuser.

Renn, O. and B. Rohrmann (2000). Cross-cultural Risk Perception. A Survey of Empirical Studies. Dordrecht, Kluwer Academic Publishers.

Rescher, N. (1983). Risk: A Philosophical Introduction to the Theory of Risk Evaluation and Management. London, University Press of America.

Rose, A. (2004). Economic Principles, Issues, and Research Priorities. in Hazard Loss Estimation. In Y. Okuyama and S. E. Chang (eds.). Modeling Spatial and Economic Impacts of Disasters. Berlin, Springer.

Rossi, P. H., J. D. Wright, S. R. Wright and E. Weber-Burdin (1978). "Are There Long Term Effects of American Natural Disasters? Estimations of Floods, Hurricanes, and Tornadoes Occurring 1960-1970 on U.S. Census Tracts in 1970." Mass Emergencies 3: 117-132.

Russel, D. T. (1999). It's A Disaster. The Money and Politics that Follow Earthquakes, Hurricanes and Other Catastrophic Losses. Los Angeles, Silver Lake Publishing.

Samuelson, P. A. (1947). Foundations of Economic Analysis. Cambridge, Harvard University Press.

Sarewitz, D., R. A. Pielke and M. Keykhah (2003). "Vulnerability and Risk: Some Thoughts from a Political and Policy Perspective." Risk Analysis 23(4): 805-810.

Sheaffer, J. R., F. R. Roland and G. W. Davis (1976). Flood Hazard Mitigation Through Safe Land Use and Construction Practices. Chicago, Kiefer & Associates.

Sheaffer, J. R. and F. R. Roland (1981). Evaluation of the Economic, Social and Environmental Effects of Floodplain Regulations. Washington DC, Federal Emergency Management Agency.

Shrader-Frechette, K. S. (1991). Risk and Rationality. Berkeley, University of California Press.

Shrader-Frechette, K. S. (1997). "How Some Risk Frameworks Disenfranchise the Public." Risk: Health, Safety & Environment 8(1): 1-8.

Siegel, P. B., J. Alwang and S. L. Lorgensen (2003). "Rediscovering Vulnerability Through a Risk Chain: Views from Different Disciplines." Quarterly Journal of International Agriculture 42(3): 351-370.

Skoufias, E. (2003). "Economic Crises and Natural Disasters: Coping Strategies and Policy Implications." World Development 31(7): 1087-1102.

Slovic, P., B. Fischhoff and S. Lichtenstein (1979). "Rating the Risk." Environment 21(3): 14-20 & 36-39.

Slovic, P. (2000). The Perception of Risk. London, Earthscan.

Smith, K. (1996). Environmental Hazards. Assessing Risk and Reducing Disaster. London, Routledge.

Spence, R. (2004). "Risk and Regulation: can improved government action reduce the impacts of natural disasters?" Building Research and Information 32(5): 391-402.

Stiglitz, J. E. (1999). Economics of the Public Sector. New York, W.W. Norton & Company.

Stoppa, A. and U. Hess (2003). Design and Use of Weather Derivatives in Agricultural Policies: The Case of Rainfall Index Insurance in Morocco. Agricultural policy reform and the WTO: Where are we heading? Capri.

Susman, O., P. O'Keefe and B. Wisner (1984). Global Disasters: A Radical Interpretation. In K. Hewitt (eds.). Interpretations of Calamity from the Viewpoint of Human Ecology. Boston, Allen and Unwin.

Swiss Re (2002). Europe in focus: Non-life markets undergoing structural change. Sigma 3/2000, Zurich, Swiss Reinsurance Company.

Swiss Re (2002). Natural Catastrophes and Man-Made Disasters in 2001. Sigma 1/2002. Zurich, Swiss Reinsurance Company.

Swiss Re (2004a). Understanding Reinsurance: How Reinsurers Create Value and Manage Risk. Zurich, Swiss Reinsurance Company.

Swiss Re (2004b). Natural Catastrophes and Man-Made Disasters in 2003. Sigma 1/2004. Zurich, Swiss Reinsurance Company.

Swiss Re (2005a). Natural Catastrophes and Man-made Disasters in 2004. Sigma 1/2005. Zurich, Swiss Reinsurance Company.

Swiss Re (2005b). Innovating to Insure the Uninsurable. Sigma 4/2005. Zurich, Swiss Reinsurance Company.

Thieken, A.H., M. Müller, L. Kleist, I. Seifert, D. Borst, and U. Werner (2006). "Regionalisation of asset values for risk analyses." Natural Hazards and Earth System Sciences 6(2): 167-178.

Thompson, P. B. and R. D. Wesley (1996). "Competing Conceptions of Risk". Risk: Health Safety and Environment 7(4): 361-384.

Thomson, A., P. Jenden and E. J. Clay (1998). Information, Risk and Disaster Preparedness: Responses to the 1997 El Nino Event. ESCOR Research Report AG1215. London, Department for International Development.

Trobe, S. L. and P. Venton (2003). Natural Disaster Risk Reduction. The Policy and Practice of Selected Institutional Donors. Teddington, Tearfund Research Project.

Turner, B.L, R.E. Kasperson, P.A. Matson, J.J. McCarthy, R.W. Corell, L. Christensen, N. Eckley, J.X. Kasperson, A. Luers, M.L. Martello, C. Polsky, A. Pulsipher and A. Schiller (2003). "A Framework for Vulnerability Analysis in Sustainability Science." PNAS 100(14): 8074-8079.

Twigg, J. and M. R. Bjatt (1998). Understanding Vulnerability: South Asian Perspectives. London, Intermediate Technology Publications/ Duryog Nivaran.

UNDHA (1992). Internationally Agreed Glossary of Basic Terms Related to Disaster Management. Geneva, United Nations Department of Humanitarian Affairs.

UNDP (2004). Reducing Disaster Risk. A Challenge for Development. New York, United Nations Development Programme.

UNDRO (1991). Mitigating Natural Disasters, Phenomena, Effects and Options. A manual for Policy Makers and Planners. New York, UNDRO.

UNISDR (2004). Living with Risk. A Global Review of Disaster Reduction Initiatives. United Nations.

UNISDR (2006). Terminology: Basic terms of disaster risk reduction. 'http://www.unisdr.org/eng/library/lib-terminology-eng%20home.htm'.

Unnewehr, D. (1994). The Legacy of Hurricane Andrew: What Price Life, Safety and Community? Insurance Institute for Property Loss Reduction. Boston.

Wharton, F. (1992). Risk Management: Basic Concepts and General Principles. In J. Ansell and F. Wharton (eds.). Risk: Analysis, Assessment and Management. Chichester, Wiley and Sons: 1-14.

White, G. F. (1974). Natural Hazards: Local, National, Global. New York, Oxford University Press.

WHO (1995). Coping with Emergencies: WHO Strategies and Approaches to Humanitarian Action. Geneva.

World Bank (1994). World Development Report 1996: Infrastructure and Development. Oxford, Oxford University Press.

World Bank (1995). "Emergency Recovery Assistance. World Banks Operating Manual OP8.50."

World Bank (2001). World Development Report. Oxford, Oxford University Press.

World Bank (2004). World Bank Development Indicators. Washington DC.

World Bank (2005a). Managing Agricultural Production Risk. Innovations in Developing Countries. Washington DC, World Bank.

World Bank (2005b). World Bank Development Indicators. Washington DC, World Bank.

World Bank (2005c). World Development Report 2006. Equity and Development. Washington DC, World Bank.

Yokomatsu, M. and K. Kobayashi (2001). The Catastrophe Risk and Economic Valuation of Disaster Prevention Investment. Proceedings of the Second EuroConference: Global Change and Catastrophe Risk Management: Earthquake Risks in Europe, Laxenburg, Austria, July 6-9, 2000, IIASA.

Appendix: Risk management approach and user interfaces

The proposed approach for risk management on the country level was introduced in chapter 2.4. According to figure 2.2, the following steps need to be performed in the risk management process:

1. Direct risk assessment.
2. Financial vulnerability assessment.
3. Macroeconomic risk assessment.
4. Risk management.

The risk management process is shown in the following with the help of the user interfaces built in the GUI environment in Matlab. The whole model was translated into a stand-alone application, so that the simulations also can be performed outside the Matlab environment. Because of printing issues, not all user interfaces can be shown. Furthermore, the user interfaces were simplified (no color, simple structure) because of printing issues. The data of Honduras is used.

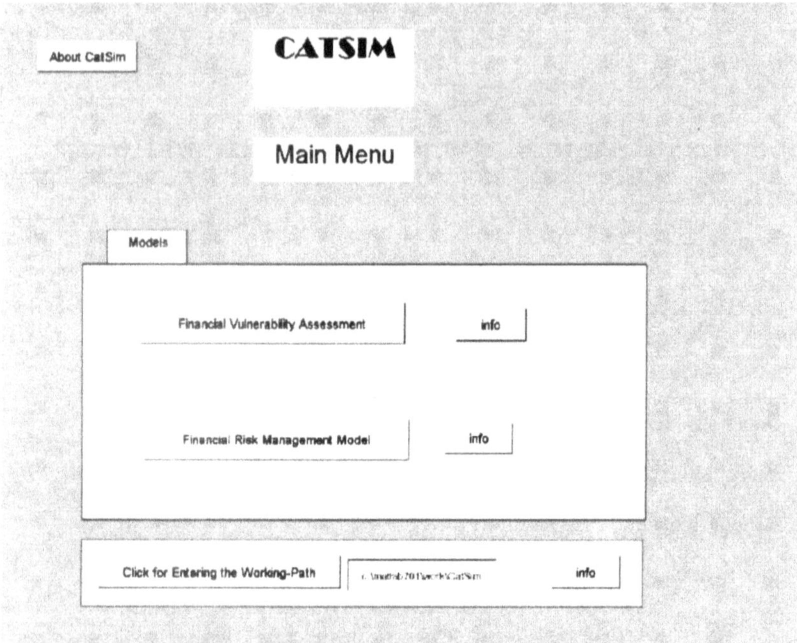

Figure 1: CatSim: Main menu

Figure 1 shows the starting point of the analysis. The financial vulnerability of the public sector should be assessed first. This will open figure 2. Dependent on the selected experiment the macroeconomic risk management model opens figure 9 or figure 10.

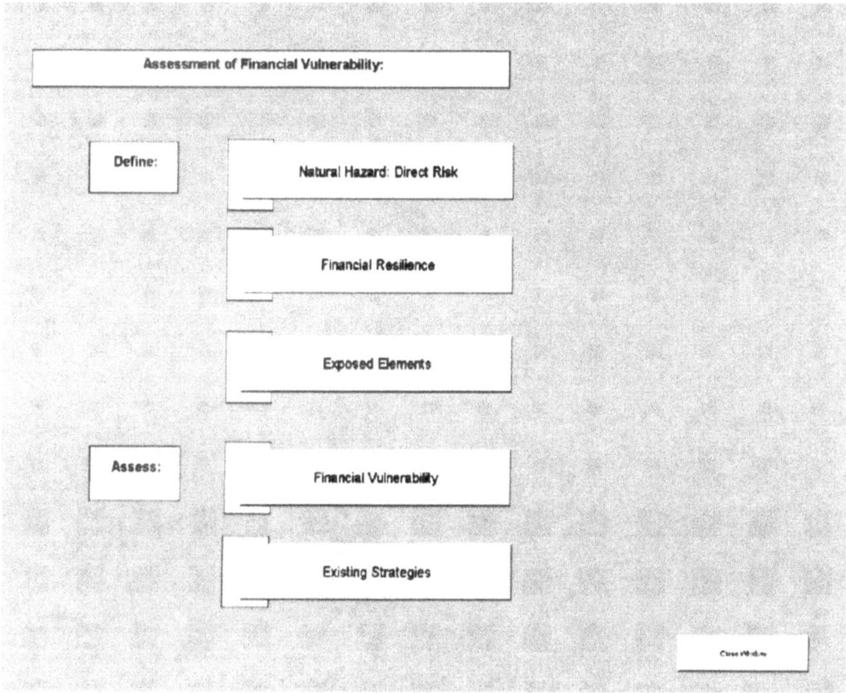

Figure 2: Catsim: Financial vulnerability assessment menu

Here, the direct risk (figure 3), the financial resilience (figure 4) and the exposed elements (figure 5) are needed as input files. There is also the possibility to use more detailed modeling approaches, presented in section 6.1 to assess the direct risk. Afterwards, the financial vulnerability can be evaluated (figure 6) and possible loss financing schemas can be looked at (figure 8).

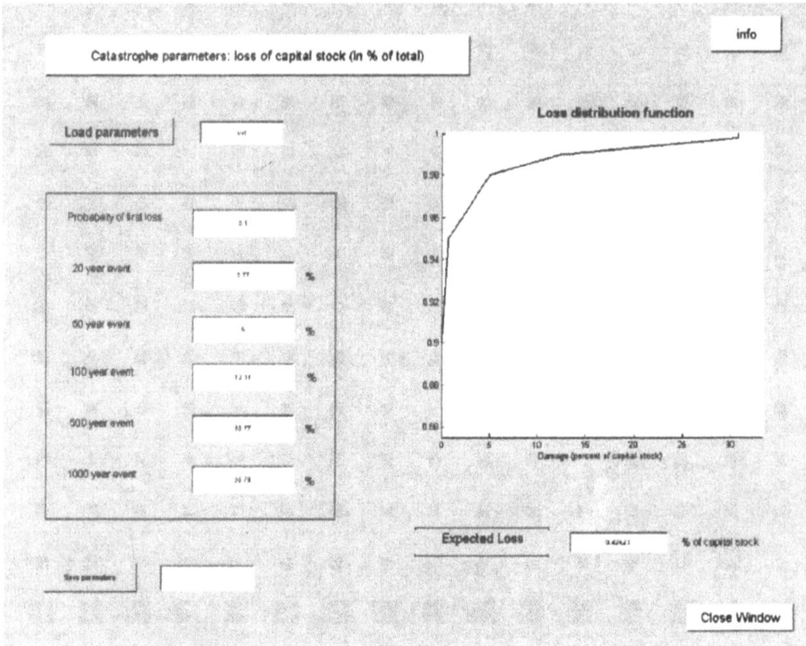

Figure 3: CatSim: Direct risk

Here, on the left hand side the catastrophe parameters in terms of selected year events and percentage of capital stock destroyed are entered. In standard mode the probability of first loss as well as the 20-, 50-, 100-, 500-, and 1000 year loss events are needed. The loss distribution is then shown on the right hand side (linear approximated or estimated using an extreme value distribution). Furthermore, the expected annual loss is calculated via integration or Monte Carlo simulation and is shown on the right hand side below the distribution. After the loss return periods are entered or loaded from a file, these parameters can be saved.

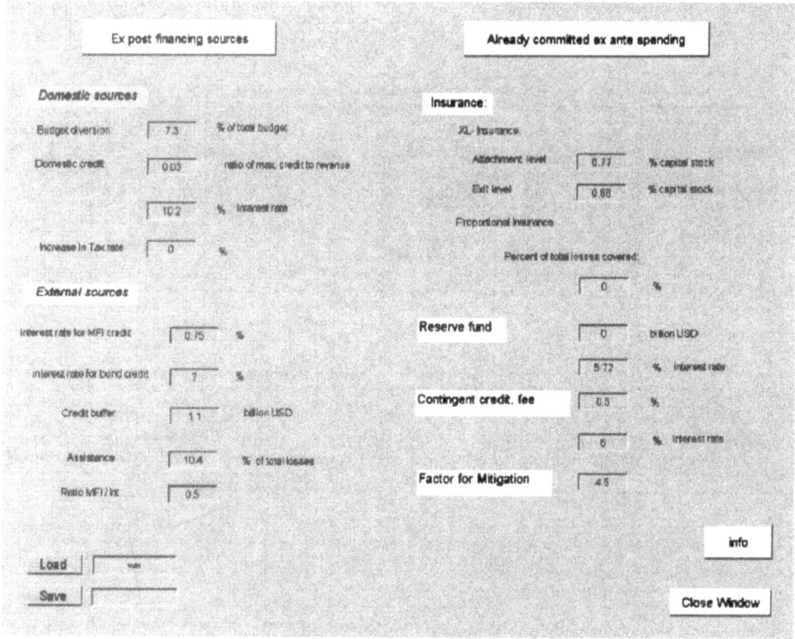

Figure 4: CatSim: Financial Resilience

In figure 4, the financial resilience is determined through the available ex-ante and ex-post measures (see chapter 5). Ex-post measures (left hand side) include domestic sources like budget diversion, domestic credit and tax rates as well as external sources like assistance, MFI and bond credits. Ex-ante measures (right hand side) include XL-insurance, reserve fund arrangements, contingent credits and mitigation. Again, the data can be saved for later studies.

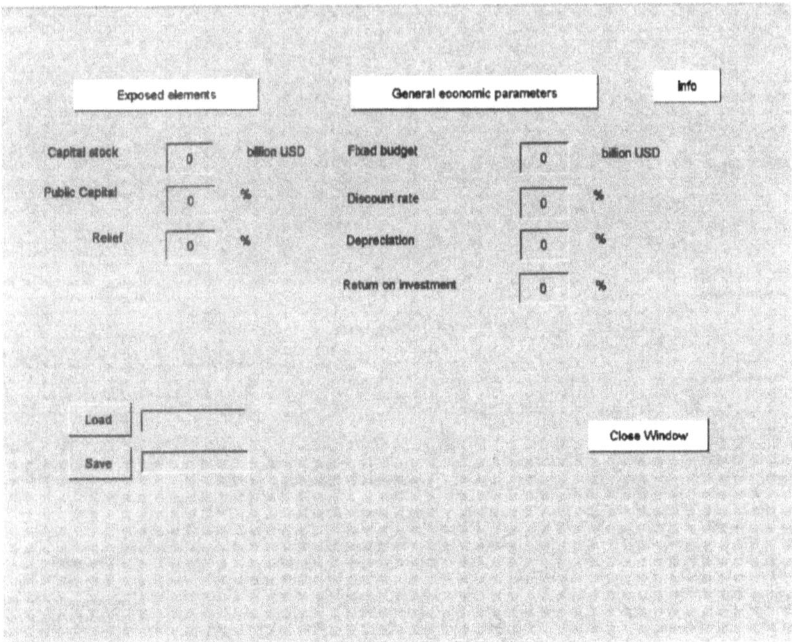

Figure 5: CatSim: Exposed elements

Figure 5 shows the user interface were the exposed elements are defined (in standard mode).

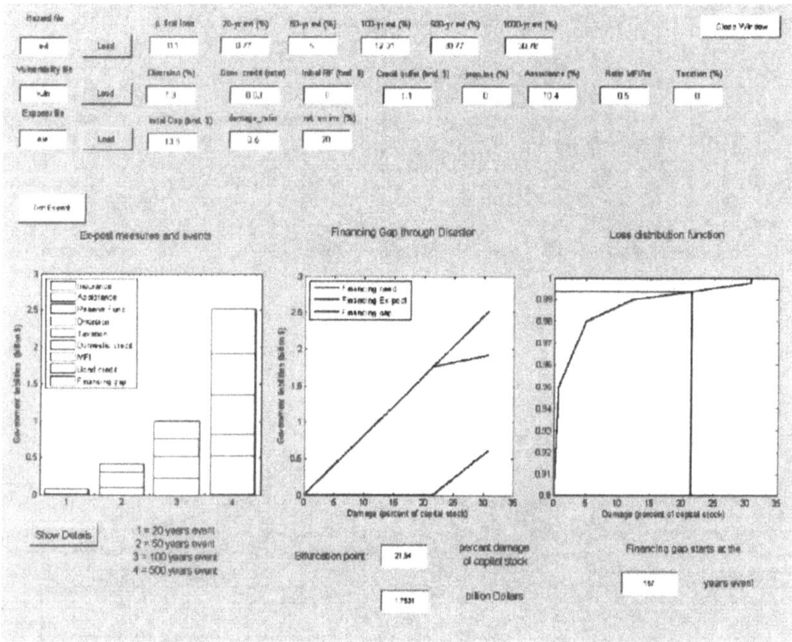

Figure 6: CatSim: Financial vulnerability

Here the financial vulnerability is calculated. On the top various parameters regarding the hazard (probability of first loss, year events), the exposed elements (capital stock at risk, public and private sector risk), and the financial resilience (available ex-post measures) can be loaded. The financial vulnerability is measured through the financing gap concept. Financing schemes (see also figure 7.2) for the 20, 50, 100 and 500 year event (left hand side), bifurcation points of needed and available capital (middle) and the critical return period (right hand side) are shown. For Honduras the critical return period is the 157 year event. However, as an example, one can ask the question how much dependent Honduras is on external borrowing (see figure 7).

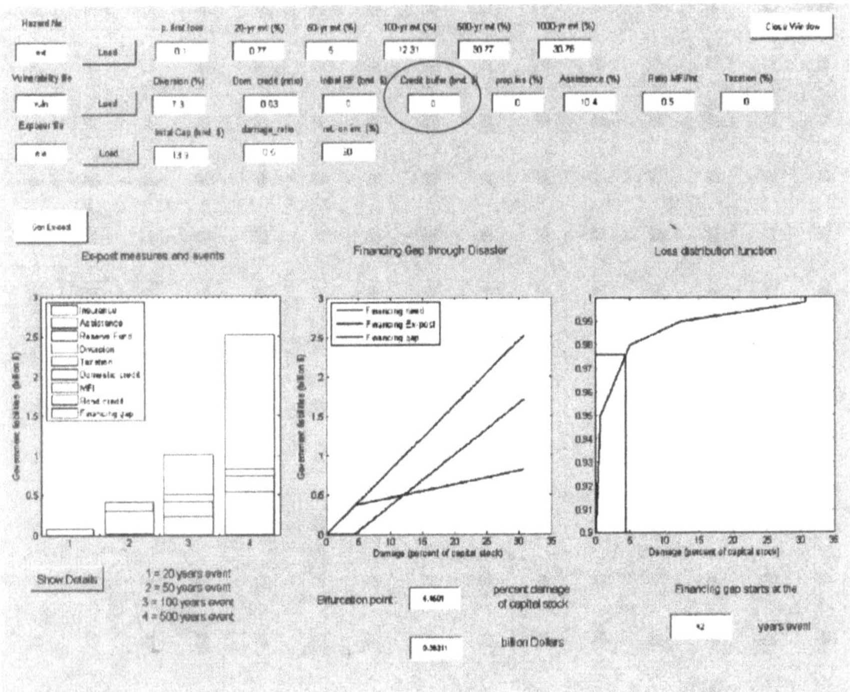

Figure 7: CatSim: Financial vulnerability

Here, the same parameters are used but the possibility to borrow is limited, e.g. the credit buffer is set to zero. The critical return period is now the 34 year event which indicates the dependence of Honduras on external financing resources and a low level of domestic financial resilience.

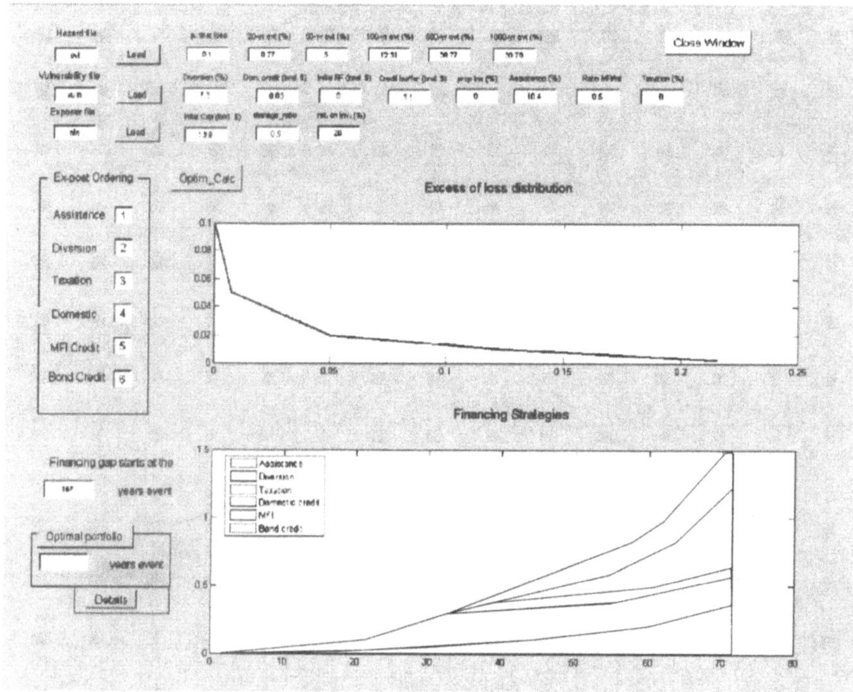

Figure 8: CatSim: Existing strategies

While in figure 6 and 7 the financial vulnerability is calculated, in this user interface the financing scheme for events lower than the critical one is shown. Again, on the top various parameters can be loaded and changed. The upper right hand picture shows the loss exceedance curve and the lower picture the financing schemes for the events depending on the order of the ex-post measures used (defined on the left hand side). Due to printing issues no colors are shown and therefore the presentation here is only on the conceptual level (see also figure 7.3). Furthermore, it is possible to look at financial schemes in more detail for specific events (left hand side on the bottom of the user interface).

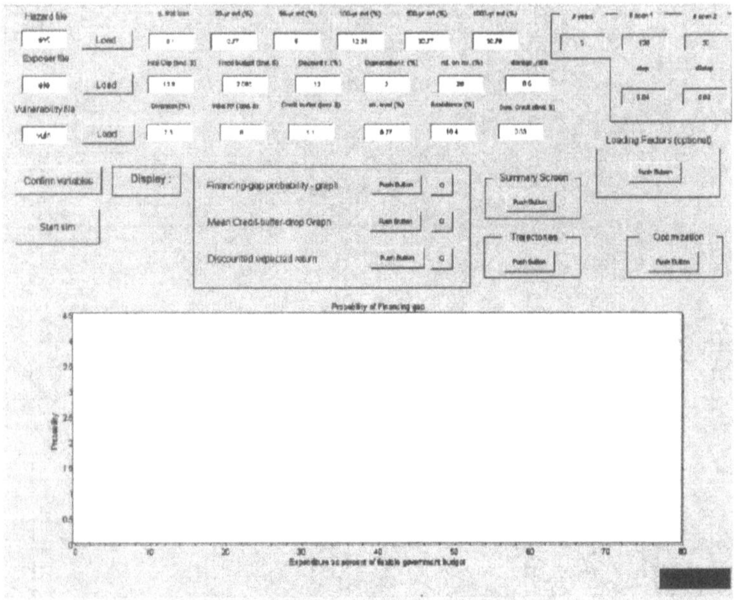

Figure 9: CatSim: Risk management

Here, the user interface for experiment 2 is shown. The different ex-ante financial strategies and tradeoffs can be compared in the middle picture (similar to the figures in the case studies). The user can change interactively the parameters and look at the outcomes. Also the upper confidence interval for the response variables can be shown. Some other windows can be opened here for further investigations (not shown here) including, (i) a summary window to compare the different risk instruments in more detail, (ii) a window were loading factors can be changed and specific layers and their premiums can be calculated, (iii) a window were trajectories over the whole time horizon for important macroeconomic variables can be compared with and without risk management strategies.

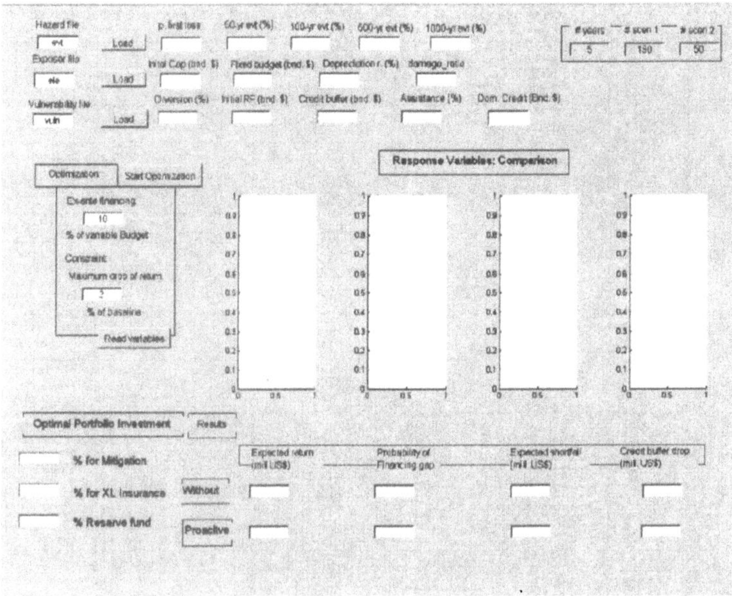

Figure 10: CatSim: Optimization

In this figure experiment 3 is performed. The results of the (local) optimization are compared with the baseline case without ex-ante instruments. The optimal portfolio is shown on the lower left hand side, whereas the response variables are shown on the lower right hand side as well as a graphical representation in the middle. The objective and constraints are determined on the middle left hand side.

FSC
www.fsc.org
MIX
Papier | Fördert gute Waldnutzung
FSC® C083411

Kolibri 360 GmbH
Ferdinand-Jühlke-Straße 7
99095 Erfurt, Deutschland
produktsicherheit@kolibri360.de